Also by Henry Stewart

True Crime Bay Ridge

How Bay Ridge Became Bay Ridge

More True Crime Bay Ridge

Also Edited by Henry Stewart

Old Sleuth, the Detective; Or, the Bay Ridge Mystery
by Harlan Halsey

THE STREETS

OF BROOKLYN

E. R. G.

Edited by Henry Stewart

Introduction and annotations, copyright 2024 by Henry Stewart.

These chapters were first published in the Brooklyn *Daily Eagle*, 1886–87.

> bklyn.newspapers.com
> henrystew.art

Cover design by Michael Verdirame for Silent Salesman.

Photo shows North Elliott Place, looking north from Myrtle Avenue, 1887, photographer unknown. This block was subsumed by the Walt Whitman Houses complex in the 1940s.

CONTENTS

Introduction, i

Notes on the Text

Streets

1. Sackett Street, 1

2. Flatbush Avenue, 11

3. Bond Street, 23

4. Sands Street, 33

5. Hicks Street, 45

6. Pierrepont, Montague and Remsen streets, 57

7. Fulton Street, 69

8. Furman Street, 81

9. Clinton Street, 95

10. Clinton Street, Part II, 107

11. Columbia Heights and Columbia Street, 121

12. Red Hook Lane, 133

13. Myrtle Avenue, 145

14. Court Street, 155

15. Washington Street, 167

16. Smith Street, 179

17. Fifth Avenue, 189

18. Navy Street, 199

19. Washington Avenue, 211

20. Lafayette Avenue, 225

21. Baltic Street East, 237

22. Baltic Street West, 247

23. Adams Street, 257

24. Henry Street, 267

25. Union Street, 279

26. Atlantic Avenue, 289

Pedestrian Pleasures

27. Third Avenue, Ridge Boulevard and Shore Road, 299

28. Prospect Park West and Fort Hamilton Parkway, 309

Sources and Acknowledgements

THE

STREETS

OF

BROOKLYN

"Keep your woods O Nature, and the quiet places by the woods,
Keep your fields of clover and timothy, and your corn-fields and orchards,
Keep the blossoming buckwheat fields where the Ninth-month bees hum;
Give me faces and streets—give me these phantoms incessant and endless along the trottoirs!"

Walt Whitman
"Give Me the Splendid Silent Sun"
(1867)

"Not one pedestrian in a thousand
has eyes for the things around him."

E. R. G.
"Prospect Park Birds"
(1886)

INTRODUCTION

In the late 1880s, the Sunday edition of the Brooklyn *Daily Eagle* ran sixteen broadsheet pages, each filled with seven columns of small type. The front page was filled with local news, while inside there was gossip from across the river in New York, small items about local people and events, reprinted articles from other papers around the country and the world, classified ads, commercial advertisements and various columns. George Hope's dealt with local politics, and he signed it by name, but typically these were bylined at the bottom with a penname, such as Recluse or Saunterer (who wrote a recurring feature called "Walks About the City"), or the writer's initials.

We know very little about the writer who signed his columns E.R.G.—just the occasional biographical details dropped in passing throughout his modest œuvre. He was a man and a bachelor; he called himself a journalist and an art critic; he possessed deep knowledge of architecture, trees and the history of Brooklyn; and he was well-educated and knowledgeable about the arts, quoting Shakespeare and *The Mikado* (when the latter was just two years old). He was also well traveled, mentioning travels through Europe, the Middle East, the Caribbean and the midwestern United States.

He published his first column in the *Eagle* on July 4, 1886. It was about the birds of Prospect Park, a favorite location to which his early columns often returned. Over the next forty-two weeks, he published more than forty pieces, almost always on Sundays, usually almost two columns in length—about three thousand words each. At first, he wrote about the city's parks, as well as its arts, history and educational institutions, even a long walk to Fort Hamilton from his home in what we'd now call Carroll Gardens or Gowanus.

But then, on September 27, he published an article about life on his street, which he does not name but abundant clues reveal to be Sackett Street, west of the Gowanus Canal, in what was then known as South Brooklyn. From then on, he mostly wrote profiles of other streets in Brooklyn and what were then still neighboring towns—famous ones and humble ones, tony ones and seedy ones, historic ones and modern ones—from Downtown to Fort Hamilton, the Heights to Flatbush. He chronicled their histories but also the street life along them, creating indelible portraits of what it felt like to live and move along these thoroughfares in the late nineteenth century. He was a reporter, an architecture critic and a sociologist with a novelist's eye—an ambling chronicler of whatever interested him, which was usually buildings and groups of people.

Brooklyn at that time was an independent city; it would not consolidate with New York and become a borough for another twelve years. The western tip of Long Island had long been home to the Lenape, settled at various points by the Canarsee. Europeans first moved onto their land in the seventeenth century, establishing towns that were mostly Dutch; they eventually became Brooklyn, Bushwick, Flatbush, New Utrecht, Flatlands and Gravesend (the only English one). The village of Brooklyn was established in 1817, the city in 1834; by 1851 it had absorbed Bushwick and the young city of Williamsburgh; in 1886, when E.R.G. published his first column, it had annexed the eastern portion of Flatbush, then called New Lots. (In 1894, Flatbush, New Utrecht and Gravesend would become part of Brooklyn, and the last holdout, Flatlands, came aboard two years later, making Brooklyn and Kings County coterminous.)

In 1880, the population was close to 600,000, having increased each decade. In 1870, it had been close to 420,000; in 1860, 280,000. By 1890, it was close to 840,000—far from the almost 2.7 million in the 2020 census but also a fraction of the land. It was bustling. In 1886, almost four thousand new buildings were erected, and in 1887 almost another four thousand.

But it was still a young city, human in scale. The Statue of Liberty was new—still a brilliant copper, not yet an oxidized green—and E.R.G. criticizes it from various vantage points around Brooklyn; the dense urban development of today was still to come, and "the Bartholdi statue" was visible from the highlands of Flatbush Avenue to the lowlands of Shore Road. The Williamsburgh Savings Bank Tower didn't open until 1929, and the Hotel St. George, newly opened, had not yet become the skyscraping colossus it would.

Most of Brooklyn's institutions were still in their adolescence: the Brooklyn Academy of Music was still on Montague Street, and Grand Army Plaza not only had yet to have that name (bestowed in 1926) but also had no Brooklyn Museum or library, which opened in 1897 and 1941. Mount Prospect Park was still a reservoir, supplying the city's water from Ridgewood. Brooklyn was growing, but gradually, into an underdog rival to its big sister across the river.

Brooklyn long had a reputation for its "churches and homes," a moral and domesticated corollary to New York, cemented by celebrity preacher Henry Ward Beecher in the pulpit at Plymouth Church in the Heights. He died while E.R.G. was writing these columns. But the two cities had recently begun a freer exchange of people and commerce. Under construction since the 1860s, the Brooklyn Bridge had finally opened just a few years earlier, in 1883. "In Brooklyn ... it [had been] said the bridge would make Brooklyn important, that it would make Brooklyn prosper," David McCullough writes in *The Great Bridge*.

> Property values would soar. [Bridge designer John] Roebling the alchemist would turn vacant lots and corn patches into pure gold. Everybody would benefit. Brooklyn was already expanding like a boomtown, and the bridge was going to double the pace, the way steam ferries had.

McCullough adds later, "[The bridge] did everything its proponents had promised. It stimulated growth, raised property values ... It put Brooklyn on the map." E.R.G. documents the early years of this colossal transition—before trolleys, before the Dodgers, before the subway, before the Williamsburg and Manhattan bridges, before consolidation, before expansive growth, before twentieth-century decline and superblock redevelopments, as the "Brooklyn spirit" soared ever upward.

Once centered on what we now call Brooklyn Heights and Downtown Brooklyn, with some industry down in Red Hook, Brooklyn had begun to urbanize and spread out. The Hill district (now Fort Greene and Clinton Hill) was the most fashionable place to live at the time these columns were written, with its handsome villas, but it was soon to be rivaled by what became Park Slope; the brownstone neighborhoods on the other side of the canal were losing their middle class to workers and immigrants. Monotonous rowhouses popped up in what we now call Prospect and Crown Heights.

Black people would not move to the borough in large numbers until World War I, during the Great Migration from the South. But there were already small settlements. Weeksville had been home to a free Black population since New York State had abolished slavery in 1827, one of the largest in the country—but it might have been too much of a schlep for E.R.G.; he barely travels in these columns farther east than the Hill district. But he visits smaller Black communities on Navy Street and a long-forgotten street in Gowanus called Cleveland Place.

E.R.G. was racist, as you could expect from a nineteenth-century white man; his prejudice takes the form of aloof condescension. In the chapter on Navy Street, he rubs his hand on the heads of Black schoolchildren and is surprised that they don't appreciate it. He's confused as to why Black women don't seem to like him. And he uses language that's very offensive. But if he's not a pioneering integrationist or civil-rights advocate, he does reject stereotypes of the time, such as that Black children were prone to stealing.

There's also a great deal of classism in E.R.G.'s columns. He argues that the middle-class Black residents of Cleveland Place, and the working-class Black residents of nearby East Baltic Street, are superior to their white-ethnic neighbors, because they keep their homes with more dignity and pride. He identifies more with them. He expresses sympathy for the poor Irish living in shanties in a column on Columbia Street. "I believe that the citizens of Shantytown, barring the dirt, are living more natural, honest and comfortable existences than if each family had three rooms in a lofty tenement of the finest brick and terra cotta," he writes. "Are we not too much in the habit of concealing our dirt and making believe that it has been removed? Do we not in effect throw it under the table, where the cloth hides it? Is our sewage system an undoubted success, so that we can afford to look down at Paddy in Shantytown, who lives in the unleveled region where there are no sewers?"

He reserves most of his vitriol for Italian Americans. In his column on Washington Street, he writes, "Sometimes a door swings open and lets out a vile, pestiferous odor, partly from the rags that the Calabrians are shifting and sorting, partly from the Calabrians themselves. They appear to be very degraded citizens indeed and are more animal and less rational than is safe in a republican country." Such sentiments recur throughout; he never writes about other races or ethnicities with such animosity.

He has many wild and wrong theories about Native Americans, especially their languages. He can wander off on interminable etymological digressions, and I would encourage readers to skim or skip these paragraphs. They are included here for completism, and because they offer a window, for anyone interested, into nineteenth-century thinking about Native history that is so vastly different from our own. He barely uses the name "Lenape," instead referring to the Brooklyn Natives as Algonquin (of which the Lenape were a part), as well as asserting there were also Iroquois here, though they lived much farther north.

His racial attitudes offer insights into his time, but such anachronisms are not the draw of these columns. It's their wealth of lived details—a study of Brooklyn that progresses with logical linearity, down one street till the end of its story, where it picks up another and follows that one before circling back to find another. You can't really tell the story of Pierrepont Street before you tell the story of Hicks Street, and it'd make more sense if you knew the story of Sands. You won't understand Fifth Avenue until you know Smith Street, and it'd be better if you already had an impression of Columbia Heights.

Some of Brooklyn's streets were ancestral, such as Fulton or Red Hook Lane, and others took shape in the early nineteenth century as parts of planned developments, such as Hicks and Henry streets. But the majority were established at the stroke of a surveyor's pen. The state hired civil engineer John Stoddard to lay out the entire city, beyond the 1819 map of the village of Brooklyn (parts of Brooklyn Heights, DUMBO and Downtown), from Marshall Street in modern-day Vinegar Hill to 60th Street in modern-day Sunset Park, from Furman Street in Brooklyn Heights to Stone Avenue (now Mother Gaston Boulevard) in modern-day Brownsville. Stoddard worked from 1835–8 and released his map in 1839; out in the fields, he and his team placed stone markers at the streets' future locations, and blocks were opened gradually, as wanted or needed.

E.R.G. begins exploring these streets haphazardly, starting with Sackett Street before moving to Flatbush Avenue, perhaps inspired by his column weeks earlier, chronicling a walk to New Utrecht, another of the outlying towns. But then he finds his rhythm and structure: he begins in Brooklyn

Heights, where modern Brooklyn begins, and branches out as the city did—to Downtown, and to Red Hook. From there he wanders into developing districts, what today we call Carroll Gardens, Cobble Hill and Boerum Hill, and then what we call Fort Greene and Clinton Hill, then to booming Park Slope. And then he returns to the streets he missed back in the city center, such as Henry and Adams, before concluding near where he began—at Union, Sackett's neighbor—for a satisfying symmetry.

Quotations from these block-by-block portraits have been included in local histories in recent years, including Robert Furman's *Brooklyn Heights* (2015), Joseph Alexiou's *Gowanus* (2015) and my own *How Bay Ridge Became Bay Ridge* (2019). Each specialized researcher has found the column that pertained to their hyperlocal focus, but no one till now has collected them in their entirety—as an opus worthy of exploration on its own, not just in part but in sum, a look not at individual streets and neighborhoods but at Brooklyn itself.

This book is reminiscent of *Walt Whitman's New York* (edited by Henry M. Christman), a compilation of the poet's "Brooklynania" columns in the Brooklyn *Daily Standard* in the 1860s, which explored the history of the old village and town. But E.R.G. outdoes Whitman, both in the thoroughness of his narratives and the colorfulness of his language. Whitman's columns come alive when they become personal, from his boyhood meeting of the Marquis de Lafayette to his yawps in the wilds of Montauk. But E.R.G. thrives in the subject itself, in the vestigial memories of a clover-covered Brooklyn Heights or the suicidal swayings of mournful grasses on Furman Street.

Whitman edited the *Eagle* forty years earlier, and during that time he walked the streets of Brooklyn and watched them from his office by the ferry. Sometimes he wrote up what he saw, but these have not been adequately collected for a general audience.

"Editor Walter Whitman was a traveled man—in Brooklyn and its rural environs, in New York, and on the East River," writes Thomas L. Brasher in *Whitman as Editor of the Brooklyn Daily Eagle* (1970).

> After business hours, and often during them, he strolled the streets or rode the omnibuses, stages, ferries, and sometimes the Long Island Railroad. Some of his rambles were aimless saunterings to see what he could see up some street or down another; others were purposefully directed toward an exhibition, a picnic, a ship launching, or a parade. In the *Eagle* Whitman told his subscribers what he had seen on these excursions. And since the *Eagle* was a Brooklyn paper, the Brooklyn scene predominated greatly over the New York scene in those accounts.
>
> As the editor of a local paper, Whitman was perforce a Brooklyn booster. He spoke for the superiority of Brooklyn over the "Gomorrah," as he frequently dubbed New York, on the opposite side of the river.

By E.R.G.'s time, Brooklyn was in transition, and so too was the *Eagle*. Its powerful longtime editor, Thomas Kinsella, instrumental in getting the bridge built, had died two years earlier; Raymond Schroth's comprehensive history *The Eagle and Brooklyn* (1974) basically skips over the period of E.R.G.'s tenure, as the paper found its footing under new leadership. But Whitman's and Kinsella's hyperdriven Brooklyn boosting was an inherent part of the paper. E.R.G. was a consummate *Eagle* man.

"The *Eagle*'s main efforts had been to reinforce the community identity of an urban community that was changing so rapidly and so radically that perhaps a sense of community was no longer possible," Schroth writes, later adding:

> This [book] has stressed the importance of a community's need for a clear image of itself and the importance of people's feelings about their surroundings. The *Eagle* understood to an extraordinary degree that its readers had to relate in a familiar way to neighborhoods, to dead heroes, and to sturdy old buildings. It knew that some kind of face-to-face relationship and some kind of public acknowledgement for otherwise forgotten men, women and children was imperative for humans living in a rapidly changing urban milieu.

That's this book to a tee. Whitman's "Brooklynania" provided a more traditional history of Brooklyn, moving through its lineage subject by subject, from courthouses to fire companies. The poet's city was not one of many streets; in *Leaves of Grass*, the word usually only comes up in connection to "Manahatta!" Between 1850 and 1890, roughly Whitman and E.R.G.'s *Eagle* heydays, the population of Brooklyn had grown sixfold, meaning many more streets for many more homes, businesses and institutions. This was no longer Francis Guy's village, as depicted in his quaint 1820 painting "Winter Scene in Brooklyn," but our modern metropolis as it more fully took shape.

E.R.G. instead hits on a novel structure, moving through the streets themselves to open up the histories contained therein. Curiously, he never ventures to North Brooklyn, ignoring the streets of Williamsburg and Greenpoint, and just barely reaches some of Bedford–Stuyvesant and Bushwick. He doesn't go out to Coney Island, then still outside the border of Brooklyn and not yet quite the amusements Mecca it would become. It was known for its hotels but not its streets. It was also probably too far to walk.

E.R.G., proudly, walks everywhere. "No one can properly appreciate Brooklyn who is not fond of walking," he writes, as true today as it was in 1886. It's part of why these columns are so valuable, their pedestrian-level view, the city not seen from a rollicking horse cart or a blurring railcar window. He stops to study, to observe, to interact. This is not a portrait from someone on the outside looking in but from the inside looking out, at the people, buildings and street life all around him.

Reprinted here are also two columns about long walks to Fort Hamilton, in modern Bay Ridge, the first down Third Avenue and Shore Road, the other by Fort Hamilton Parkway, through modern Kensington, Borough Park and Dyker Heights when they were mostly undeveloped. They are especially long walks, six or seven miles one way.

When I first began reading these columns, I assumed E.R.G. was elderly, given his knowledge and enthusiasm for Old Brooklyn. But then I wondered, would an older person have been so eager for long hikes up and down poorly or unpaved roads, out into raw country?

Was E.R.G. a younger man?

I tried everything I could think of to figure out his identity. No staffing records from the *Eagle* seem to exist, certainly not from the nineteenth century. I settled on City Directories from the time but found no newspapermen with the initials E. G., and no likely suspect living on Sackett Street. But I did come up with one candidate.

Like E.R.G., Edward Rowland Greene (1861–1928) was a bachelor. Greene was closely involved in Trinity Church, on Clinton Street, which E.R.G. writes in Chapter 10 needs "more money than *we* have" (emphasis mine). He also almost always used his middle initial, appearing in the newspaper record for his business affairs as "Edward R. Greene."

From there it gets fuzzier. His address is listed as 99 Henry Street, his father's house, and not some building on Sackett, though one could imagine his home address was officially listed as the family residence while the young man rented his own room elsewhere. (At the end of his column on Columbia Street, he describes renting a room.) He was a lawyer, not a journalist, though the latter may have been something he dabbled in before practicing. (Greene eventually became a partner at Stetson, Jennings & Russell, where Grover Cleveland had once been a partner.) If Edward R. Greene had been a newspaperman living on Sackett Street, I would have put his name on the cover.

He was educated: Greene graduated from Columbia Law School in 1882 and passed the bar in 1884. He does not appear in local directories until 1887. Perhaps he traveled in the intervening years on his successful father's dime, picking up some of the firsthand knowledge of the world that E.R.G. exhibits. The Greenes were noted residents of the Heights, the neighborhood to which E.R.G. seems most closely connected and in whose history he's so deeply steeped. Perhaps Greene picked it up from his father, Lyman (who probably moved to Brooklyn from Rhode Island in the 1850s), perhaps also from some of the old timers who would have been his neighbors.

Lyman Greene died in 1904. He was by then retired, having once been a partner in a coffee and tea firm, then the president of the Eagle Warehouse and Storage Company, whose notable building on what's now Old Fulton Street was landmarked in 1977. He was well known in local business circles and in the Heights, where he was a longtime resident, closely involved with Trinity Church, where he was a vestryman for more than thirty years. Edward succeeded him in that role.

Edward R. Greene was living with his father at the family home at 99 Henry Street in 1892, and after his father died, he remained at the house for most of the rest of his life, sharing it with his half-brother, Arthur Vogt. Greene died on November 2, 1928, and was buried in the family plot in Green-Wood Cemetery, next to his mother and father, from which you can see 37th Street, near the corner of Ninth Avenue.

The house on Henry Street remained standing until the 1960s, when it was torn down as part of the Cadman Plaza redevelopment. A New York *Times* article from 1964, about preservationists raiding homes slated for demolition for "old fireplaces, mantles, mirrors, doorways, doorknobs and chandeliers," describes 99 Henry as a "decayed building."

I found one photo of Greene, in the obscure 1914 reference work *Empire State Notables*, held by Columbia University.

EDWARD R. GREENE
Stetson, Jennings & Russell, Counsellors-at-Law
New York City

Whether Greene wrote these columns is irrelevant. Their value is not in who wrote them, like Whitman's "Brooklynania," but in the writing itself.

Parts of Brooklyn, such as Williamsburg and Downtown, have become unrecognizable in the past few decades, torn down and redeveloped at gargantuan scale amid gentrification. The Williamsburgh Savings Bank Tower, at the edge of Fort Greene, once owned the Brooklyn sky; it's now almost crowded out of sight. We rely not just on traditional histories but also ground-level accounts—films such as Diego Echeverria's *Los Sures*, Kelly Anderson's *My Brooklyn* and Amy Nicholson's *Zipper*, novels such as Ernest Poole's *The Harbor*, Paule Marshall's *Brown Girl, Brownstones* and L.J. Davis's *A Meaningful Life*—to remind us of what once was, physically and culturally. E.R.G., too, was reporting at the cusp of a great transition, on what had already been lost, what remained and what he envisioned was to come.

Few writers of his era stood on street corners and hid in hallways, recording the movements and conversations of the well-to-do and disadvantaged alike. E.R.G. ties them together through their churches, storefronts and homes, from great Gothic cathedrals to quaint country chapels, from fancy shops to sidewalk peddlers, from hilltop villas to canalside shanties, fashioning the great, complex mosaic that is Brooklyn—as seen from the streets.

Henry Stewart

NOTES ON THE TEXT

I transcribed these columns from digital scans, occasionally making copyedits for clarity, uniting what are now compound words (eg. "every one"), adding or cutting commas and updating archaic usage, especially of prepositions (e.g., we now say a building is *on* a street, not *in* a street). I intend this text to be readable, not a record of the spelling and grammatical eccentricities of the nineteenth century.

However, I have retained certain idiosyncrasies, such as his use of the open-mid front rounded vowel, as in Phoenician, because I find them charming.

1

Sackett Street

OUR STREET.

Glance at a Characteristic Brooklyn Thoroughfare.

An Obstructive Canal—How Its Condition Might Be Bettered—Customs of Some People.

Monday, September 27, 1886

Ours is not a famous street; neither historic nor aristocratic associations have entwined themselves about the name that designates our thoroughfare[1]. We are not even a thoroughfare, now that I come to think of it, for midway in our career from the Hamilton Ferry[2] to the Park Plaza[3] progress is intercepted by an evil-looking and foul-smelling ditch called a canal[4]. We are like a snake cut into two pieces, and that part of us which debouches into the plaza scorns our humble name and calls itself a place[5]. But nevertheless, we are satisfied with our street and have the proud consciousness that someday we may be historical. Strangers may visit us in the future and ask to be shown a particular house. For be it

---

[1] Sackett Street was named for Samuel Sackett (1754–1822), a local advocate for public education and the poor.
[2] A major ferry terminal, connecting Red Hook to Whitehall Street, from 1846 to 1942, at the waterfront, where Hamilton Avenue and Sackett Street converged west of Van Brunt Street.
[3] Renamed Grand Army Plaza in 1926.
[4] The Gowanus.
[5] East of Fifth Avenue, Sackett Street becomes Berkeley Place, after the Irish philosopher George Berkeley.

known unto all men of Brooklyn that the great landscape painter of this continent, who is believed by the best judges to be a genius rivaling those great Dutch painters Ruysdael and Hobbema and Cuyp, is one of us, and has been for very many years[6]. We are too close to the men of our own time to distinguish closely and discriminate between the truly great and those who are great for the moment. The popular preacher, the popular actor, the popular politician, the popular journalist, are during their heyday of renown very great men, but no sooner is the breath out of their bodies than they are forgotten. Their work was ephemeral, and therefore their reputation is that of ephemerides. Not so the artist. In his lifetime on his own street the boys are impudent to him, and on our street the boys have a faculty of impudence that passes belief. While he is alive the neighbors speak of him respectfully if he pays his way, and the reverse if he is dilatory in settling accounts with the butcher and the baker and their tribe. But when he is dead and the hand lies torpid that spread deathless colors upon imperishable canvas, then they learn in a score of years to speak of him with bated breath as a superior being and to feel that their street is immortal because he, who is one of the immortals, lived on it.

    I have surveyed with curious eye the length and breadth of our street and am constrained to say that from its source in the what-is-it place to its finality at the Hamilton Ferry it contains not one section that can be called fashionable or aristocratic. It has a neighbor that is far more so[7], and that would be a splendid thoroughfare and the finest driving street in Brooklyn were it not for the canal. For it is the natural driving outlet of the Heights, and the Parkway on the other side of the Plaza[8] is really a continuation of our neighboring

---

[6] The minor Hudson River School painter William Hart lived at No. 407. The columnist profiled him for the *Eagle* almost two months earlier, visiting his "comfortable, handsome house on Sackett Street."
[7] Union Street, the next block south.
[8] Eastern Parkway.

street. There is not in all America such a noble drive as this would be, were it not for the canal. It is true that this ditch is crossed by a turn bridge[9], but it is constantly out of repair, and those who drive on our neighboring street are compelled to describe a circumbendibus. When it is supposed to be in working order there is a frightful delay every time a schooner arrives loaded with bricks, because there is not space enough for the passage of anything but canalboats. Much lamentation, many tears and groans are occasioned in our street by the oppressive character of this canal, for we are forced to use the bridge of our neighbor, not having one of our own. Neither are the men, women and children of our street protected from falling into the canal by any wall or railing or fence, so that of Christmas nights absent-minded men, who after a glass of apple toddy, or two or perhaps three, become oblivious to the points of the compass, are exposed to great peril of their lives. It has been whispered among the women of our street that in such a case a poor widow could not collect insurance money from any company, as the failure to ask and insist upon adequate protection would be construed as constructive *felo de se*. No. Our street is not fashionable. The best section is that which contains the artists' house, and this can only be described as well-to-do respectability. The other sections may be classed as respectable. It is true that in one part of our street there is a row of white marble houses[10], but these were erected when the knowledge of stone masonry in Brooklyn was more than limited, for these structures evince a decided inclination to moult, to shed their lintels and

---

[9] A turn bridge could be rotated to allow ships to pass. The modern Union Street Bridge, which can be raised, opened in 1905.

[10] Five marble-front homes stood at or near probably the southwest corner of Hicks. "These were beautiful houses when first finished in 1854," the *Eagle* reported in 1888. But "the yards look deserted, while some of the houses bear the notice 'Floors to Let.' The corner house has been turned into a liquor store." Many if not all would have been in the way of the BQE in the 1950s, if they weren't replaced sooner.

brackets and jambs and other architectural features. We have another row of brick structures, which are surmounted by copings that appear to imitate battlements or machicolations. But the necessity for these fortifications has never been quite apparent to the denizens of our street, no creature more formidable than a cow ever appearing in it. She, dear animal, is perfectly tame and pastures upon the grassplot between the sidewalk and garden wall of a highly respected citizen, whose house is situated on the neighboring street before mentioned, but whose enormous garden reaches to our street, occupying a large part of one section. She reclines upon the grass and chews the cud with perfect contentment, and, it is believed, furnishes milk for the table of the old citizen who is much beloved and revered in this city by reason of his connection with Prospect Park[11]. Other architectural features have we none save our grand church, which is named after St. Agnes, and which is indeed a beautiful structure. The cornerstone is inscribed 1881, and the interior has just been commenced[12]. When this building has been completed, we have hopes that those who are connected with it will stir up the authorities to build a wall in front of the canal, which is very close at hand. The tower of this church is quite a landmark, and those who survey the city from the height

---

[11] James S.T. Stranahan, a longtime Brooklyn parks commissioner regarded as the father of Prospect Park, lived at 269 Union Street. His land occupied the whole east side of Clinton Street between Union and Sackett—the equivalent of about fifteen lots, which at the time (as now) was an unusually large piece of land in this neighborhood. Today, it's occupied by nine apartment buildings.

[12] St. Agnes was dedicated in May 1888. On July 2, 1901, it was hit by lightning; fire destroyed the roof and interior and badly damaged the walls. A man died, overcome by heat and smoke, trying to help the priests save the sacred vessels, and several others were injured, including two firefighters who were given last rites. The present church, on the same northeast corner of Sackett and Hoyt streets, was dedicated in 1913, with a spire that still dominates the local skyline.

of the reservoir[13] have often observed it and admired its bold outlines without knowing that it was on our street. It is our only church. We cannot consider our street as being of a commercial character, for we have but one factory—a saleratus mill[14]. We have a coal yard down by Hamilton Ferry[15], and we have another coal yard down by the raging canal[16], and I shrewdly suspect that it is for the benefit of the latter that the authorities have neglected to protect us by a wall. For the coal barges come alongside our street and dump their cargoes upon the cobblestones of our pavement, so that in this particular section our street is a gratuitous wharf for the benefit of the parties connected with the coal yard. These are our industries. Beyond these our street is occupied by dwelling houses, owned in our best section almost entirely by the occupants. We have at nighttime a bright and animated appearance, for the windows are all ablaze with light, and a piano is banging away for dear life in every parlor, and the sidewalks are filled by schoolgirls, big and little, exchanging confidences, and the pavement near the curbstones is dotted by small campfires, which the boys of our street have a passion for lighting. Whether they play at soldiers, Indian fighters or bold and bloody pirates upon the raging main, the first and chief consideration is a campfire. They are good boys, but when it comes to campfires they have not that due consideration for the property of others that ordinarily marks the good boy. Woe to the housekeeper who leaves out of doors an ash barrel. It would itself become ashes in no time. A hardy band of Mississippi rangers only the other evening

---

[13] Modern Mount Prospect Park, one of the high points in Brooklyn, was once the site of its reservoir, built in 1856 and torn down in 1935.
[14] The main ingredient in baking powder.
[15] There was a coal yard on Van Brunt, between Sackett and Degraw, as well as a coal shed on the waterfront, belonging to the Union Ferry Company.
[16] There were, in fact, four coal yards, on both sides of the street, between Bond and the canal.

discovered that a wash tub was left in an area where coal had been dumped and where the flagging had been washed down subsequently. The band, waving flaming torches composed of superannuated brush brooms, kept alight by being constantly whirled around the head, rushed into the area and carried off the spoil with hideous yells and were about to break it up when they were vigorously charged by the boy of the despoiled house who had rallied part of his own band by giving the whistle of distress. The wash tub was rescued, although the rescuers were stigmatized loudly as tender foot and dough heads, and unworthy of belonging to the brave banditti of our street. When itinerant venders of fruit come with their wagons into our domain, they have to guard their baskets strictly or they will be whisked off to feed the sacrificial fires. But no boy of our street would steal their fruit.

With that circuitous inconsistency of reasoning that marks the boy of all times and all countries, while it would be considered dishonorable if any buffalo hunter or Indian fighter in our street were to rob a fruit dealer, or to pilfer from the overflowing hoards of the grocerymen that dot the neighboring corners, the robbery of a garden that contains peaches, and that abuts upon the sidewalk of our street, is held to be an act of prowess of the highest class. It is in the parlance of our street boys "the taking a big Injun scalp." The patience displayed and the perils encountered are not small. The owner of the garden, wishing probably to preserve his peaches, has studded his fence with nails of the most taking character, but the boys are equal to the emergency. I saw three engaged in the nefarious act of robbery the other day. The stoutest boy bore upon his shoulders the skinniest, who was, beside his leanness, the happy owner of a suit of clothes that fitted him snugly, to put it mildly. With patient ingenuity the skinny one pounded through the nails two bits of wood stout enough to support his weight. Then raising himself he placed his feet upon the shoulders of his friend and supporter, and after bracing himself for the effort, delicately hoisted one leg over the nails, bringing one knee down upon one bit of wood and then repeated the process with the other, balancing himself with his friend's head. Then he deliberately plucked every peach within reach and with a business-like air chucked them to the third boy who, with an equal air of business, caught them and deposited them in his cap. When the latter was full, he announced the fact, and the boy on the fence withdrew from his awkward position and slid down his human ladder. Then the three marched off with an elated air but composed countenances, leaving the bits of wood to tell the story of their guilt.

From time immemorial the streets of Brooklyn have been playing grounds for children, particularly for girls, and our street is by no means an exception. When it is warm and sunny one can hear sweet voices in the singing games like "sing a ring a rosy." When it is cold then tag becomes the great institution. The very little girls will insist upon joining in, thinking that the big girls ought not to touch them, and when they become tag they generally refuse to accept the responsibilities of the position, and that brings the game to an abrupt conclusion. There is a cunning little tot of 7 whose mother dresses her usually in a tight-fitting basque with a cape and places on her pretty head a broad brimmed hat with a steeple crown very much like those that witches are supposed to have worn in the days of Cotton Mather. It is a wonderful sight to see this little maiden run after the big girls in loyal endeavor to catch them, and one might feel alarm that the little legs would break short off if the elasticity of youthful limbs were not proverbial. Then, when experience has proved to her that she cannot catch them, she walks up the steps of her mother's house in a dignified way, refusing utterly to listen to any proposal that the game should be commenced anew, and that they should count for tag. The most popular game for the girls in our street is keeping school, and the greatest adept at playing teacher is a little woman whose fondness for not going to school is well known. As the fated hour arrives she generally contrives to have a headache or an earache or an incipient gathering in her eye. As soon as she has obtained from parental authority what in college is known as an "aegrotat[17]," she emerges upon our street with a white handkerchief bound round her head and proceeds to gather in all the little ones who do not go to school. She arranges them upon the steps of high stoops and then begins to do the active business of mock teaching. Mabel, a girl of 4, who adores her, is generally rewarded for her devotion by being made to stand up for talking in school, although she is an intensely silent child. Then this young teacher flies up the steps at double quick step and, playing that the street door is a blackboard, covers it with imaginary words in seventeen syllables for the spelling class. Among the big girls there is a charming free masonry with regard to infants, and they lend the babies of their households to each other with touching sisterly feeling. Proud, indeed, is the big girl of No. 6,006 when she has borrowed the baby of No. 6,024[18], and her delight is unbounded when her special chum from across the way has also borrowed the baby from four doors up the street. The young ones are carefully tucked in their respective perambulators, and then the friends make a double team and march up and down, telling each other thrilling experiences of their respective schools. The passerby can generally hear fragments of "I said to Miss Jones," or "Mary Jane went up to the teacher in No. 4," or "Would you believe it, she kept me in for an hour."

Our street would be truly happy if something could be done about the canal. We recognize that the people connect-

---

[17] A dated Britishism for a certificate indicating a student is ill.
[18] These house numbers don't exist today, nor do they appear on insurance maps drawn the year this was written. Perhaps he refers to the sixth and twenty-fourth houses on the sixth block of Sackett Street. Counting up at the time from the waterfront, that would be between Clinton and Court, the same block that abutted Stranahan's garden—perhaps the block where E.R.G. was living.

ed with it have vested rights, and vested rights, though hard to explain, are, as everybody knows, as sacred as Scripture, and as inalienable as a Jew's nose. Some of young men of our street are employed in various capacities by the canal firms, and no one wishes to take away their bread and butter or to injure their employers. But two things are patent; first, that the streets abutting on the canal ought to be protected by high walls; secondly, that the bridge upon our neighboring street ought to be a fixture and not a turn bridge. It is too narrow for the passage of schooners, and every time that one attempts to pass there is a jam, which not only causes unparalleled delays to the people who wish to pass but also throws the bridge itself out of gear. If our street and its grand neighbor are willing to accept the presence of the canal as a finality, then those who are interested in the canal ought to be willing to concede that schooners should not be brought below the last bridge. If the present crippled turn bridge were replaced by a permanent iron structure, which could be done at very little expense, the barges could pass as freely as ever, and the great bulk of the commercial activity of the canal is done through them, and there would be an immense gain to the neighborhood, and especially to our grand street, which then would become throughout its bounds one of the finest streets and best drives in Brooklyn. The canal firms that use the streets as their private wharves may be opposed to protecting walls, but this is a matter in which our street and its neighbors have legal rights and can compel the authorities to protect them. If the city chooses to turn these street ends into wharves it can do so, perhaps, but certainly the people who do business along the canal have no such power. Our street finally observes that it is a good street, and has the welfare of Brooklyn at heart and wishes to be well thought of, and it therefore prays those who are in authority to consider its present lamentable case and listen to its anguish[19].

E. R. G.

---

[19] Today a barbed-wire fence no one could miss, no matter how many Christmas toddies they'd consumed, separates Sackett Street from the Gowanus Canal.

2

Flatbush Avenue

ANOTHER OF OUR STREETS.

Flatbush Avenue a Survival of the Old Ferry Road.

What May Be Seen from Its Highest Point and in the Course of a Stroll from End to End.

Sunday, October 10, 1886

The avenues and streets of Brooklyn are for many reasons more interesting than those of the sister city[1]. The chief cause of this is undoubtedly to be found in the fact that ancient avenues of communication on Manhattan Island have not been maintained but have been completely obliterated or have been metamorphosed. But they never were so various and so interesting as those on Long Island, even in the days when the Bowery extended all the way to Harlem and the old post road to Boston ran through Madison Square[2]. The most interesting avenue in those old days was probably the road that led along the North River[3], and which was a sort of English rival to the Bowery, which was essentially Dutch as well in character as in name[4]. The sturdy burghers of Nieuw Amsterdam had their boweries or country seats along

---

[1] Manhattan did not unite with surrounding counties to form the five-borough New York City until 1898.
[2] A winding road from Wall Street to Boston used to deliver mail. It only survives today in Manhattan as portions of other streets.
[3] An archaic name for the Hudson River.
[4] Bowery is an Anglicization of the Dutch *bouwerij*, meaning farm.

this road, for they were men who lived in better style and with far more refinement and culture than even the proud cavaliers of Virginia. The English conquerors of Manhattan Island found that, to retain their supremacy, it would be necessary to introduce a higher element of British colonists than those who had come to New York as soon as the Cross of St. George was hoisted on the Battery. They therefore gave many patents to the younger sons of the landed aristocracy of England, granting forty acres and fifty acres of land upon Manhattan Island itself, and upon these the newcomers erected villas in the English style along the Hudson or North River. But, from some reason not to be explained at this late day, there was a belief both among the English and the Dutch that New York was unhealthy during the great heats of the Summer and the beginning of the Fall, and very many of the best families established their country seats on Long Island. The British were partial to the region about Hempstead plains, and at a very early date had a racecourse there and villas at Roslyn and its neighborhood. The Dutch, at an equally early time, located themselves in Flatbush, the "level country[5]."

Flatbush Avenue is undoubtedly the genuine survival of the road to the old ferry at Brooklyn, and here there was not only a well-frequented ferriage, but there was a sort of sporting community, where shooting and fishing parties were accommodated. There was on Fulton Street at the time of the Revolutionary War a tavern noted for its fish dinners, and the British officers belonging to the army in New York used to come across regularly for recreation and frolic[6]. It is a well-known law in physics that the dog wags his tail and that it is not the tail that wags the dog. A logical application of this great truth will show why Flatbush Avenue does not

---

[5] "Flatbush" is derived from the Dutch *Vlacke bos*, or flat woodland.
[6] The King's Head Tavern—or Brooklyne–Hall, after the war—had been a popular spot for royalists at the foot of Fulton Street (now Old Fulton).

now go right down to the ferry, and why it is, so to speak, absorbed by Fulton Street. The latter was the highway of all coming from New York to Long Island, going straight to Jamaica and then to all points eastward, and therefore was of much greater importance than Flatbush Avenue, which only led to the other cluster of villas or boweries where the burghers planted their fine trees and their beloved tulips. Each of these great avenues of transit, however, has faithfully preserved its old line, and tells the story of its past with distinctness, reminding the people of the present day who are sometimes inclined to feel badly over the haughty airs of New Yorkers that Long Island and Brooklyn and Flatbush especially were, as far back as history goes, known by everyone to be more salubrious, with better soil, with better natural drainage, with finer verdure and trees than Manhattan Island. Had there been a count and a king in these United States, there can be no doubt that the royal habitation would have been built somewhere near Brooklyn, if not upon the Heights. For Colonel Nichols[7], who took the Island of Manhattan from the Dutch, immediately inaugurated the practice of spending half the year on Long Island, and the Governor was dutifully followed by the gubernatorial courtiers.

The tail end of Flatbush Avenue, the Village of Flatbush, has changed but little since the days when the British troops quartered themselves there and emptied the cellars and set fire to the villas in their drunken frenzy. Flatbush, indeed, is a beautiful example of the manner in which time lingers in some localities. It is as quiet and composed as if the great American nation were phlegmatic and self-possessed, like the old Hollanders. Possibly the roadbed is better constructed than in the days of the Dutch Governors, and the lighting and the streetcars and the water supply are of modern date.

---

[7] Richard Nicolls led the British naval squadron that blockaded New Amsterdam in 1664 before the Dutch surrendered the colony. He served as governor of the newly English colony until 1668.

But the houses are for the most part of the most respectable antiquity and stand in the midst of grand old forest trees, which the old Dutch had the good taste to plant upon their lawns. The inhabitants of Flatbush were, however, not all Hollanders, for there in the Crooke place[8] there is a magnificent English walnut planted by an English possessor. It is of stupendous girth and its enormous branches stretch halfway across the avenue. It is, however, not quite as large as the one at Roslyn, which was indubitably planted in 1713[9]. But this grand tree is not alone, for Flatbush Avenue at this point is series of splendid lawns and gardens in which are most noble trees and many exquisite flowers. The eyes of Americans have never beheld anything more magnificent than the begonia rubra on the lawn of Colonel Lefferts' old house, one of those that was fired by British soldiers after the Battle of Long Island[10]. There were two of them, 110 feet high, and each plant had two stems, each of which was a perfect cascade of scarlet flowers. On every side of these splendid specimens of floriculture are fine trees, principally tiriodendrons. On Clarkson Place there are just as notable examples of fine forest trees, mingled with tall elms that have unfortunately fallen victim to the galeruca beetle[11]. In fact, the Flatbush

---

[8] Philip S. Crooke, a brigadier general in the Civil War, lived on an estate the size of four square-blocks between Ocean and Flatbush avenues, Caton and Woodruff. Crooke Avenue, which ended at the western edge of his estate, is named for him.

[9] This ancient tree, on William Cullen Bryant's Cedarmere estate in Roslyn Harbor, Long Island, was the defining example of its kind in America, cited whenever the subject of walnut trees came up.

[10] South of what's now Lincoln Road (then East New York Avenue), John Lefferts and his family had several homes on 240 acres. The oldest was moved in 1918 to Prospect Park, where today it's a museum. The main residence was at the southeast corner of what's now Flatbush and Maple Street.

[11] Probably the Xanthogaleruca luteola, which eats the leaves of elm trees. A nonnative insect, it was introduced accidentally to Baltimore in the 1830s and soon spread throughout the continent.

Avenue car runs through an avenue of character unmatched on this Continent. There may be, among the young giant cities of the West, avenues of villas that cost far more money; but there are none that are so marked with the trees of two centuries of refinement. In the days of Richmond Hill, when there was a Village of Greenwich[12], perhaps the old West Side road of New York could have rivaled it; but every particle of that epoch has been obliterated, and even the fact that Aaron Burr had a villa there is known only to a few bookworms.

When the car arrives at the Prospect Park depot of a charming little railroad that runs to Brighton Beach, Flatbush Avenue enters upon a new stage of existence[13]. Hitherto it has been the scene of the most perfect quiet, of great beauty, great antiquity and innumerable proofs of blue blood in its best sense. Now Flatbush Avenue becomes noisy and excitable, and a trifle vulgar. For it becomes here one of the avenues of transit to the racecourses of Brighton Beach and Sheepshead Bay[14], and the hangers on of the racing world, black and white, loaf considerably in the neighborhood of the little depot, seeking for some patron whom they may strike for a dollar or so in return for some stable rumor about

---

[12] Richmond Hill was an eighteenth-century estate in Manhattan, used at one time as a country home by Aaron Burr. It occupied twenty-six acres around the modern intersection of Varick and Charlton streets, in SoHo, just south of Greenwich Village (when it was actually a village).

[13] This route was incorporated into the modern-day B and Q subway lines, and the old depot was where Flatbush and Ocean avenues meet. Today this is roughly the Prospect Park station on Lincoln Road.

[14] The Brighton Beach Race Course opened in 1879, the Sheepshead Bay Race Track in 1880. The former occupied roughly seventeen square blocks, between roughly Ocean Parkway, Neptune, Coney Island and Brighton Beach avenues; the latter was even larger, very roughly between approximately Ocean Avenue, Avenue V, Brown Street and Avenue Z. Both closed in the early twentieth century due to the fallout from the Hart–Agnew Law, which illegalized gambling in New York State, and the sites were later developed mostly as private housing.

a favorite horse. While waiting about for this chance they loiter around the saloons that flourish in some numbers hereabouts, but which rely for their profits upon a far different order of patronage. For we are close here to one of the great entrances to Prospect Park[15], and as the refreshments inside the Park are not liked by very many, these saloons minister to the internal wants of families visiting the great playground of Brooklyn, providing them with sandwiches of bologna sausage and Swiss cheese and with glasses of foaming lager. Once past the Willink entrance to the Park, Flatbush Avenue becomes a causeway. It is higher than the level of the Park, though this is concealed by the adroit manner in which the sides of the causeway have been planted with bushes and trees. And upon the other side there is considerable descent, and the ground is broken and desolate in appearance. The soil appears to be gravel mixed with boulders, and it is covered with a thin, green carpet of stunted grass, which a few cows perseveringly try to graze upon. The drainage is so excellent, however, that malarious and typhoid complaints seem impossible, and we wonder why this part has not been built upon. When the soil has been enriched with vegetable mould from eastern parts of Long Island it becomes admirable for gardens, and there is no reason why the Flatbush Avenue stretch of the park should not be faced by a line of villas framed in lovely gardens[16]. There is one drawback—the huge water pipe which belongs to the Flatbush supply system[17], and which is odiously ugly. The day will come when people who want to have homes of their own will discover what it means to have a natural gravel foundation.

---

[15] Willink Plaza, on Flatbush Avenue, north of the intersection with Ocean Avenue and Empire Boulevard, today near the carousel and Lefferts house.

[16] This instead became, in 1911, the Brooklyn Botanic Garden.

[17] A private concern that supplied reportedly brackish and salty water to Flatbush. The neighborhood would not receive water through the city, from the Catskills reservoir, until 1947.

What it saves families where there are young children in doctors' bills cannot be estimated. But it must be owned that in fair Brooklyn there are many localities beside Flatbush Avenue where the soil is gravel.

The site of the reservoir[18] marks the highest point of Flatbush Avenue, and here the observer will begin to realize what a glorious city Brooklyn is bound to be. Before him is the plaza, on his right is the noble Parkway[19], and on his left the splendid drive of Union Street connecting with the aristocratic quarter of Brooklyn Heights. Beyond the plaza lies the long stretch of Flatbush Avenue, very broad now and grand in its third and last stage. In the extreme distance one can see the towers of the bridge[20], and beyond these the heights of Hoboken, and the clustering turrets of the Passionist Monastery[21]. Looking down Union Street the perspective gives the blue, hazy masses of Orange Mountain in New Jersey[22]. The plaza is alive with vehicles dashing into it from all directions, the long, homely bodies of the street cars consorting oddly with splendid victorias and elegant rockaways, and fast double-team buggies, and spider-like sulkies[23] drawn by equine celebrities booted in true trotting style. The two horsecar lines wheel around the fountain and cross each other's tracks, and then, in nautical language, hug the coastlines of the Park[24]. The driving teams are mingled with mar-

---

[18] Today, Mount Prospect Park, on the east side of Flatbush Avenue, which opened in 1939 after the demolition of the obsolete reservoir.
[19] Grand Army Plaza and Eastern Parkway.
[20] The Brooklyn Bridge, which opened in 1883.
[21] The Monastery and Church of St. Michael, built in West Hoboken (now Union City) from 1864 to 1875, once dominated the New Jersey skyline. It still stands, but it's no longer visible from Brooklyn.
[22] Approximately seventeen miles away, as the crow flies. Before dense development, high ground in Brooklyn afforded spectacular views.
[23] These are different styles of carriages.
[24] Horse cars were passenger cars pulled on tracks by horses, a precursor to electric trolleys (which largely replaced them in the 1890s). One line traveled the length of Flatbush Avenue, from Fulton

ket wagons loaded with produce from Canarsie and Flatlands and the environs of Flatbush[25]; with huge vans containing the entire furniture of houses, evidently from Summer storage, and taken from darkness to the light of home; with wagons loaded with dry goods, and every other conceivable kind of merchandise. For Flatbush Avenue is the main artery of a part of the city that is growing up with startling rapidity, and the plaza is a good diverging point. Here, too, one's conveyance meets with funeral processions going to the Cemetery of the Holy Cross[26]. Much of the life of Brooklyn in its everyday form is exhibited on the plaza.

When we follow Flatbush Avenue to its third stage, we immediately become cognizant of the fact that the city grew and was not planned. The streets and avenues on the right hand and left hand of the avenue do not correspond, and the consequence is that there is an unusual number of gores of all sizes[27]. Some of these have been built upon; some are still vacant. The latter offer opportunities to the billposters, which have been embraced with avidity. Many of the board fences of these gores are ornamented with theatrical signs of the most lurid character, in which the thrilling excitement of the melodrama has impressed itself most forcibly. Two plays in particular have color tones that reveal positive genius. The gentleman who planned them is obviously a true impression-

---

Street past the Park, while another traveled on Vanderbilt Avenue, from Park Avenue, near the Navy Yard, then down Ninth Avenue, now Prospect Park West. The two lines crossed at what's now called Grand Army Plaza.

[25] The rural towns of Kings County were at the time still growing vegetables on some farms, or "market gardens," though not for much longer.

[26] It was Brooklyn's premier Catholic cemetery since the mid nineteenth century, less than a mile east of Flatbush Avenue.

[27] He refers to the odd triangular lots along Flatbush, from the Plaza to Atlantic Avenue, created by the awkward juxtaposition of the Park Slope and Prospect Heights street grids.

ist, for he is able by the mere choice of his pigments to give a faithful foreshadowing of the harrowing effect upon the nerves that will be brought by the plays themselves. And it is to be remembered that all the people who drive on Flatbush Avenue must see at least half of these signs, for, as stated above, the streets on the two sides of the avenue do not match, and consequently the gores are evenly distributed. If the billposter does not fetch you with his right barrel his left catches you infallibly. Some of the permanent advertisers have taken a hint from this state of things and have painted enormous signs upon the sides of the houses that the gores leave exposed. These gentlemen, however, are deficient in the high pictorial sense that marks the decorators of the board fences, and their signs are painful to the eyes instead of being wellsprings of delight.

There are a few vestiges here and there of a far-off time when this third part of Flatbush Avenue was not the rattling, noisy thoroughfare it now is. These are chiefly in the form of trees, old Paulownias and silver poplars. They are as healthy as can be expected under the changed conditions of their lives and seem infinitely more sturdy than the more recently planted maple trees, which are anything but robust. There are some old houses that, like the trees, preserve the air of other days. Two of these have been united into a tavern of the old kind[28]—a place where gentlemen can meet and enjoy themselves as they would in a club house. Doubtless this tavern is to the inhabitants of this new and constantly growing part of Brooklyn a veritable clubhouse. About this point the granite block gives place to a splendid concrete pavement[29], which was probably laid for the benefit of the park-

---

[28] Possibly what were then 138 and 140 Park Place, at the southeast corner of Seventh Avenue—the only buildings on an 1888 map that fit this description.

[29] Flatbush Avenue was paved with granite block from the Plaza to Park Place, where it became asphalt until Fifth Avenue, according to a 1907 street-pavings map.

going community on wheels. At the present time a certain amount of vehicles going to the drive does come up Flatbush Avenue, but this can only be considered temporary. There are unmistakable signs that Flatbush Avenue, from Fulton Street up to the Plaza, will be a succession of singularly high toned and stylish retail stores. Even now, although the major parts are connected with house building and furnishing, yet those for provisions are already of a distinct character. This is specially the case with the fishmongers, which are marked by more cleanliness and delicacy than will be found in very pretentious[30] stores in New York. The different kinds of fish are displayed on clean, white plates in an appetizing and asymmetrical way. If these things are so, it is not because the people who own these stores are different from others, but it is because their patrons can only be secured by this attention to their feelings. The refined women who do their marketing in this part of Flatbush Avenue are propitiated and like to come to these stores. In this way, however, a style is being developed which will become characteristic and habitual. It is certain that the big grocery firm that is building a palatial store near the point where Flatbush Avenue is absorbed by Fulton Street[31] is acting upon this thought and proposed to have an establishment as attractive and as refined as any in New York.

What will be the effect upon Flatbush Avenue when Brooklyn is made the terminal point of the Long Island Railroad instead of Long Island City[32]? It is to be hoped that Mr.

---

[30] Used without the pejorative connotation it has today.
[31] No. 10–22 Flatbush Avenue, at the southwest corner of Nevins Street, occupying less than a quarter of the triangular block. The whole block is now occupied by a modernist monolith built in 1971, with stores on the ground floor and offices above, which replaced another building from the 1920s, which had probably replaced this old market.
[32] The Long Island Rail Road stopped at the corner of Atlantic and Flatbush avenues since the 1830s. The first proper station was built in

Corbin[33] will, before he builds an adequate depot, consult someone possessed of a sense of beauty in architecture. There are two eyesores upon Flatbush Avenue; one is the Gospel Pavilion[34], near the Plaza, which looks like the barracks of a slave trader on the Guinea coast: the other is the Long Island Railroad depot. This last is atrociously ungraceful, nor does the façade contain one single line that is beautiful or forcible. Everything is tame and insipid, and it is as bad as the Fifty-second street depot in New York, which is saying volumes for its ugliness[35]. The situation is a grand one. Atlantic Avenue, Fourth Avenue and Flatbush Avenue all come together, beside some streets of a subordinate character. The three main arteries are of splendid width, and the position, fine as it is, could be improved still more if the city would purchase that impudent little gore that raises its head so proudly and displays all the glories of its drug store and insurance company[36]. It is the misfortune of New York that it is everywhere cramped and confined and has no approaches. It is the great merit of Brooklyn that its approaches, its avenues, grew up naturally, and its municipal guides had the good sense not only to retain them but to enhance them.

1877, and a modern Atlantic Terminal was built in 1907. It was torn down in 1988 and replaced with the present depot in 2010.

[33] Austin Corbin, railroad magnate and robber baron, was the father of the Long Island Rail Road and the original developer of Manhattan Beach.

[34] The Y.M.C.A. held Sunday services from 1877 to 1892 where Flatbush and St. John's Place form a point, just before the Plaza. It evolved from a tent to, at the time this column was published, a wood-frame pavilion.

[35] This may be a misprinted reference to Grand Central Depot, on 42nd Street, later replaced by Grand Central Station. He writes in the next chapter of his special disdain for the Depot.

[36] The traffic island formed by the intersections of Fourth, Atlantic and Flatbush avenues today houses the Times Control House, a terra cotta kiosk built in 1908 as an entrance to the IRT subway lines.

If Mr. Austin Corbin, whom everyone praises[37], wants to have a statue to his memory as the great railroad man of Long Island, let him build on Flatbush Avenue at this meeting place of the avenues a depot that shall be a thing of beauty and joy forever. Then shall Flatbush Avenue rejoice and sing pæans in his praise from Fulton Street to its leafy beginning in the sweet shades of Flatbush.

E. R. G.

---

[37] He was a fierce anti-Semite.

3

Bond Street

COURSE OF BOND STREET.

From the Y. M. C. A. to Gowanus Canal.

Architectural—Business Men Who Think They Own the Thoroughfare—Typical Toughs of Brooklyn.

Sunday, October 17, 1886

Almost everyone in Brooklyn knows where the Young Men's Christian Association building is, near the corner of Fulton and Bond streets[1]. No doubt it would have been at the corner had not that particular spot been preempted. In consequence of this state of things, that part of the Association building that does not appear on Fulton is cruelly separated according to appearances from the rest of the structure, and the whole force and glory of the façade is upon Bond Street. This street, therefore, is well known to those who are pained at the irreligion of modern life and sympathize with the earnest efforts that crystalized in the formation of the Young Men's Christian Associations in every city of importance[2]. Bond Street to the religious man living away from Brooklyn means

---

[1] Built in 1885, this Downtown YMCA, at 11 Bond Street, was abandoned by the organization in 1915 for a larger building on Hanson Place. Department of buildings records suggest the building on Bond was replaced that year, or shortly thereafter, with the building that's still on Bond and Fulton today (though much remodeled).
[2] The YMCA was founded in 1844 in response to the depraved conditions of Industrial Revolution-era London.

the Young Men's Christian Association and recalls memories of a structure that has much that is artistic, much that is noble and yet totally devoid of pretentiousness. But Bond Street to the Brooklynite proper, the citizen within the gates, means dirt and filth and municipal corruption, greed of rich men, want of self-respect in poor ones; slatternly girls at the corners, swarms of vicious and mischievous boys around the wharves, grimy, sore-eyed cats sneaking out of coal yards, wooden structures ready to fall with the next strong gale, strings of wagons loaded with coal, wood, produce, bricks and bales of tobacco for the great tobacco house, whose factories are in neighboring streets[3]. Bond Street is like Sin as Milton described her in *Paradise Lost*—very fair and loveable at the beginning, but exceedingly foul lower down, for this forlorn and thrice unhappy street has the misfortune to be for nearly one-half of its length a side partner of the famous or rather infamous Gowanus Canal.

Poor Bond Street, that commences with such bright auguries! For the Association Building has genuine architectural merit, and it is a pleasure to look upon an American structure where brick has been used with such telling effect. Brick as a material is gaining favor, especially for large buildings, but it is seldom used artistically, and those traveled men who had seen the market square at Bologna and the leaning tower of Zaragoza in Arragon were very apt to despair when they looked at the Church of the Holy Beefsteak, in New York, upon Fourth Avenue, sometimes called the Holy Ze-

---

[3] Probably a reference to Buchanan and Lyall, which operated a tobacco factory at 344–360 Carroll Street, between Bond and Hoyt, from 1879 to 1899; it remained a tobacco factory until 1912. It was "one of the best-known buildings in South Brooklyn, and one of the landmarks of the section," the Brooklyn *Eagle* reported in 1916. "A number of picturesque old residences were demolished to make room" for it. In 1899, the company employed 1,500 people. Today the site is home to the Mary Star of the Sea apartment complex, constructed in 1985 to provide senior housing.

bra[4], the Forty-Second Street Depot[5], and other intolerable monstrosities of brick work. The building of the Long Island Historical Society[6] was the first sign that architects in this country had begun to comprehend brick. Then followed the Produce Exchange in New York[7]. The structure on Bond Street is thoroughly worthy of comparison with these and belongs to the same high plane. The façade consists of a central tower with two unequal wings, the inequality being due to the Schniderian obstinacy of the vendor of fine brandies and old rye whiskies. The main entrance is adorned by a salient portico surmounted by a terra cotta pediment in the Neo-Hellenic style, with the inscription "Association Hall" upon the frieze. The pilasters on each side are unobtrusive in character, but sufficiently massive to be in harmony with the structure. The ponderous oak door, Renaissance in form, is set well back beneath the arch supporting the pediment and is reached by a flight of eight wide granite steps rising from a sidewalk broad and splendidly flagged with large stones. The brick of the arch is noteworthy, evincing a complete mastery of the material and an evident knowledge of what can be accomplished with it. The lamps on each side of the entrance have fine bronze shaftings.

An artistic little entresol peeps just above the imposing pediment of the portico, and the spandrils, or what would be spandrils had the windows been arched, are heavy masses of brown sandstone in modernized Renaissance. The capitals of the pillars between the windows are of terra cotta, and of

---

[4] The All Souls Unitarian Church, built in 1855 at the corner of what's now Park Avenue South and 20th Street, featured bands of red and white bricks.

[5] Cornelius Vanderbilt's Grand Central Depot, on Fourth Avenue, opened in 1871 and was superseded by Grand Central Terminal in 1913.

[6] Now the Center for Brooklyn History, opened in 1881 and still on the corner of Pierrepont and Clinton.

[7] First opened on Bowling Green in the 1860s and demolished in 1957.

graceful form, and the shafts are of polished gray granite. Above the sandstone bounding comes a string course of terra cotta dividing the stories. It is simple but elegant. The story succeeding this is surmounted by a mezzanine window, and then comes the attic crowned with a terra cotta gable, which is of the Tudor style, passing into the Queen Anne, or in other words a blending of pure Tudor with the debased rococo Renaissance, which King William brought from Holland with him. Whatever purists may say, this mingling is perfectly correct in form and spirit, for common sense shows that the classic pediment does not differ one whit from the so-called Tudor gable. This is probably Britannic in origin, older than Julius Caesar, and was certainly known in ancient Gaul. It may be Phœnician, but it is difficult to conceive of a wooden building without gables, and both Hellenic temples and Tudor colleges drew their first inspiration from wooden houses and timber-bonded rubble structures. This final gable juts out from the peaked belfry. The wings offer nothing noteworthy save the attic story, which repeats the gable form, although in a less ornate way, making a truly artistic line against the sky. The windows are in double sets, and on one story the archivolts and the arches are thoroughly Byzantine in character. The windows of the ground floor are very large and harmonize well with the massive portico. They may be classed as modernized English Renaissance or Tudor with wooden divisions instead of stone.

    A sense of light and beauty accompanies one down the street for several blocks, and yet one sees nothing but dwelling houses, offering nothing special to the observer save a type of wooden house of great beauty and essentially suitable to wood. These structures are in thorough preservation, but it is the fate of wooden houses to disappear from great cities, and these will, no doubt, not be an exception[8]. As one goes

---

[8] Between the YMCA and Atlantic Avenue there were many brick-lined wooden buildings that do not seem to have survived.

southward the dwellings become less and less indicative of refinement, and by the time Atlantic Avenue is reached, the neighborhood and the street seem to be changed. At this point we find the United Presbyterian Church[9], a low, quaint structure of brick, inartistic in construction and feebly Gothic in style—the Gothic of a deacon's fancy or a presiding elder's imagination. On we go along Bond Street, the houses being less and less pleasant to look upon and the people more and more careless, dirty and slatternly, until we come to Douglass. We have now arrived at the plague spot of this part of Brooklyn, for at the foot of Douglass Street is the canal. Here is the establishment of P. G. Hughes, who deals in brick, lime, laths and other building material. Part of his stock in trade blocks up both sidewalks and the pavement and kindly prevents the passerby from falling into the canal. The next street that crosses Bond Street and goes down to the canal is Degraw. Mr. Murtha is engaged in the coal business on one side of the street and Mr. Nelson on the other. A canal boat is disgorging its black diamonds on the pavement of the street, and the sidewalks on both sides of the street are heaped several feet high with the fine dust of coal. Sackett Street reveals a precisely similar state of things, but the canal boat that is discharging its cargo is not loaded with coal but with bales of tobacco for the great firm of Buchanan & Lyall. These millionaires back their wagons to the edge of the canal. The boat is furnished with tackling, and two men handle it easily and drop the bales comfortably into the wagons. The business could not be done more expeditiously if Buchanan & Lyall owned the canal and the street. The firm does not own either, but simply uses gratuitously the facilities for which it ought to pay the city roundly. The coal wharves on either side be-

---

[9] The Second United Presbyterian Church, at 401 Atlantic Avenue, first appears in the newspaper record in 1867. It's now home to the Belarusian Autocephalous Orthodox Church, which bought the building in 1957.

long to W. H. & J. W. Vanderbilt, and they also use the street and canal as if they owned them.

At Union Street there is a turn bridge, and the public rights have to be respected. The maker of packing boxes[10] however is determined to follow the good example set by the millionaires, and his wares blockade the sidewalk on the north side, and his men actually make their boxes there. Such an astonishing disregard of public rights would be inconceivable if Buchanan & Lyall, the rich tobacco firm, did not do the same thing. Next comes President Street, where there is no bridge and consequently an utter and complete seizure of public rights by private individuals. The end of the street is blockaded with piles of lumber and of bricks[11]. There are no sidewalks, and the street is unpaved, and the fine dust flies in clouds whenever a wagon goes or comes, which is very frequently. On Carroll Street there is a bridge and consequently a marked improvement. Nothing can prevent these harpies from using public property without paying for it, so strong is their ring. But the erection of a bridge upon every street would utterly spoil their game. After Carroll comes First Street, and here the Vesta Oil Works[12] are doing their very best to provide the City of Brooklyn with a widespread and terrible conflagration. Beside their works they have toward the canal an immense pile of empty barrels, which it is to be presumed have contained coal oil. On the other side of the street and on the street itself a lumber firm[13] has stored its lumber. A flash of lightning from an angry sky, and there would be a fire that would leave far in the rear those of Chi-

---

[10] On the north side of Union, abutting the canal, was Dykeman's Box Factory.
[11] On the north side of President was Lidford's Coal and Wood Yard; on the south side, John Morton and Sons Lime and Brick Shed.
[12] Occupying the entire south side of First Street, between Bond and the Canal.
[13] Watson and Pittinger Lumber Yard, on the north side of the street.

cago and Boston[14]. The train is laid all along the canal. There is every element necessary to start a ruinous conflagration—rickety old houses that are so much tinder, seasoned lumber, oil works, gas works, coal dust and hay and feed stores, and paint shops sprinkled around judiciously.

On Second Street there is a wonder, a miracle. For here we find a firm doing business on the canal that scrupulously respects the public rights. The name of this phœnix is Shaw & Truesdell, dealing in grain, feed, etc. They have nothing on the street, and their sidewalk is neatly paved with small cobblestones. All their goods are elevated by steam from the canalboats to their storehouse, and the wagons are loaded with them upon the street as they have a perfect right to be. But Mr. Christian on the other side of the way, who deals in building materials, piles up his bricks upon the street and sidewalk in the usual Gowanus Canal fashion. On Third Street, there is a bridge, and public rights are unscathed from end to end. Bond Street ends a little way beyond Third Street, the canal executing a graceful curve, which brings it at right angles with the poor street that has moved beside it for so many blocks. The Ridgewood Ice Company are upon one side[15] and appear to respect public rights. On the other side is a lumber yard[16] upon whose fence is a notice in large characters to captains of vessels and others not to place obstruction within twenty-five feet of that fence. No attention is paid to this request, for it is a favorite unloading place for schooners loaded with brick, and the bricks are piled up on the street and sidewalk and against the fence itself. The wagons come for the bricks when there is leisure and opportunity, and the author of that notice is laughed to scorn.

---

[14] Of 1871 and 1872, respectively—relatively recent memories for E.R.G.
[15] The west side, No. 436, right up against the Canal's graceful curve.
[16] A. Lippitt's Planning Mill and Lumber Yard, on the east side, No. 401–27, also up against the Canal.

Apparently, a theory exists that the ends of these streets are wharves for public accommodation. In some instances, this is so, but in others the owners of the wharves alongside use the streets and sidewalks as their own, from the mere fact of contiguity. Were they to be questioned as to their right, they would base it upon the above-mentioned theory. One can imagine such a claim in a new settlement where there is no discrimination between public and private rights, and where there are no taxes. But in Brooklyn, a city of enormous population, with immense municipal expenditure and an abnormally high rate of taxation, it is madness to permit such a state of things. Wharfage is one of the few methods by which the city can add to its income. Wharfage is a public right. The City of Brooklyn having to meet so huge an expenditure resulting mainly from the enormous extent of its streets and the heavy expenses of public schools planned upon far too liberal a basis requires every dollar that it can honestly obtain. It would be justified in using its right of eminent domain to purchase the entire property along the length of the canal, to close the canal side of Bond Street completely, to divide the space so required into wharfing privileges and wharves and to lease these year by year. At present, under a loose system of administration, the canal can hardly be called a source of revenue to the city; but it is a source of petty criminalities, and a constant menace of fire. Ask the police force which is the worst district in Brooklyn, and they will tell you that, though not a vicious quarter, Bond Street boasts the greatest toughs of Brooklyn. These canal rats dive into the cabins of the barges and steal everything in the way of eatables they can lay their hands on. They pelt the police officers and everybody who attempts to arrest their molestations with small pieces of coal, which they constantly keep as ammunition in their pockets. When hard pressed, they jump into the oil-bespangled waters of the canal and swim to the other side. They are hard cases, and are easily led into criminality if tempted, because it is their ambition to be toughs, to be terrors—the tigers of Bond St.

This sort of thing would cease if the canal side of Bond Street were to be enclosed and leased by the city. Now the rats can readily pass from one yard to the other and dodge their pursuers between piles of lumber whose intricacies are to them what the lava beds were to the Modocs[17]. Then all this would cease, and they could only enter when the gates were opened for the passage of wagons, nor could they pass from one yard to the other unless they could get to the canal itself and run from barge to barge as they do now. It is necessary to reclaim Bond Street from the condition of things that is springing up in our midst. The canal may be and probably is a necessity, but it ought to be as much hidden as the Regents' Canal in London, which actually passes through much of the city and skirts one of the parks without ever showing itself[18]. It is necessary—first, for the city's safeguard, because now conflagration is actually invited; secondly, for the Christianization of the young boys and girls of Bond Street, who are practically young heathens; and thirdly, for the city's revenue, which ought to receive a notable income from the Gowanus Canal. So tenacious, however, are men of the illegitimate profits that circumstances sometimes enable them to make, that it is doubtful if any movement will be made or any change affected until there is a terrible fire. Then, of course, outraged public sentiment will speak out in unmistakable language, and a system will be devised akin to that previously mentioned. But it would be far better if the change should be made before a third part of Brooklyn is in ashes, nor is it judicious to force patriotic citizens to pray that an avenging spark from heaven's own fires should fall upon

---

[17] Native Americans in California who fought a war against the U.S. army in 1872–73 on their native lava beds, which are now a national monument.
[18] Completed in 1820, the 8.6-mile waterway runs just north of central London, including past Regent's Park.

some oil tank and communicate its billowy flame to all the lumber and coal in that region.

E. R. G.

4

Sands Street

SANDS STREET'S HISTORY.

Its Early Grandeur and Its Later Decay.

A Fashionable Thoroughfare After Vinegar Hill Days—
The High-Toned People Gone, but Their Well-Built
Houses Standing.

Sunday, October 24, 1886

There is a certain grandeur in a ruin, which appeals irresistibly to the human heart. We are softened when we think that the owl hoots in the ruined palaces, and the spider builds her web in the halls of Afrasiab[1]. The mind dwells with tenderness and interest upon the past scenes of princely splendor that brightened those walls and loves to re-create the throngs of courtiers and attendants and soldiers whose sandaled footsteps pressed the bright tiles of the floor. But it is not so with those places that, having been scenes of grandeur, sink by almost imperceptible degrees into inferiority and degradation. There is a feeling of oppression that is almost pain when in some American city we contemplate a house that was once the comfortable, the splendid mansion of some family whose personal history is associated with the beginning of the city itself, and see it fallen from its high estate and degraded into a restaurant. These ideas rush tumultuously into the brain of anyone who may chance to stroll down

---

[1] A Turan king, archenemy of Iran, from the Persian epic *Shahmaneh*.

Sands Street. The first steps do not pain one in spite of the French proverb[2], for the bridge and bridge railway are such preponderating objects that no one can think of anything else when near them[3]. It is only when one gets to the corner of Washington Street[4] and sees that old wooden mansion stripped of its surrounding garden, painted gaudily and adorned with signs relating to its present career as a restaurant, oyster and ice cream saloon, that the mind takes in the situation[5]. It then for the first time becomes apparent to the inner sense that one is treading the pavement of a street with history.

"Tell me your story, old man," said a philanthropic rambler to a knifegrinder with a very expressive face. "Story! God bless your Honor for the quarter, but story I have none to tell." He meant that he had passed through no thrilling scenes, had killed no one, had undergone no perilous voyages and had done nothing save suffer, love and endure[6]. So with Sands Street. There is not and there never was any house that was once occupied by George Washington as his headquarters. There never was any hand-to-hand fighting with the Hessian mercenaries of the British invaders over its cobblestones[7]. One cannot stop at some corner and say with awe, "Here the heroic General Two Stars fell." Long Island, indeed, bore a conspicuous part in the sad annals of the

---

[2] *Le premier pas est le plus difficile*—the first step is the most difficult.
[3] Sands Street began at Fulton Street (now Cadman Plaza West) and passed east underneath tracks that brought Brooklyn Bridge railcars from sheds on the north side of the street to repair shops on the south. This whole section is now part of Cadman Plaza.
[4] Now Cadman Plaza East.
[5] No. 30–34, a wooden, boxy, three-story building on the southeast corner marked on an 1887 map as "hotel." It's now a parking lot.
[6] A reference to George Canning's poem "The Friend of Humanity and the Knife-Grinder," whose political satire E.R.G. seems to have missed.
[7] For the Revolutionary War, the British hired 30,000 German troops, collectively known as Hessians, many of whom fought in the Battle of Brooklyn in August 1776.

Revolution, and her sons and daughters felt the heavy hand of tyranny. But Sands Street was then in the mist cloudland of uncreated possibilities and was, indeed, part of Vinegar Hill, a bold bluff that rose up from the shore almost perpendicularly and whose summit was crowned with a gigantic tulip tree. Mr. Stiles, in his history of Brooklyn[8], believes this to have been a magnolia, but he is a better historian than botanist, for it was a liriodendron, one of our own Long Island forest trees, and far more majestic and beautiful than any magnolia. The South may take exception if it chooses. There was, at the time of the Revolutionary War, a noted tavern somewhere up the hill, where the British officers had bouts of punch drinking and fought mains of cocks and got up races. It may be that now and again some British hero, overcome by the fumes of Jamaica rum, may have slept under the shade of its spreading branches, but when the war was over and white-robed peace brought in her train commercial enterprises and manufacturing energy, the tulip hill tree became a rendezvous for engaged couples and those whose intentions went that way, and a syllabub house rose to accommodate the fair sex. Ice cream was not known to our grandmothers, but our grandfathers were not let off any more than their descendants, and had to pay for syllabubs, which were some kind of whipped cream[9]. About this time the first house was erected on Sands Street, on the corner of the Brooklyn Ferry Road (now Fulton Street)[10], and it was a factory for the manufacture of oilcloth. The enterprise was a failure, and the building was removed.

Sands Street did not really enter upon its career until the Brooklyn Ferry Road was a bustling line of business houses. Prior to that time, it had been a short cut to Flushing[11] for those who knew how to navigate around the Wallabout

---

[8] *A History of the City of Brooklyn,* by Henry Reed Stiles, 1867–70.
[9] They're old English dairy desserts, made with sweet wine.
[10] Now Cadman Plaza West.
[11] Flushing Avenue.

marshes. A plank causeway was made across the Wallabout to the great convenience of everybody, and the two brothers Joshua and Comfort Sands[12] sold the waterfront to the United States Government for a naval station[13]. The front part of Vinegar Hill was scarped to give dock facilities, and residents of Brooklyn began to see their way to affluence by commercial pursuits. They could afford themselves fine mansions, and they began to build them. Front Street was at first the scene of operations, but Sands Street followed so closely after that the palmy time of one was also the grand time of the other. Sands Street, if not the elder, was certainly the more fashionable of the two, and it owed this preeminence to the Episcopal church St. Ann's, which was torn down to make way for the bridge[14]. It was roughly built of limestone, and had small, narrow windows and was unsightly and awkward in the extreme, from an architectural point of view. But it was a rallying point for the Episcopalians, and soon after its erection Sands Street was adorned with finely built wooden villas, each one standing within its own garden. All the names illustrious in the history of Brooklyn will be found connected

---

[12] The Sandses were wealthy merchants, ropemakers and landowners in old Brooklyn. Joshua was also a politician, renaming what had been Congress Street "Adams Street" for the president who had appointed him to the powerful position of Collector of the Port of New York.

[13] The Brooklyn Navy Yard, on Wallabout Bay, in use from 1806–1966, was actually built on land sold to the government by John Jackson, who bought it after the Revolutionary War and started building ships there. The Sands brothers bought 160 adjoining acres in 1784, encompassing modern Downtown Brooklyn, Vinegar Hill and DUMBO.

[14] St. Ann's today is in Brooklyn Heights, on Montague Street. But the Episcopal congregation formed in 1778, meeting first in Joshua and Ann Sands's home, then in John Middagh's barn before building a proper church in 1795 on Washington Street, with a neighboring graveyard on Sands. By the 1860s, St. Ann's (named for Mrs. Sands) was in the way of the coming Brooklyn Bridge approach, and the congregation moved to 161 Clinton Street, at the corner of Livingston. Built from 1867–69, the gloriously Gothic structure still stands. See Chapter 10.

with Sands Street or Front. Mr. Joshua Sands lived on the latter street, but on the former were the mansions of the Tuckers, Jack Moore, General Swift, Mr. Treadwell, Mr. Clarke, Mr. Sackett, Mr. Ellison, Mr. Cole, Mr. Petit, Mr. Van Buren, Mr. Hunter, Mr. Sullivan, Mr. Hudson, Mr. Worthington, Mr. Stewart, Mr. Patchen, Mr. Gable, Mr. Cornell, Mr. Middagh, Mr. Hicks, Mr. Carter, Mr. March, Mr. Spooner, Mr. Bach, Mr. Waring, Mr. Van Nishard and last, but by no means least, the Pierreponts.

Of their houses perhaps two are still extant. One is a restaurant, where young Spriggs wastes his substance upon the ice cream and Amanda Jane[15], and this is supposed to be the veritable house built by Major Fanning C. Tucker[16], and the other is No. 86[17]. The latter is less transmogrified than the former, whose metamorphosis has been so irritatingly ludicrous that nothing save a word unblessed by the dictionaries will meet the exigencies of the case. No. 86 may be the bachelor home of Jack Moore[18]. It is near Jay Street, and it may be remarked that the fashionable part of Sands Street never went farther than Jay Street. The descent of the hill toward the United States Navy Yard wall is gentle, but as the bottom of the hill was occupied by a colony of jolly Dutch negroes, who were much given to exuberant whooping, and general rampageousness at holiday times, it may be that these circumstances prevented the further progress of fashionable building. No. 86 is in excellent condition, is covered with shingles and has an elaborate cornice surmounted by balustrading, through which is seen the cupola or lantern observ-

---

[15] He is hung up again on young men's social obligation to purchase ice cream for young women. "Spriggs" and "Amanda Jane" are probably meant to be generic names.

[16] A descendant of Joshua Sands (1837–78), a "gentleman of kindly manner and refinement," according to his Brooklyn *Union* obit.

[17] In the middle of the south side of the street, between Peal and Jay.

[18] John Moore was a lawyer and prominent citizen of Brooklyn in the early nineteenth century.

atory on the roof. It is exceedingly probable that the brick basement and high stoop are of later date, concessions as it were to the succeeding style of architecture. The observing eye will notice the excellence of the carpentry work and the obvious fact that this old house is as good as new and infinitely better than the majority of houses that are going up today in every part of the city like exhalations. They are merely shells, and when one thinks of the frozen winds from the west that blow upon Prospect Heights[19] one shudders at the thought of the cold time people are going to have in their fine-looking houses. The same wind has been blowing for nearly a hundred years upon Jack Moore's house, and yet the odds are that it is one of the warmest buildings in Brooklyn. But in those days people built their own houses. Nowadays speculative men forestall the legitimate growth of the city, buy up lots in good localities and erect trumpery houses on them, so that the man who wants to be in a certain location is in a measure forced to buy one of their hastily run up structures. As soon as circumstances indicate the probable opening up of a new locality, these speculators rush to the front. In this manner many men who would build their own houses are deterred from doing so, and the choicest parts of Brooklyn are covered with badly built, uncomfortable houses that are always needing repair.

The fact that further progress on Sands Street was stayed at Jay gives the reason for its downfall as a fashionable center. The new generation that wanted houses had to go elsewhere, and they stole across the Brooklyn Ferry Road to Hicks Street, which in its inchoate stage had been a part of Clover Hill[20]. This was the beginning of Brooklyn Heights, and also the decadence of Sands Street. It still remained the scene of splendid, refined hospitality, the home of a society possessing the geniality of New York with the culture of Boston, but it

---

[19] What we would call Park Slope, then bourgeoning and fashionable.
[20] An eighteenth-century name for what we now call Brooklyn Heights.

was felt to be, as it really was, old fashioned. But it was a good fashion nevertheless, and it gave to Brooklyn an impress of ideas that has never been lost, and perhaps never will fade from the minds of Brooklynites. It set a style that may be called distinctively Brooklynite. The fault of New York society ever has been that it has constantly paid too much respect to American money and to foreign rank. It was hospitable, it was genial in the past generation, but it was ostentatious, and its doors were always open to the rich of other cities, no matter how their money was acquired, and it was always ready to bow the knee before a British lord or a French count. The fault of Boston society has been that its high ideal has ever been a professor or a schoolmarm, both of whom are awkward and unpleasantly unpracticed in the ways of the world. Its ideals may have been wise, but they were uncouth; and the Boston Brahmin of Beacon Hill, the real B. B. B., never can rid himself of the consciousness that the Bostonian standard is one of mind. He always has had the foolish idea that this conferred intellectuality upon himself. This has made Boston bookish; for everyone can read, although few can understand; and the average Bostonian, therefore, affects to have everything, unconscious that he knows nothing. On Sands Street, an ideal was developed of splendor and aristocratic feeling in the manner of living, without ostentation, and of literary culture, without bookishness. Sands Street gave rise to a strong public opinion. A man in New York society can do what he pleases, for public opinion, that is to say, of his own set, is too weak to rebuke him. In Boston, and in Brooklyn, no man can be happy who defies the public opinion of his own circle. We owe much to Sands Street, but this is greatest boon of all.

Sands Street was after all the fashionable center during the lifetime of its founders, perhaps thirty years. As they died it became the abode of men who were comfortably well off, principally professional men, but not exactly the leaders of the social world. Neither can it be quite believed that they built for themselves. On each side of Adams Street, there are two houses, forming a group of four, which are precisely alike[21], and which are conspicuous by the ruined splendor of the iron railings and the iron work on each side of the high stoop for the support of gas lamps. These houses are of brick, solid, substantial and of a comfortable size and appearance, but they no doubt were the result of a speculation on the part of some builder. There are on other blocks pairs of houses and triads which seem to belong to the same epoch, from forty to fifty years ago. Then came an era of wooden houses of respectable appearance. Mixed in with these are two one-story wooden houses, with garden behind and grass plot in front, on which are two fine maple trees[22]. They are nearly opposite Charles Street[23], and they ought to have a history, though perhaps they have not. The imagination suggests that they have been improved, while the old mansions with which perhaps they are coeval have been degraded. There is an undeniable air of gentility about them, yet they are too distressingly small to have been occupied by gentlefolks in the old time, and they moreover are down the hill on the immense block from Jay to Bridge Street. Below the latter street we come into what was the quarter of Dutch negroes and which is still inhabited by colored people, though many white people are mingled with them. Some person with no idea of congruity has erected here an enormous chewing gum factory[24], profusely decorated with not-very-artistic terra cotta.

---

[21] Nos. 47 and 49, 48 and 50, on the western corners of Adams.
[22] Nos. 168 and 170, a few doors down from the corner of Gold Street.
[23] A short block once between York and Sands, parallel to Bridge and Gold. It was roughly in line with the alleyway, between the China Mansion/former YMCA and the Farragut houses, that connects Sands to Prospect Street today. There were many such narrow streets and alleyways throughout what's now DUMBO, since demapped and built over.
[24] The Adams & Son factory, No. 150–54. Thomas Adams is regarded as the father of chewing gum. Because he used chicle, the latex of the

It stands among the poor wooden shanties like a Triton among the minnows and no doubt in the near future it will be the source of happiness to myriads of schoolgirls. However, there is another equally incongruous building on the corner of Jay Street[25], a stupendous pile of brick upon a substructory of massive granite. It looks like a fortified mansion of a nobleman at the beginning of the sixteenth century, but in reality, it is the store of a wholesale grocer.

Prior to the building of St. Ann's Church, the Methodists of Brooklyn in the year A.D. 1791 erected a church upon Sands Street. It was exceedingly small and, about five years after the erection of St. Ann's, was torn down and rebuilt. It was painted white and was known as the white church. In 1842 it was again rebuilt but was in a year or two destroyed by fire, and the present building was erected in 1848. It is maintained in spite of the fact that its parishioners have all departed, but it is now a free church and a notification to that effect is posted upon one of its gloomy pillars, for it is in the severest classical style and it may be noted that classical architecture requires considerable elbow room. When it is crowded on one side by a pawnbroker's and on the side by a small hotel, its pylon becomes cavernous and accumulates dust at a fearful rate. One cannot but sympathize with the feelings of the congregation who maintain it at their own expense, although they worship elsewhere. It is the mother church of the Methodists in Brooklyn. And although it is a pity that it is not a block or two lower down on Sands Street yet, even where it is, close to Fulton Street[26], it must in time supply a real religious want. It is the only church on Sands Street, and it is clearly the fate of this old street never to be commercial. It is now a great resort of doctors, but ulti-

---

sapodilla tree, he called his product Chiclets, which were made on Sands Street until 1903.
[25] 96 Sands Street, on the southeast corner.
[26] No. 14–20 Sands Street, between Fulton and Washington. A five-story hotel was under construction at the time at the corner of Fulton.

mately it will be occupied almost entirely by boarding houses. Young men doing business in New York will be too glad to obtain rooms in these large, well-built brick houses that mark the third epoch of Sands Street. For their sake there ought to be one church at least on Sands Street. Whether this ought to prevent a license being given to the aspiring publican and sinner at the corner is another matter.

E.R.G.

POSTSCRIPT

The late references in this column to a pawnshop, hotel and rooming-house suggest the street's future. The church was sold in 1888, and the congregation used the money to dig up and move the bodies in the adjoining graveyard and build a new house of worship—the Sands Street Memorial Church, opened in 1891 at the corner of Clark and Henry streets, in Brooklyn Heights. (It was torn down in 1947.) Construction of the Manhattan Bridge began in 1901, cutting across Sands. But more significantly, the Sands Street Gate to the Navy Yard opened late in the summer of 1896, supplanting the entrance at York Street. "The new gate has had the effect of closing nearly all the saloons on York Street near the Navy Yard," the New York Sun *reported at the time, "and now their proprietors are looking for accommodations over on Sands Street."*

"It is seldom that a gate has as much to do with real estate prices," the Brooklyn Citizen *added, "but the completion of the Sands Street gate sent rents up on Sands Street and pulled down rents on York Street. Nearly all the liquor stores on York Street within two blocks of the old gate have been closed, and 'To let' signs meet the eye at every glance. Many of the York Street wine merchants have established themselves on Sands Street, and the character of that street has greatly improved within the past few months. It is well paved and well lighted and presents an animated appearance at night."*

Sands soon became notorious for its saloons and brothels, catering especially to men from the Navy Yard, who could walk out the Sands Street Gate into a sea of strong drink and sex, as well as those slumming it. There was a strong gay subculture here, too. It was in the 1920s a favorite cruising spot of the poet Hart Crane, who lived in Brooklyn Heights on Middagh Street, almost a straight shot to Sands. From the Brooklyn Bridge to the Navy Yard, it "was a dangerous erotic playground [with a] reputation for debauchery," Hugh Ryan writes in When Brooklyn Was Queer *(2019). "Sands Street was so synonymous with the gay sex trade that when Charles Demuth painted a watercolor of a businessman picking up two sailors there [ca. 1932], he simply entitled it* On 'That' Street, *certain that his audience would know which street he was referencing."*

After World War II, the street's culture was expunged by urban renewal. Most of its buildings were acquired and torn down for the Farragut Houses, a public-housing complex that opened in the 1950s, while other chunks were lost to the Brooklyn–Queens Expressway, Cadman Plaza and other projects. Today, no building seen by E.R.G., and almost none seen by any of the Navy Yard men who followed him, remain.

Sands Street, literally, is not what it used to be. —Ed.

5

Hicks Street

STREETS OF BROOKLYN.

The One Named by the Hicks Brothers.

A Study of an Old Map—Rise and Fall of a High-Toned Thoroughfare—Houses of the Past and Present.

Sunday, November 7, 1886

Fulton Street and Hicks Street were to Brooklyn what Broadway and Fifth Avenue are to New York. Fulton Street is still our Broadway, but Hicks, poor Hicks, has fallen from its proud prominence. The antiquarian pursuing his researches among the ancient streets of this city is somewhat surprised when he enters Hicks from Fulton[1]. There is nothing here that indicates to trained eye either antiquity or high repute. The grocery store where they sell the celebrated Pasi and Revellon cherries, the hotel where single men can have rooms for a quarter[2], the Bethel of Plymouth Church[3], a saloon, and the laundry of Fung Kau Charley are not exactly what one looks for in a street that once rivaled New York's famous Fifth Avenue. But the fact is that Hicks started in the

---

[1] Today, Old Fulton Street. You can't get very far onto Hicks from here anymore because of the Brooklyn–Queens Expressway.

[2] At the southeast corner of Fulton, No. 1–5. It was still a hotel in 1929, but the corner was destroyed by the BQE in the 1950s.

[3] The Bethel Mission, No. 15–17, a Sunday School adopted by Plymouth Church in 1867, the year the cornerstone for its new meeting hall and reading room was laid on Hicks Street. By 1929, the lot was home to a factory, and the block was later subsumed by the BQE.

middle. Though upon paper Hicks Street existed from Fulton to Clark, with all its cross streets exactly as they are now as far back as 1806, yet there were only two houses upon it for years and years. One of these was a stone house fronting on Fulton Street, or as it was then called, the Brooklyn Ferry Road, and the other was the residence of the founder of the Clark family, who had upon what is now Clark Street a very well-known ropewalk[4]. From the ropewalk to the Ferry Road, north and south and from Hicks Street to the river, was the old Middagh farm, and this passed by marriage to the original Hicks[5], who was the father of Jacob Middagh Hicks and his brother, and these two lived in the old stone house upon the Ferry Road. It was this old Hicks, though his name does not often appear in the annals of the past, who seems to have comprehended the future destinies of Brooklyn, and to have promulgated his ideas so thoroughly in his family that the two brothers were inspired by it. In the year 1806 Jeremiah Lott, surveyor, executed for them a map of their property, in which the present arrangement is distinctly shown with the identical names for all the cross streets[6]. While the poor benighted rich men of Brooklyn were building their fine villas and laying out their gardens upon Front and Sands streets, this map, big with all the promise and potency of the future, slumbered peacefully in a cabinet drawer in the old stone house. I can imagine the Hicks brothers taking it out upon occasions and talking over prospects as the news came that

---

[4] A long path where strands of material would be laid to be twisted into ropes. Captain William Clark's stretched at least three modern blocks, southeast, from just past the corner of what's now Columbia and Clark, past Willow and Hicks, off toward Henry.
[5] Jacob Hicks, son of English immigrant John Hicks, who crossed the ocean in 1642.
[6] The Center for Brooklyn History has digitized this map, which shows a portion of the ropewalk as well as Hicks, Willow and Columbia streets, and Poplar, Middagh, Cranberry, Orange, "Pine Apple" and Clark streets.

another fine house had been put up on Sands Street. They must have discussed often and often the grave question whether the time had not yet come to show their hand and develop the glory of Clover Hill, and lay out Hicks, Willow and Columbia streets and the cross streets to the river, Poplar, Middagh, Cranberry, Orange, Pineapple and Clark. The map ended there. Beyond the ropewalk extended the far away region of the Bedients' land, afterward the property of Henry Waring[7]. Beyond that was the Pierrepont estate, beyond that a corner of Remsen farm, and still Sands Street and Front grew and prospered, and Hicks Street and Willow and Columbia lay in the womb of the future.

Suddenly Jacob M. Hicks resolved to commence the great work. He abandoned the house on the Ferry Road to his brother John and built himself a new house on the corner of Pineapple, where his son Edwin, whom he used to call Adewine, speedily made friends with Captain Clark's pretty little daughter, and the two children surveyed the wonders of ropemaking or sat under the willows and talked about what they would do when they grew up. Adewine had also two little sisters, and, no doubt, the four had famous times. Jacob M. Hicks and his brother had laid out the property in lots of 25x100, and the house on the corner of Pineapple, with its garden, occupied four lots. Circumstances indicate that the West End Flat[8] was built over the site of the Hicks House, and the kindergarten children now play pretty much where the Hicks and Clark children played. Of the four corners on

---

[7] Bedient was a merchant in eighteenth-century Brooklyn, doing business with a Mr. Hubbell and then a Mr. Kimberly. Kimberly went into business in 1791 with Henry Waring. His house, the Waring Mansion, on Fulton Street (now Cadman Plaza West) near Johnson, was a local landmark at least into the mid nineteenth century.

[8] No. 97, on the northeast corner, which seems to still be standing. Also known as 55 Pineapple Street.

Pineapple, one is occupied by D. H. Lamke[9], one is the original house built by Admiral Stringham[10], who married one of the daughters of Jacob M. Hicks, another one is a substantial brick mansion of some antiquity[11], and the fourth is the flat. This was the true beginning of Hicks Street, which started in the middle and worked its way north and south. Mr. Lamke's house is an old clapboard frame building with old-fashioned quarter windows on the side of semi-ecclesiastical character, with a hip roof, and a patched-up old chimney. No. 101, which was the Stringham house, is cased on the outside with cedar shingles, and has dormer attics with fan transoms to the windows[12]. There are quarter windows on the sides. The chimney is very tall and of brick, and strikingly well built. All the houses in the vicinity are of much later date, but are solid and handsome, and give full evidence of what Hicks used to be in its palmy time, which was subsequent to 1835. But at the corners of the next cross street, which is Clark, we come upon very interesting spots.

The house No. 121, which is now occupied by Mr. H. M. Peckham[13], is covered with cedar shingles like Admiral Stringham's, and has dormer attics and a hip roof[14]. It has two tall chimneys, and these are united by a wooden balus-

---

[9] Daniel Lamke was a grocer who lived at No. 102, on the northwest corner. In 1894, he received a permit to build a five-story brick building for nine families and a store—the building at that address today.
[10] Silas Stringham was a celebrated Navy veteran in the nineteenth century who retired with the rank of Rear Admiral. When he died in 1876, naval stations and ships flew their flags at half-mast. He lived at 124 Hicks Street, at the corner of Clark, after he moved from No. 101.
[11] No. 104, on the southwest corner.
[12] The house occupied what's now part of the footprint of the St. George Tower, 111 Hicks Street, completed in 1929. In 1887, the hotel occupied just eight lots between Pineapple and Clark, Henry and Hicks, but would eventually take over the entire block.
[13] Henry Peckham was a coal dealer. He died in 1889.
[14] This was at the northeast corner of Hicks and Clark, also later subsumed by the St. George Hotel complex.

trading, obviously put there for the protection of the men occupied in sweeping off snow from the roof in wintry weather. An old maple tree rears its tall form in front of this house, which tradition connects with Jacob M. Hicks, but incorrectly. On the opposite side of the way are three brick houses built very plainly, with brownstone trimmings, with dormer attics and heavy cornices, one of which is a fine specimen of carving[15]. These three are in a remarkable state of preservation for American houses, and it is doubtful if their equal can be obtained for love or money nowadays. On the southwest corner is No. 124, a fine mansion of Ohio sandstone[16]. This was built by Admiral Stringham, who sold his first house on the corner of Pineapple. This house is still owned by his widow, who leases it to Henry Ward Beecher[17]. This block from Clark Street to Pierrepont is exceedingly long and marks what may be called the flood tide of the fortunes of Hicks Street. There are many good houses on it. No. 130 is a double house of Ohio stone, now occupied by Dr. H. C. Hutchison[18]. By all appearances it was built prior to the erection of the Stringham mansion. A queer, grand house is No. 159, a frame house of clapboards, painted white, with green shutters[19]. It has an overhanging cornice of ornamental cha-

---

[15] Probably Nos. 118, 120 and 122, on the northwest corner. The apartment building now there, at 35 Clark Street, was built in 1922.

[16] Demolition permits were issued for this property in 1922, and the apartment building that goes by 32 Clark Street was built shortly thereafter.

[17] Beecher, who died just a few months after this column was published, was one of the most prominent citizens in Brooklyn if not the country. The pastor at Plymouth Church, on Orange Street, he was a noted orator, abolitionist, social reformer and scandal maker, accused of adultery.

[18] A demolition permit was filed in 1944, and a new-building permit, for the apartment tower now there, was first filed in 1948.

[19] Today, the site of No. 155–57. It's unclear when it was torn down. The address last appears in the newspaper record in 1888, when it was the home of the Brophy family.

racter and stands in its own little garden. No. 150 is also an old frame house, with dormer attics, which seem as if they had been an afterthought, for they appear to have been pressed out of the line of rectitude by the elaborately carved wooden cornice, with its brackets and frieze[20]. The new houses, with their bright brick and terra cotta and their mingling of styles—Byzantine Renaissance and Queen Anne—and their decorations of Tiffany Glass in the spandrils of the windows agree well enough with the old stagers on the street. The only thing that jars is the huge flat.

It may be said the Mansion House, which is on this block, is just as big as any of the flats that so spoil the appearance of the Heights[21]. But the Mansion House has a great frontage, and this carries off the weight of one of the wings. Beside this the center is of considerable age, and great care was taken that the addition should be in harmony with the first part. This central portion, which is now half hidden by the quaint wooden portico, was originally a seminary. In the days when old Joshua Sands was president of Brooklyn village, receiving a salary of $300 for his services, in the year 1827, a meeting was held to discuss the founding of a Female Collegiate Seminary upon Clover Hill, and the undertaking seemed so certain of success that it was immediately carried out. In those days two things were impressed strongly upon the public mind. One was the healthiness of Brooklyn and the other was the comparative unhealthiness of New York. The founders

---

[20] Now a tall and slender white-brick apartment house, built around the turn of the twentieth century.

[21] A hotel at 139–153 Hicks, occupying more than six lots, which was one of the great Heights landmarks. It began as the Waring family's villa, then became a series of private schools and finally the hotel, which added several buildings to the original. It remained an old-fashioned hotel until it closed in 1930, unable to compete with the St. George and its swimming pool, ballrooms and radios in every room. In 1935, a developer announced he would build an apartment building there, also called Mansion House, which still stands at No. 145.

of the seminary do not seem to have relied much upon home support, but they thought their collegiate institution would be largely patronized by families from the sister city and from the South. The patronage of the South was then the glittering prize which dazzled men of speculative minds. The enterprise was a failure, and the building was eventually sold to General Edwin Yale[22], who converted it into a quiet family hotel, such as it has been ever since. It was much used by Southerners in the heated term and was quite a feature in the life of Brooklyn. To one individual however it was a source of heartburning and anger. Edwin Hicks, when he grew to man's estate, married the pretty Clark girl and built for himself a house on Clark Street, or, perhaps, only enlarged the old Clark house. His gardens went back to the Mansion House, and he was constantly annoyed by finding on his choice beds of tulips pieces of paper, torn up letters, etc., which the boarders of the hotel had thrown out of the windows, and which the wind blew upon his flowers. This is one of the traditions of the Mansion House but is obviously untrue. Mr. Hicks used to raise grapes in great abundance, as his father had done, and the probabilities are that the help in the hotel used to steal his fruit and that he complained about it, and that henceforward there was trouble between the neighbors. Probably to this source may be traced another ludicrous story about him. His father, when the son dutifully acquainted him with his desire to marry Miss Clark, said that he was satisfied but would like to see him engaged in some business first. Edwin said he would think about it. A short time afterward old Jacob M. accosted him with the query, "Well, Adewine, have you thought about the matter?" "Yes, father," he replied, "I have, and, upon mature consideration, I have come to the conclusion that I will follow your business." Old Mr. Hicks was more ornamental than useful, had never

---

[22] A Brooklyn lawyer remembered really only for having been the proprietor of the Mansion House.

had any occupation[23], and was known as Gentleman Hicks all his life. So that the son's retort was a square hit. But probably this story is no truer than the other.

I pause. A sympathetic little thrill goes through my mind as I contemplate the coming fall of Hicks Street. Hitherto Hicks had been the great street of Brooklyn, and its progress was uninterrupted until it came to Pierrepont Street, the beginning of the Pierrepont property. This extended as far south as Remsen Street. Just as the Hicks brothers had a cruel map waiting its time to come out and crush Sands and Front, so Hezekiah B. Pierrepont, the father of Henry E. Pierrepont, had a map stowed away, biding its time to come out and crush Hicks[24]. His system of laying out his lots was diametrically opposed to the prosperity of Hicks. His idea was to make the cross streets of the first importance, to fence his lots upon them, and to reduce Hicks Street to the condition of a back street containing nothing but garden walls. There was courage as well as calculation in this, for he was running counter to the received opinion of Brooklyn society. The curious traveler who wanders up Hicks Street finds as soon as he arrives at Pierrepont Street a new system, another air, and it must be confessed a grander conception. The charm of the Heights was in the view of the bay, of Staten Island and Hoboken and the purple hazes of the distant

---

[23] Other sources say Jacob and his brother John operated the ferry between Brooklyn and New York.
[24] Hezekiah moved to Brooklyn in 1803 and reopened Philip Livingston's distillery at the foot of what's now Joralemon Street, making a fortune off his Anchor Gin. He bought up real estate in Brooklyn Heights, from about modern Pierrepont to Remsen streets, Fulton to the water, planning for its development. He also invested in Robert Fulton's steam ferry. His son Henry unified the city's disparate ferry companies and operated bonded warehouses on the waterfront, using his profits and inheritance to become a leading citizen in Brooklyn, laying out the city's street grid and founding both Green-Wood Cemetery and the Long Island Historical Society (now the Center for Brooklyn History), among involvements in other civic organizations.

mountains of New Jersey, of the glittering sails and puffing steamers. The Pierrepont system made the most of this beyond all question, but it ended the career of Willow Street and Columbia and gave a mortal stab to the prosperity of Hicks. Yet all who examine must see that the houses upon the Pierrepont part of the Heights are grander and more palatial than anything in that part of Brooklyn.

A curious instance of the new order of things is visible in 47 Pierrepont Street, the house on the northeast corner of Hicks[25]. The brick wall of the kitchen, offices and garden is surmounted by peculiar tiles of green porcelain, evidently from China. They are perforated, or else they are in pieces and were cemented together. They are of a strange style of decoration, a four-legged zigzag, set in a hexagonal frame surrounded by square scroll work. At first sight these look like stanniferous, glazed tiles, but a more careful examination shows that they are really porcelain and that a small amount of manganese was mixed with the petuntse or feldspar glaze. This gives the peculiar transparency to the manganese, which, as ordinarily used, is a rich, opaque glaze. The original builder of this house must have been one of the old ten merchants for whom Brooklyn was famous. There was a coterie of merchant princes in those days in this city who formed its public opinion and who laid the foundations for its present greatness. To them Brooklyn owes its great shipping interests. Though the list of foreign steamer companies will not compare with that of New York, yet the tonnage of sailing vessels coming to the docks and warehouses of Brooklyn is surprisingly large. So long as that element interested itself in public matters, there was a provision of unmatched sagacity. But of late years the same interest in the welfare of Brooklyn is not shown, and for want of a little foresight, nuisances grew up at Newtown Creek and around the Gowanus

---

[25] This site is presently occupied by a large and somewhat magnificent apartment building, 187 Hicks, built ca. 1929.

Canal and at Brighton Beach, which are bad for the interests of the city and injurious to its morals[26].

Hicks Street was crushed. The Remsen property commenced at the south side of Remsen and extended to Joralemon Street, but it was not thought expedient to build upon it, for the old Joralemon property barred the way, lying across from Hicks Street like a sleeping lion. Joralemon was a Hollander from Flatbush, in which charming village he had followed the occupation of a wheelwright[27]. He had a little money and he invested it in this property, which had a bad repute. It had been used as a hospital for English soldiers in the Revolutionary War, and Flatbush negroes had seen headless Hessians with glaring eyes as big as billiard balls[28]. Joralemon Street, however, was bound to a main thoroughfare, for it was an Indian trail—one of the paths by which they carried their canoes to the river[29]. Joralemon after his purchase went into the business of a milk peddler and made money and reared a family of seven children. To all propositions about opening up Hicks Street the milkman gave an emphatic "Nein." When he died his seven children agreed tumultuously to open the street and each built a house on Hicks Street beyond Joralemon. But the public fancy had strayed elsewhere in the meanwhile, and Hicks had fallen, never to rise again. Changed in flank by the tremendous attacks of the Pierrepont cross streets and brought to a halt by the obstinacy of old Joralemon, speculation in Hicks Street lots was dead, and this drove the attention of purchasers into other directions. Even the subsequent building of the Episco-

---

[26] He refers to the industry around the Creek and Canal, which he believed bred criminality, and the racetrack at Brighton Beach.
[27] Teunis Joralemon (1760–1841) bought thirteen acres of Philip Livingston's estate in 1803, south of what's now Joralemon Street. He notoriously opposed streets being cut through his property.
[28] Washington Irving's Headless Horseman was a Hessian, decapitated at the Battle of White Plains, 1776.
[29] The Natives who lived in Brooklyn Heights called it Ihpetonga.

palian Grace Church[30] and the opening up of Grace Court in rear of the gardens of the Remsen Street houses had little or no effect. The structures on Hicks Street between Remsen and Joralemon are chiefly stables, and the six brownstone houses[31] on the corner of Joralemon were evidently built to be sold, according to the present order of things. Hicks Street on this block is Hick Streets no more, but a mere ghost of itself. The true, the famous, the historic Hicks ends with Pierrepont Street. After that, the tide runs out, and its course is bound in shallows and in miseries. It goes, indeed, down to the Bay of Gowanus, and it terminates in a slip, named Hicks, but it is the Hicks Street of the directories, not of the hearts and memories of old Brooklynites[32].

E.R.G.

---

[30] No. 246, built 1847–48 in the Gothic Revival style.
[31] On the northeast corner, Nos. 255–265 Hicks Street still stand.
[32] Today, Hicks Street runs more than two miles, from Old Fulton to Red Hook Park. Less than a mile runs alongside the Brooklyn–Queens Expressway in Cobble Hill and Carroll Gardens; less than a mile runs through Brooklyn Heights.

6

Pierrepont, Montague and Remsen Streets

HEART OF THE HEIGHTS.

The Cross Streets of Hezekiah B. Pierrepont Not Accidental.

How the Hand of the British Was Heavy on Brooklyn— They Transformed the Fair Face of Clover Hill—The Later and Lasting Influence.

Sunday, November 21, 1886

Brooklyn Heights are the heart of the city, and Pierrepont, Montague and Remsen streets are the heart of the Heights. How curious, how unusual, is the state of things existing here, where one finds the grandest houses of all Brooklyn in close proximity to the great thoroughfare—Fulton Street! Generally, in the growth of a community from the condition of a village to that of a metropolitan city, the quarter where the wealthy citizens live is pushed farther and farther off, until at length it is many miles away and completely divorced from the business and financial streets. It has been so in New York. There was a time when the Strand, or State Street, as it was afterward called, was the home of all that was refined and distinguished in our neighbor, and from this point the good quarter crept round the island to Hanover Square, where now the cotton men congregate, and thence it advanced to Franklin Square, known all over the world as the location of the Harper publishing house[1]. But the antiquarian has a deeper interest in it, for he knows that it was here that the Walton House stood, the home of the wealthiest merchant in America[2], who furnished the model for Mr. Wharton, one of the characters in Fenimore Cooper's "Spy."[3] Thence the polite part of the town crept up always on the East Side until it reached Second Avenue, where many good old families still persist in living. Then it deserted the East Side and went over to the West Side and established itself on Bleecker Street and worked northward until it created Washington Square. Then Fifth Avenue was born, and the rich have gone north and still north until they are now on Washington Heights and Fordham Heights. There has been a continual migration, until now the businessman must go to his business place by the elevated road, for he has passed beyond the capacity of his coach horses. Wall Street, Broad Street and the lower part of Broadway form the financial part of New York, but between them and the heart of the fashionable world there is an immense gulf bridged by the speed of iron horse alone[4].

How different is the state of matters in our own city, where one finds existing still that concentration which belongs to the infancy of a city. Here in November, 1886, the wealthy merchant of Brooklyn has no farther to go to his business than he had in 1815, or than the wealthy Mr. Wal-

---

[1] Once the intersection of Pearl, Dover and Cherry streets in lower Manhattan, Franklin Square was named for Benjamin Franklin. It was eliminated in the twentieth century by the growing tangle of highways on and around the Brooklyn Bridge.

[2] William Walton, Jr., built in 1752 one of the most impressive houses in the city on what's now Pearl Street. It was terribly damaged by fire in 1853, but survived until about 1881, when it was replaced by a factory.

[3] A historical novel published in 1821, *The Spy: A Tale of the Neutral Ground* is set in and around a Westchester estate, owned by Mr. Wharton, during the Revolutionary War.

[4] "Iron horse" was slang for a steam-powered locomotive. New York businessmen lived so far from downtown they had to take the train to work.

ton had to go in 1767 in New York[5]. And as we see in a rising town in southwest Missouri (the garden spot of America, east of the Rockies) the Lyceum where the itinerant lecturer thunders forth the story of the lost arts cheek by jowl with the First Methodist Episcopal Church, next to which is the First National Bank, next to which is the clapboard mansion of the bank president, next to which Mr. Whackboy's Institute of Engineering, and so on. So we discover in the cross streets established by Hezekiah Beers Pierrepont the same mingling. The financial houses of Brooklyn, the banks and insurance companies, are a broad fringe on Remsen, Montague and Pierrepont streets; farther on are the palatial mansions of our old families mixed in with splendid churches, academies, and historical societies and clubs. It is as if there had been some mighty spell muttered, some tremendous charm spoken when these streets were first opened, which allowed them to grow in magnificence but did not permit them to change. They have not changed, and all the signs that reveal to observant eyes the future of localities point unerringly to the prediction that they will not change. Some differences for the better or for the worst may come to Hicks and to some of the lower cross streets on the Heights—Orange, Cranberry, Pineapple, etc. But upon those cross streets on which Hezekiah Beers Pierrepont set the seal of his genius there will come no blight. Even the towering flats are powerless to harm them.

Before telling the story of these cross streets it may not be amiss to endeavor to recast the eidolon or appearance of the Heights when the region was known as Clover Hill, away back to these days when Mr. Walton built his splendid home in Franklin Square, and before the British army of occupation commenced their ravages and devastations on Long Island. Sufficient stress has not been laid upon the dreadful

---

[5] It's less than a mile down Pearl Street from old Franklin Square to State Street.

setback to Brooklyn caused by the British army. At that time part of Furman Street was occupied with stores, and Mr. Livingston had a distillery upon the waterfront, foot of Joralemon Street, and a grand mansion on the Heights which was afterward purchased by old Joralemon[6]. Mr. George Cornell had a very splendid mansion (afterward the Pierrepont mansion)[7] on the site near the house of A.A. Low[8], and Mr. Nicholas Bamper had the stone house on Fulton Street, or Brooklyn Ferry Road, which was afterward the property of the Hicks brothers[9]. The Middaghs had a house on their farm, which was south of Mr. Bamper's gardens and west of it and north of it. The Remsens' property adjoined the Cornell property[10]. The Ferry Road was the King's Highway, and stretched eastward to Jamaica, but was for much of the way upon the old track from the bottom lands of Flatbush to the Brooklyn Ferry. The whole slope of the Heights from Fur-

---

[6] Philip Livingston owned forty acres of Brooklyn Heights, from roughly the waterfront to Boerum Place, Joralemon to State Street. His house was approximately on Hicks Street, and Garden Place was once a path through his gardens. Teunis Joralemon bought the property in 1803.

[7] A landmark of old Brooklyn referred to as "the Four Chimneys" for its four chimneys. Stiles writes that it was built by *John* Cornell, a son of Whitehead Cornell, a British loyalist during the Revolution who reportedly faced no repercussions for his politics. The family was "among the most respectable citizens of old Brooklyn," Stiles writes.

[8] Abiel Abbot Low's house still stands at 3 Pierrepont Place. Low was a prominent businessman and citizen and the father of Seth Low, a mayor of both Brooklyn and the consolidated, five-borough New York.

[9] Stiles mentions a Lodewyck Bamper, who had a country home at the corner of Clark and Willow in the mid eighteenth century. (Another source places the Bamper Estate south of Clark, from the waterfront to Henry.) He was a wealthy immigrant who started a glass factory on State Street, between Hicks and Columbia. Stiles reports he had two daughters. See Chapter 5 about the Hicks house, which was on the southeast corner of Fulton (now Old Fulton) and Hicks.

[10] In short: west of Fulton Street, from the Ferry to Livingston, there were a few families with large land holdings, living in scattered houses along scant roads.

man Street was overgrown with stunted cedars, while the top was level ground in clover and grass, save where the gardens blossomed and smiled around the mansions. Behind the gardens there were great stretches of orchards filled with fruit trees, apples, pears, plums, apricots, cherries and grapevines that reached to the Flatbush trackway or spoorweg, which was itself beyond question founded upon an Algonquin trail[11]. Beyond the Flatbush spoor and along the King's Highway stretched the primeval woods of Long Island, cedar and pine in the sandy parts, and hard woods in the bottoms, while around the Wallabout and Gowanus swamps flourished the maple, the sweet gum and the pepperidge. Red-leafed sumachs grew everywhere. The mansions were of wood with an inner casing of brickwork and were of that severe classical style that in spite of criticism is in reality more suited to wood than it ever was, or could ever be, to stone, even in the days of Phidias[12]. Much elaborate carving adorned the façades, which looked upon the bay. And if anyone believes that there were more comfortable houses then, in any part of the habitable world, or finer gardens, or a more glorious outlook, that person is mistaken. Mr. Livingston was the head of the Low Church party in America[13], one of the brightest spirits of the Revolution[14], and his mansion was the headquarters of the patriots of New York and Long Island[15]. There was no place on the Island of Manhattan that gathered together so many eminent men in the cause of liberty.

---

[11] The road to Flatbush was more or less modern Flatbush Avenue, just not as rigidly straight. It is believed to follow a Lenape trail.
[12] Fifth-century BCE Greek sculptor whose Statue of Zeus at Olympia was one of the Seven Wonders of the Ancient World.
[13] The more liberal, less Catholic wing of the Anglican church.
[14] He signed the Declaration of Independence—the only Brooklynite to do so. He also financed "at least fifteen separate slaving voyages," according to the Brooklyn Public Library.
[15] Philip Livingston's magnificently large colonial country house was located approximately at today's 277 Hicks Street.

This old Joralemon House, where the Flatbush negroes used to see headless Hessians, was one of the cradles of American independence, and when the heirs pulled it down for the continuance of Hicks Street, they did no good to the latter, which was dead, and they demolished a building that should have been dear to every American heart.

The British came, and through a series of misunderstandings and fatalities, won the Battle of Long Island[16]. Their wounded were in the deserted mansions, their officers were billeted upon the houses of Flatbush and Brooklyn, and the men were encamped in tents. They established their commissariat and quartermaster departments in Brooklyn, or, as they called it, Brookland, and the inhabitants of Long Island were assessed for hay and forage, grain and firewood. They commenced building a fort upon the Heights[17], in the vicinity of Pierrepont and Henry streets, and the unhappy Long Islanders had to furnish fascines and gabines for the interior slopes of the earthworks. Then when Fort Stirling was finished, barracks of wood were erected within the enceinte, and this necessitated further requisitions for building timber. In this way the western end of Long Island was stripped of its valuable woods, only those trees being left that were the property of enthusiastic Tories[18]. When the British evacuated Long Island they left behind them an almost ruined country[19]. The splendid orchards had been cut down, the forests had been annihilated, the fisheries had been abandoned, the rising commerce around the ferry had given place to the low haunts of dissipation and debauchery that clung upon the rear of every army[20]. But the recuperative energies inherent in Long Island enabled it to survive the blow. And

---

[16] Also now called the Battle of Brooklyn, August 1776.
[17] Fort Stirling was built by the Americans, who soon lost control of it.
[18] American colonists loyal to the British.
[19] The British evacuated in 1783, and the Americans dismantled Fort Stirling. Today, its former site is occupied by Fort Sterling Park.
[20] Likely a reference to the King's Head Tavern. See Chapter 2.

in this Brooklyn was far happier than Newport, in Rhode Island, which never recovered from the shock of British occupation.

I think it may be counted as a remarkable piece of good fortune that just at the time when Brooklyn was beginning to stand once more upon its feet, Mr. Hezekiah B. Pierrepont became one of its citizens[21]. He was a very remarkable man, uniting keen observation and an intense love of nature with great business capacity. Generally, a businessman despises the beautiful and sees nothing but the main chance. But the first Pierrepont of Brooklyn was a man of far finer strain, and had been a traveler and a bold, adventurous merchant, risking much, gaining much, enduring much in the troubled years of the great Revolutionary War. In 1802 he planted the tree of his fortunes in Brooklyn by the purchase of the Benson estate. This property reached from the Debevoise farm[22] to Remsen Street. He had previously married Miss Constable[23], and with his father-in-law[24] was interested to an immense pecuniary extent in the wild lands of Northern New York. In 1816, fourteen years afterward, he bought from Robert Debevoise fourteen acres that lay between the Benson property and Love Lane, thus rounding his possessions to a compact estate of sixty acres[25]. The Cornell mansion was on the Benson property and here he took up his residence, and when in 1819 the Village of Brooklyn was incorporated, he became one of the trustees and gave to the care of his trust all the resources of his fine mind. Living upon the Heights, he very soon discovered that though the Four Chimneys was

---

[21] He moved to Brooklyn in 1803.
[22] The De Bevoise land stretched from about the waterfront to Fulton Street (now Cadman Plaza West) between roughly Love Lane and Pierrepont Street.
[23] He married Anna Maria Constable in 1802.
[24] William Kerin Constable, a prominent New York businessman.
[25] Sixty acres is roughly the size of a rectangle from the waterfront to Fulton, Love Lane to Livingston.

a fine object from the bay and commanded a fine view, yet it did not obtain proper ventilation in the heated Summer term, which lasts a long while. The Four Chimneys, as his mansion was called[26], faced east and west and therefore received no benefit from the cooling breezes which blow in the Summer from the southwest in the morning and from the southeast in the afternoon. He built, therefore, an L addition to his house upon the south wing, which was faced south and north, and the coolness which ensued during the hot months convinced him that all houses ought, if possible, to be faced that way in Brooklyn.

Jeremiah Lott, the surveyor, had made for the Hicks Brothers a map in 1806, in which their property was laid out in streets and cross streets in blocks 200 feet square as it is today, and the Brooklynites were greatly disposed to take their arrangement of streets as the model. But Mr. Pierrepont was dissatisfied. He pointed out the facts as he saw them with regard to ventilation, declared that the Hicks' streets, which were only forty feet wide, were too narrow, and had not sufficient space for front yards, and that the blocks were too small. At his own expense he purchased the lots on both sides of Hicks Street and widened Hicks Street from Cranberry Street to his line, making it fifty feet. Hicks Street was opened in 1819, and in 1825 Mr. Pierrepont made the proposition that a public promenade 150 feet in width should be established along the front of the Heights. He engaged Mr. Silas Ludlam, now City Surveyor, to map out his proposed promenade. But old Judge Radcliffe[27], who had built his house on Columbia Street, one of the Hicks' streets, made such a violent opposition to it because it went in front of his house that Mr. Pierrepont very handsomely withdrew his proposal. And although he had the survey and plan of the

---

[26] A plaque in a stone at the foot of Montague Street marks the former location of this famous house, where Washington quartered during the Battle of Brooklyn.
[27] Peter W. Radcliffe, a prominent New York lawyer.

proposed promenade made while he was Village Trustee and Chairman of the Street Committee, he paid for the survey and map out of his own pocket. He said that though he was convinced that it was of the utmost importance to the public and that, the Hicks Brothers being in favor of it, there would be no opposition save that of Judge Radcliffe, yet he valued the friendship of that gentleman and would not persist against his wishes. So Brooklyn lost a promenade that would have been grand and unique among cities, and a source of constant gratification to all cultured minds to whom the beauties of nature give the highest possible enjoyment[28]. Mr. Pierrepont loved the Heights with an intense feeling, and he longed to secure to his fellow citizens in perpetuity what was to him a constant wellspring of delight. His highest happiness was to pace up and down watching the panorama of the clouds, and the water, the ships and bustling ferryboats, the Battery point, the ridged hogback of Staten Island and the curving shores of New Jersey. He died in 1838.

But before he died, he had created the heart of the Heights. He opened Pierrepont Street in 1829, Constable Street some time afterward, in 1830, Clinton the same year and Remsen, or part of it, in 1835. In Pierrepont Street, Constable (afterward called Montague[29]) and Remsen streets, he carried out thoroughly his ideas with regard to ventilation. Pierrepont was sixty feet from curb to curb, ten feet from curb to court wall, making it eighty feet wide, or the same as Broadway. He never would sell a lot unless with the condition that the purchaser should put upon it a good brick or stone house. The consequence was that he could not at first sell his lots, because he was in advance of his time, for he realized the future of Brooklyn as his fellow citizens could not,

---

[28] This idea was resurrected in the 1940s, during planning for the BQE, and the modern Promenade opened in 1950–51.

[29] After a different Pierrepont relative, Lady Mary Wortley Montagu, a writer, inoculation advocate and early feminist.

not having the same brains. One of his friends, Rev. Evan M. Johnson[30], remonstrated him on the strictness of his ideas. "Mr. Pierrepont," he said, "why don't you sell your lots without conditions, as other gentlemen do? See how briskly the Hickses are selling their lots on Hicks and Willow and Columbia, and the Middaghs upon John Street (afterward Henry)!" "Why," said Mr. Pierrepont, "Johnson, don't you see that every good building which goes up on my lots increases the value of the remainder, whereas every small building that goes up on a lot has the opposite tendency? Speculative ardor may for the moment increase above its value property anywhere, but the true value of building lots will always be based upon the buildings on the adjoining lots." And he advised Mr. Johnson not to sell to anyone whose intention was to put up a wooden house. Finding that the public was slow to comprehend him, he built two large brick houses at the corner of Pierrepont and Henry streets. This last street was opened by the Middaghs, who called it John, but when it came upon Mr. Pierrepont's streets he insisted upon calling it Henry, after his son, the present Henry Evelyn Pierrepont, and this name survived[31]. Then Thomas March[32] built a brick house on the opposite corner, and next Cyrus P. Smith[33] erected a large mansion. The first house, however, of remarkable appearance was built by Henry Young[34] and is now occupied

---

[30] Evan Malbone Johnson moved to Brooklyn in 1824 and built St. John's Church, at Washington and Johnson streets, on his farmland (now part of Cadman Plaza). Later he established St. Michael's Church, on High Street, near Navy Street (now part of the Farragut Houses), to minister to the poor. He died in 1865 at home, on Pearl Street, near Myrtle Avenue (now part of Metrotech).

[31] Historians believe Henry Street was named for the Middaghs' family doctor, Thomas W. Henry, but this strikes me as more plausible.

[32] One of the foremost wine merchants in New York at the time.

[33] The mayor of Brooklyn, 1839–42.

[34] A successful New York merchant.

by John T. Martin[35]. Then Samuel Boyd[36] built a fine house on the corner of Hicks and Pierrepont streets. The house was afterward bought by Mr. Henry E. Pierrepont as a dwelling for his mother when, in 1846, her residence, the old mansion called the Four Chimneys, had to be pulled down to open Montague Street to Wall Street Ferry[37]. Monsieur St. Felix[38], a rich French gentleman, built the double house in the middle of the block on the north side of Pierrepont Street[39], and about that time Dr. Bethune's church was built[40]. The first occupant of the house built by Mr. Pierrepont on the corner of Pierrepont and Henry streets was Arthur Tappan[41]. To tell who lives upon the Heights now would be simply to transfer to the columns of the EAGLE the pages of the Elite Directory.

E.R.G.

---

[35] This was No. 28 Pierrepont. A massive front garden, circled by a drive, led to the front of a colonnaded and well-terraced square house, crowned with a one-windowed room. Martin (1816–97) was a wealthy factory owner invested in real estate, railroads, banks and especially trust companies. He was known for his art collection.

[36] A physician (1805–60) who moved to Brooklyn in 1823. He served many years as the city's health officer (like a health commissioner).

[37] This line operated from 1853 until 1912, when it could no longer compete with surface-level transit options over the Brooklyn Bridge.

[38] John Reynaud St. Felix (1790–1854) appears in the newspaper record hundreds of times, in assessment rolls, legal proceedings and real estate transactions, but never for personal or professional reasons, aside from a brief notice of his death (there was no full obituary) and a formal complaint to the health warden about a large amount of manure deposited near his premises. He married Anna Maltby, and they had eight children before being buried in Green-Wood.

[39] No. 71–73, torn down ca. 1925.

[40] Rev. George W. Bethune moved to Brooklyn in 1850 to take over the new Dutch Reform Church on the Heights, which opened in 1851 on the northwest corner of Pierrepont and Monroe Place. He retired ca. 1860, and the church was torn down in the 1920s.

[41] A silk merchant who devoted his life and fortune to abolition.

7

Fulton Street

BROOKLYN'S BACKBONE.

Fulton Street the Father of All the City Thoroughfares.

Its Ancient History and Varied Nomenclature. The Wretchedness of the Old Ferry in Knickerbocker Times— Brooklyn's Healthiness the Secret of Its Growth.

Sunday, November 28, 1886

One of the questions that the minions of the Civil Service Reform Commission ought to put to aspirants for Brooklyn offices should be, "Which is the first avenue or street that crosses Fulton Street?" The answer is "Navy Street." All the other streets lose their identity and become something else[1]. But, indeed, before one comes to the great open space[2] in front of the Municipal Buildings[3], there is no thought of in-

---

[1] In Brooklyn Heights and Downtown Brooklyn, streets intersect with Fulton and come out the other side with different names. (Fulton here includes what are now Old Fulton Street and Cadman Plaza West.) Middagh becomes Sands, Cranberry becomes High, Orange becomes Nassau, Jay becomes Smith, Bridge becomes Hoyt, Hudson becomes Nevins, and so on. Only at Navy Street—before the southern section of Navy was renamed Rockwell Place (see Chapter 18)—did a street's name for the first time stay the same on either side of Fulton.
[2] The open space here today is much greater. Then, there was a small triangular lot with a fountain in front of City Hall (now Borough Hall), bordered by Remsen, Court and Fulton streets. (The latter, now Cadman Plaza West, then extended all the way to Joralemon.)
[3] On Joralemon Street, directly behind City Hall (built in 1848), was the Municipal Building, whose two neighbors to the east were the County

tersecting streets, for the thoroughfares east and west belong to two different systems built without the least regard to each other, and according to the nature of the ground. At the beginning of Court Street, a good level was obtained, and it might have been possible to have laid out this part of Brooklyn with some regularity. But nothing would have been gained save an ideal symmetry, which is possible only in those unhappy cities that, like, Chicago, have been built upon a level plain. There are other cities in Illinois where the surface is so flat that the rainwater that falls does not know how to find a lower level, and in disgust remains where it is and stagnates, and breeds musquitoes and malaria. Brooklyn is not one of those, nor is there a city in the Union save San Francisco where the streets and avenues have such picturesque perspectives. This happiness of topography is the result of the city's having developed its body upon a skeleton of well-defined ancient routes. Similar ones have been completely obliterated in New York, but these have been maintained in Brooklyn, and the great thoroughfare, the backbone of the city, is the oldest of them all. This is Fulton Street.

It has had many names during its long existence. Finlit was the Indian trail from the eastern end of Long Island to Ihpetonga[4]. Then when the Dutch farmers settled on the rich bottom lands of Flatbush and Flatlands it was widened first into a cow path and next into a good road. For, as has been repeatedly pointed out, though it cannot be done too often, from the very first settlement of New Amsterdam that

---

Court House and the Hall of Records. The Municipal Building there today replaced its predecessor in the 1920s. Brooklyn Law School replaced the other two buildings in 1961.
[4] Fulton Street runs all the way through Cypress Hills to the Queens border at Eldert Lane. Its ancient path is picked up by its sister, Jamaica Avenue, both said to form a Native path from modern Brooklyn to the Hempstead Plains of Nassau County; Jamaica Avenue today connects with the Jericho Turnpike, which goes all the way to Orient Point. I found no mention of the name "Finlit" anywhere but in this column.

city largely depended on Long Island for supplies. The soil of Manhattan at the southern extremity was simply sand and was poor throughout except in a few spots along the North River. In many places it was nothing but a lava bed, holding the surface water and collecting it in great stagnant pools. The neighboring shores of Long Island were beautiful not only by contrast but in themselves, and as soon as the director of the Dutch West India Company was instructed to pay some attention to the development of agriculture as well as to the fur trade, settlers from Holland began farming in the vicinity of Brooklyn, finding an immediate market in the settlement of New Amsterdam. Two things were necessitated by this state of matters, a good road for wagons and a ferry. Fulton Street was the road, and as the ferry was established at its foot, it was known as the Ferry Road. The first ferry master was Cornelius Dircksen, who was appointed by the Governor in 1642, and his sailboat was, in fact, a scow for the transit of wagons. Each wagon drawn by two horses or oxen were charged a toll of two guilders and ten styvers[5] and each single passenger paid six styvers. The two guilders and a half were about equal to one American dollar, so that the ferry was an onerous tax upon the Long Island farmers[6]. But its worst fault was that it could not be depended upon. Whenever there was a still gale it was impossible to make the landing at Peck Slip[7], and the wagons were condemned to a long halt that sometimes lasted several days. Farmers in those

---

[5] Usually spelled *stuiver*, it's the Dutch nickname for a five-cent coin, or one-twentieth of a *guilder*.

[6] Reliable inflation calculations are not possible this far back, but $1 in 1886—or 1642—was considerably more valuable than now.

[7] Still the name of a short street that intersects with the waterfront in Lower Manhattan, just south of the Brooklyn Bridge. Dircksen owned much of the surrounding land, as well as a tavern.

days had to be exceedingly weatherwise and could no doubt have given points even to Wiggins[8].

Perhaps this was the origin of Brooklyn itself, which grew up around the ferry, for the difficulties of crossing must have suggested the propriety of locating in the vicinity of the ferry station stores for the supply of Long Island farmers. These were, of course, furnished with the establishments at New Amsterdam, a point wonderfully adapted for the trade in peltries but having no local advantages. And as it flourished and grew in numbers, so must the farming element on our side of the East River have prospered. Those who know old New York are well aware that the living part crept along the shore opposite to Long Island, while the trading part was on the North River, showing by the logic of fact that those supplies came from Long Island by which the early inhabitants of the great city were fed. And the more that Long Island was developed to respond to the needs of embryonic New York, the greater and more important grew the germ of Brooklyn around the ferry. A delay of three days in stormy weather meant barns for the horses and loaded wagons, and taverns for the teamsters, and blacksmiths' forges and harness stores. The trade that would under other circumstances have been developed at the spot where the wagons delivered their produce was by the force of things retained in Long Island and concentrated around the ferry. So that the old Ferry Road must have had at the terminus upon the East River a thriving active settlement at a quite early time. And this state of things must have lasted until the Indian difficulties around Albany and Schenectady had been arranged[9], and New York was

---

[8] Probably Joseph Wiggins, an English mariner notable for navigating routes to Siberia, starting in the 1870s.
[9] There were many "difficulties" with Native peoples throughout the seventeenth century, including the so-called Beaver Wars, a fight for economic dominance between the Dutch, English, French and various allied Native peoples, and King William's War. In 1690, French, Mohawk

able to settle its back country and feed itself. But the activity of the French and the fear of the Kono-Shioni or Iroquois Indians delayed this settlement for a very long time, so that Brooklyn obtained such a start to have grown beyond fear of competition[10]. New York might get meat and meal from other sources than Long Island, but her fruit, her vegetables and her flowers all came from the fertile lands around Brooklyn.

In the Brooklyn Directory of 1796, Fulton Street is called the Main Road. At that time, it must have resembled not a little the present main street of the beautiful village of Flushing, an ancient settlement that has its own interesting history[11]. For there were long rows of magnificent elms from the crest of the hill at Orange Street up to Court Street. When the Nineteenth Century was in its teens, Joshua Sands, and Gentleman Hicks, and the gifted, far-seeing Pierrepont were guiding the destinies of Brooklyn, Fulton Street was a beautiful turnpike road with orchards and gardens upon each side of it, and the fine old Brooklynites who lived on it were enthusiastic horticulturists. They planted mulberry trees and raised grapes in abundance and looked forward with hopeful eyes to the time when Long Island would be a great wine-producing land. And then Robert Fulton, weary of the law contests in which he was involved from efforts to

---

and Algonquin fighters decimated Schenectady, killing about half the population of the English village.

[10] The name Iroquois is French, derived from a Native name. They called themselves "Ongwanonsionni," which was sometimes rendered by colonists as "Konoshioni." E.R.G.'s knowledge of Native Americans and their history is often wildly incorrect, but his point here is that wars with the Native populations and the French north of Manhattan gave the Long Island colonists a head start in farming.

[11] The Dutch settlement of Flushing, now part of Queens, was founded in 1645.

evade his patent granted by the State[12], came to Brooklyn and was the guest of many of its leading citizens. The first thought in his brain was the application of steam power to ferriage, and a company was formed for which he built the first regular steam ferryboat in existence. It was called the Nassau and made its first trip on May 10, 1814. Very many trips did that boat make on that day, and it was voted an immense success. All the thinking men of Brooklyn were satisfied that it would develop great prosperity for their homes, which at that time had not even been incorporated as a village, although the Long Island traffic with New York must have been very great even at this time, and in gratitude the citizens gave to the old Ferry Road the name of the inventor of the steamboat, and the New Yorkers followed suit with their Fulton Street, which traverses their island, running from the East River to the North River. It is pleasant to an inhabitant of Brooklyn to reflect that the growth of the city is indissolubly connected in a personal and direct way with the invention that has transformed the world.

And now, if ever, the retail merchants of this city had cause to tremble. At last, all the contrarieties of the ferry had been overcome, and crossing the river was now an agreeable incident. It could reasonably have been foretold that men would do their buying and women the mysteries of their shopping in New York. But it did not work that way at all. Some persons, no doubt, said to their neighbors, "I do all my buying now in New York," but for these there was abundant compensation in the recruits that poured over from that city to establish themselves definitely in Brooklyn. The great truth, that Brooklyn is healthy and that New York is not, has never been forgotten by the real inhabitants. Strangers from everywhere coming to the great money center of this hemisphere know nothing about the topography of the two cities,

---

[12] Fulton filed his first patent for a steamboat in 1809, but rival inventors contested its legitimacy for several years.

nor have they ever heard of General Viele's Health map[13]. If anyone were to tell them about the past of the great twins, they would revile him as a marauder of ancient history and say with a sneer that Fifth Avenue is good enough for them. Well! Well! All along the line of Fifth Avenue, from Fifty-Ninth Street northward, there is a constant plague of malaria and diphtheria that never leaves them. The healthiest part of Fifth Avenue is in the neighborhood of Murray Hill, where the great Quaker family lived in such open-handed, friendly, generous style[14]. Their gardens came down to Madison Square, facing partly on the old post road to Boston where the strange coaches used to the thunder by, and where George Francis Train now sits and muses upon the mysteries of megalomania[15]. But close to Twenty-Third Street there was a marshy tract through which flowed a little, almost stagnant stream, and this was filled in with earth but never drained. Just such work has been done in Brooklyn in the vicinity of the Gowanus tract, but this is exceptional here, whereas in New York it was the law. The healthy spots in New York are few and far between, and the old inhabitants knew it, and they rushed over to Brooklyn and established charming and life-restoring homes for their families, as soon as the Fulton Ferry made daily transit a matter of reasonable certainty. So Robert Fulton's Nassau, instead of destroying

---

[13] Civil engineer Egbert Viele published in 1865 his "Sanitary & Topographical Map of the City of New York," which shows the original streams and marshes of Manhattan underneath the modern street grid. It is still referenced by engineers when building in that borough.
[14] Robert Murray converted to Quakerism when he married Mary Lindley. They moved to New York City in 1755 and built a house on a hill at about Park Avenue and 36th Street on a twenty-nine-acre farm.
[15] Train, a businessman and adventurer, made a fortune off the transcontinental railroad and other interests. Increasingly "eccentric" (probably mentally ill), he spent his last few years as a fixture of Madison Square Park, chatting with children and animals.

the retail trade of Brooklyn (concentrated as now on Fulton Street), gave it an enormous boom.

Then came the bridge[16] in much later days, and once more the merchants of Fulton Street shook in their shoes. The fog and ice troubles that had made transit by the Union Ferry Company a thing of terror and discomfort for two or three days in each winter were now overcome, and Brooklyn and New York were joined like the Siamese twins[17]. The cable railway was then desired, and people today fly over the waves of the East River as if they had the wings of doves, and their visits to New York are made with as much safety and comfort as from one part of New York to another. Crossing the bridge is the same as taking the elevated roads. The consequence has been another rush of New Yorkers, and another boom upon Fulton Street. The new arrivals come because homes are cheap and good and healthy in Brooklyn, and the public schools are, if anything, better than in New York, but they trembled at the thought of shopping anywhere save in New York, and proposed to come over and shop as before. They come, they see the retail stores on Fulton Street and are conquered. Incredible as it seems, things can be bought on Fulton Street as cheaply as on Sixth Avenue or Grand Street. And what is still more incredible but equally true, things that belong to higher lines of articles are just as good and just as dear on Fulton Street as on Broadway, Union Square or Fifth Avenue. We have our great jewelry houses, our faience venders, our makers of artistic furniture. Our carpet warehouses, where they toss over a hundred Smyrna rugs to please a single customer, and display to real connoisseurs Yushaks[18] that are as smooth as velvet and have

---

[16] The Brooklyn Bridge opened in 1883.
[17] Conjoined twins were popularized in the 1830s by Chang and Eng Bunker, who had been born in Siam (now Thailand).
[18] Typically spelled Ushak, after the Turkish city Uşak, traditionally a major center of carpet production.

colors that are at the same time bright, lustrous, soft and harmonious. Does the immigrant from New York, who is founding a home, desire to have artistic brass fireplaces and a tiled hearth? Twenty stores will dispute for his custom, or, if he likes, he can go to the tile factory and order his own tiles, and to the furniture factory and have his brass repoussé ware made to suit himself.

I love to lounge on Fulton Street and examine the marvels in the store windows and muse upon the changes that time has made and is making. At present the greatest number of fine establishments are upon that part of Fulton that is north of the City Hall. There is also here the greatest variety and the things most interesting to lovers of bric-a-brac and collectors. But there are ominous signs that the dry goods part of this splendid thoroughfare is destined to be concentrated ultimately upon that part of Fulton that stretches from the Hall of Records to Flatbush Avenue[19]. There are blocks here that are a line of clothing houses and furnishing stores for the replenishing of gentlemen's wardrobes, and places devoted entirely to the fascination of the fair sex. In one of these where they sell Parisian novelties the ornithological eye will detect upon two of the hats birds that were shot in the vicinity of Brooklyn (around Astoria and the Ravenswood swamp[20] in fact) and were prepared by Brooklyn feather workers, have been placed upon hats manufactured in Brooklyn. The EAGLE has taken a praiseworthy stand with regard to the shooting of American songbirds, and the girls who work at the feather trade have chosen to complain about its strictures. Their hearts must be hard, indeed, if they can palliate the wholesome slaughter of our Long Island birds for the work it gives them. If birds were not used, bonnets would still be in

---

[19] The Hall of Records was at the corner of Boerum Place. This stretch today is the Fulton Mall. The part of Fulton north of City Hall is now Cadman Plaza West and Old Fulton.

[20] A marshy section of Astoria, Queens, along the East River, across from Roosevelt Island.

vogue, and there would be just as much work for them as before. But times are so bad with working classes everywhere[21] that a selfishness is engendered which does not belong to the character of American girls and shows that there is something radically wrong in the present labor system. Under the cruel working of this error, whatever it may be, the bloom of existence is taken from the toiling woman, and she has to struggle so hard for mere subsistence that she loses sympathy even with the lovely birds of our woods, the flying flowers of the American world.

The dry-goods quarter ends at Bond Street, but the stores are still of a high grade. One feels instinctively a difference in the Fulton Street that stretches beyond the beginning of Flatbush Avenue. The Brooklyn Museum[22] marks the boundary of the fashionable and splendid part of Fulton Street, but the chain of grandeur is taken up by Flatbush Avenue. There are indications that seem to foretell that Flatbush Avenue will do for Fulton Street what Fifth and Sixth avenues are doing for Broadway beyond Twenty-Third Street in New York. Who would [have] believed it possible that Fifth Avenue would ever become a line of retail stores, or that Sixth Avenue would be the haunt of pleasure, and the home of the rounder? But as it is, we have seen the commencement, and we know that wherever commerce chooses a line she is inexorable. The Strand, in London, was a magnificent stretch of the palaces of the British nobility, but commerce claimed it, pulled down the splendid man-

---

[21] The U.S. had just emerged from an economic depression, 1882–85.
[22] Not the venerable institution of today, whose first wing opened on Eastern Parkway in 1897, but a theater, on the southern triangle formed by the intersection of Flatbush and Fulton—now the site of the luxury-apartment development 1 Flatbush. The theater opened less than a week before this column ran. In addition to its thousand-seat auditorium, it had a picture gallery, lecture room and "mechanical hall," where visitors could watch machines manufacture pins and needles— and then take one home as a souvenir.

sions, reared up the palaces of the trading nobility, and transformed the Strand into the backbone of the London retail business. So it will be with Fulton Street. The lower part, from the Municipal Halls to the bridge, will sooner or later take on a more dedicated commercial character, which time alone will reveal. Middle Fulton Street will be like Broadway from Union to Madison Square; and Flatbush Avenue will be what lower Fulton Street is now, only greater and more splendid. Then perhaps, the City Fathers will change its name and make it Fulton Street, and rechristen the upper Fulton Street, whose fortunes in the future do not seem equal to so honored a name.

E.R.G.

POSTSCRIPT

Flatbush Avenue was never renamed Fulton Street, though Flatbush Avenue Extension was built, past Fulton, in 1906, to connect the avenue with the Manhattan Bridge, which opened three years later. At the time this column was written, construction had already begun on the Fulton Street Line, an elevated railway that opened in 1888 from the Ferry and Brooklyn Bridge to Nostrand Avenue. It clattered over shoppers' heads until 1940, a few years after the modern A and C subway lines made it obsolete. The land from Prospect to Tillary streets was acquired in the 1930s; the old stores were torn down and replaced with Cadman Plaza, defying E.R.G.'s prediction that this section would become the dedicated commercial corridor. Alongside the new park, Fulton Street was renamed Cadman Plaza West. The dominant commercial corridor became the section from Adams Street to Flatbush Avenue, which in the early twentieth century was home to fancy department stores. By the 1970s, it was redeveloped and rebranded as "Fulton Mall," a pedestrian shopping strip intended to keep people from flooding to suburban malls—the way those of E.R.G.'s time feared Brooklynites would leave to shop in Manhattan. Fulton Mall became the most prosperous shopping strip in the outerboroughs, lined with independent vendors and businesses. Since the Bloomberg era, however, Downtown Brooklyn (including Fulton Street) has been overrun by gentrification and luxury development. —Ed.

8

Furman Street

UNDER THE HEIGHTS.

One of the Strangest Thoroughfares in the World.

Furman Street's Appearance and Qualities. Once Known as The Shore—The Hardships of Long Island Milkmen—How the Slope Would Have Been Handled in Genoa.

Sunday, December 5, 1886

Furman Street is by long odds the homeliest, the most picturesque, the most valuable and the least valuable in appearance thoroughfare in Brooklyn. It is traversed by a horse-car line, but there is besides a pretty steady stream of ice carts and big trucks from the warehouses that extend from the west side of the street to the waterfront. Very grim and forbidding are these huge stores[1] in external appearance. There are arched entrances through which the lounger catches a glimpse of the water's side and sees steamers and sailing vessels in all the febrile activity of loading and unloading. These arches are just high enough to admit the passage of a truck with its driver, and very prison-like indeed appears the long vista before the light comes, and the bustle and creaking of pulleys and the cries of men and the shrillness of steam whistles. These stores go back 200 feet, and as you walk along the passage you are irresistibly reminded of railroad tunnels, and your mind in an agitated way begins to reflect upon what would happen to you if a truck horse should go crazy and in-

---

[1] Storehouses, not shops.

sist on galloping down upon you. But, fortunately, the truck horses are very peaceable, nay, even affectionate in their dispositions and seem to be fondly attached to the drivers, whose enthusiasm over their calling apparently finds vent in the most sentimental names for their outfit, painted boldly on the front of the wagon where all men may discern them. I saw one called "Here We Come" turning down into one of the defiles on Furman Street, a defile with an exceedingly sugary smell. I saw others in the street entitled respectively "Little Jennie" and "The Blue-Eyed Girl," which leads me to suppose that the truckmen as a class are exceedingly satisfied with themselves, their big horses, their trucks and the general condition of affairs.

Furman Street upon the west side is altogether taken up with three monster warehouses, from Fulton Street to Wall Street Ferry[2], where a new order of things begins. Upon the east side there is more variety and picturesqueness, and there are some remains of buildings that existed when this gloomy old street was known as The Shore and was the brightest, most animated, the most delightful part of Brooklyn, or, to be more exact, the Ferry Village. For, until the incorporation of the two villages into one[3], the houses that clustered around the ferries and the hamlet of Breuckelyn were separate existences. When men ordinarily speak of old Brooklyn, they imagine a vain thing, for it did not exist in the way that people have supposed but was simply a collection of farmers' houses on what is now Fulton Street, between the Hall of Records and Smith Street, or thereabouts[4]. So far back as 1766, when Lieutenant Ratzer, of the Sixtieth Rifles, immortalized himself by making an admirable topographical map of New York and the neighboring part of Nassau (as Long Island was of-

---

[2] At the foot of Montague Street.
[3] The separate town and village of Brooklyn consolidated in 1834 to become a city.
[4] The Hall of Records was at the southwest corner of Boerum Place, just one block west of Smith Street.

ficially called by the British tyrants), the population of the hamlet of Brookland or Breuckelyn was confined to the families of a few farmers[5]. The busy, the thriving, the animated part of Nassau was the ferry station and the Shore. It must be noted that the Shore meant only that part of the waterline between the ferry and the Red Hook, and this was the scene of much activity. The sand was very fine and the approach gradual, so that the shipping merchants of New York found it a good place for a graving dock. Their small schooners and brigs were run up on the sands, and the sides supported with timber, while the bottoms were vigorously scrubbed clean of seaweed and barnacles and other marine parasites, after which heavy coats of pitch were applied, and then they were slid back again at high tide. This primitive process, however, was only practicable from Pierrepont to Joralemon Street. Here the sands were always covered by high tides, and when westerly winds lashed the waters of the bay, and made the fiddlers dance tumultuously, the waves broke strongly against the base of the Heights with a rhythmic booming and a force that made all Clover Hill tremble.

There was another source of activity on the Shore, and this was the periaguas of the milkmen who supplied New York. There was a row of posts to which the periaguas were tied. Every morning the men came down with two great cans and a wooden yoke which went across the shoulders and supported the cans and, having embarked each on his own periagua, they either sailed across to New York or paddled according as the wind served. In wintertime these milkmen suffered intensely, for the ice was much more troublesome then than now. Probably the winters are not less severe now than they were eighty or a hundred years ago, but the ice was

---

[5] Ratzer was a British officer and surveyor. His name "is invoked as something of a Da Vinci of New York cartography," as the New York *Times* once reported, and his "Plan of the City of New York," from 1770, was his "Mona Lisa." There are four known copies, one of which is at the Center for Brooklyn History.

not then incessantly cut up by the paddlewheels of big steamboats and the screws of innumerable tugs and, therefore, froze much more solidly. These poor milkmen had to labor with their sculls through masses of hummocky ice and great cakes, swirled down from the flatlands near Hellgate[6] by the fierce currents. They kept together in a squadron, so that their mutual efforts might make the task easier, and old gentlemen now living relate that old Joralemon, who was one of the milk band, used to describe how they had to beat each other with the boat seats over the back and shoulders to preserve the circulation and keep from freezing to death. Many a New York lady looking out her windows in her fashionable house on Hanover Square was compelled to announce to her family that the poor milkmen could not get across from the ferry and that the coffee would necessarily be without its usual enrichment of Long Island cream. When the milkmen did get across, they had to go stamping from door to door, bearing their cans depending from the yoke upon their shoulders, with feet half frozen and fingers benumbed from handling the icy metal. Little does the proud and vainglorious lord of a milk wagon, who sits in the rear and drives with long reins, threatening the lives of pedestrians in South Brooklyn, remember the toil and tribulation of his predecessor. And perhaps the milk is not as good now as it was then, either.

    At the bottom of Leituenant Ratzer's admirable map of New York there is a well-drawn sketch of the appearance of the city and its environs, from which it appears that so early as 1766 there were three houses on the Shore, besides Philip Livingstone's distillery at Joralemon Street. History is silent with regard to two of these, but the third appears to have the nucleus of the flint-glass works for which Long Island was fa-

---

[6] The East River tidal strait between Astoria, Queens, and Randall's and Ward's Islands.

mous in quite early times[7]. It is allowable to conjecture that of the other two, one was a tavern, and the other may have been a warehouse, erected by some New York merchant for the convenience of vessels that wanted to be graved. There was a road for vehicles along the shore at low water, not a very good one, but it was a favorable spot for fishing and for bathing, particularly between the ferry station at Joralemon Street and District Street, as it was then called, now Atlantic [Avenue]. Here a sort of bay existed before the Joralemon heirs filled it up, and this was much frequented by all the kinds of fish that thronged in the harbor, until they were driven away by dumping and by the refuse oil that is poured out upon the water by the Standard Oil Company west of Staten Island[8], and by the refineries on Newtown Creek. Such nuisances would never have been permitted in the days of Joshua Sands and Hezekiah Beers Pierrepont, but the politicians have completely driven the patriots from the field of municipal government nowadays, and they wink at every invasion of public rights for the *quid pro quo* of political support. The road wound under the Heights, which were about eighty feet above, and the sketch in Lieutenant Ratzer's map shows that the slope was densely wooded. Old inhabitants are unanimous that the trees that grew on it were cedars and locusts. But it is to be remarked that the locust is not indigenous north of Pennsylvania, and while there cannot be a doubt that the locusts were there it seems equally certain that they were planted by the hand of man. In fact, it may be stated that there was much more tree planting at an early date on Long Island than there is now, and very much of the

---

[7] I found no record of Brooklyn's being notable for flint glass until the 1850s, when Christian Dorflinger took over the Long Island Flint Glass Works, which fashioned glassware for President and Mrs. Lincoln.
[8] The company took over a refinery in Bayonne, New Jersey, in 1877.

"natural forest" part of Prospect Park[9] must be attributed the same source.

This fact is a peculiar one. Who was the man and what his nationality who in that early age had the perspicuity to plant robinias upon a slope? It is not twenty years since the French Government appointed a commission to find out what was the best method of preserving the slopes of railroad embankments, of river levees and of crumbling mountains, and after much investigation it was decided that the best method was to plant the robinia, or locust[10], not only because of its rapid growth but because there is a fertilizing principle in the fallen leaves that encourages and fosters the springing up of underwood. It has been found in practice that a glacis or slope planted with locusts is in a few years covered with weeds, briars, flowers and grass to such an extent as to throw off the rainfall and prevent the washing away of the loose earth. This was minutely explained to me, when I was in the south of France inspecting the ravages of mountain torrents, by an officer of the Forest Guards, to which force is committed the general disposition of all such matters. When it is remembered that the Heights are composed of gravel and boulders in a glacial drift fashion, and therefore particularly liable to washing, it does seem pretty certain that the genius who planted the locust tree on the slopes of Ihpetonga Heights was a man far in advance of his times who had solved the problem that tormented the French Government. Such men are often discovered by the investigations of historians, men who, as a mere matter of course, foresaw the future and comprehended the present, but whose superiority was never even dreamed of by their contemporaries. The

---

[9] The Midwood, in the center of the park, was largely untouched by designers Frederick Olmsted and Calvert Vaux.
[10] *Robinia pseudoacacia*, named for the French royal gardener Jean Robin, who in the seventeenth century planted the first black locust tree in Europe, where it has become an invasive species.

investigator finds their footprints and says reverentially, "A giant walked here."

The street was named after Judge Furman[11], who had a house upon the corner, and here his unfortunate son Gabriel lived after him[12]. The great building of the Brooklyn City Railway Company is upon its site[13], and the company uses for stabling purposes the first warehouse known to history erected upon the shore[14]. It was built by Tommy Everit[15]. It is a great red-brick house, with brownstone trimmings and a huge gabled end that faces upon Furman Street. The level of the place must have been changed somewhat, for the heavy stone archway is below the street by nearly two feet. Goods were hoisted to the upperstory by a crane, whose beam is still in its old position. This is upon the side of the structure. The next gentleman who saw remuneration in warehousing was no less a man than Samuel Thompson, Collector, in his day, of the Port of New York[16], whose son died a few months ago.

---

[11] William Furman (1765–1832), the first jurist in the county, was also a state legislator and village trustee.

[12] Gabriel (1800–54) was also a judge and state legislator, but he's best remembered for being Brooklyn's first historian, the author of *Notes, Geographical and Historical, Relating to the Town of Brooklyn* (1824). E.R.G. calls him "unfortunate" because later in life he suffered from mental illness, brought on by opium and stimulants. The Furman house, at No. 5 Fulton, was torn down in 1836 to widen the street, and Gabriel moved to 103 Willow Street until his finances collapsed. His library was sold off to pay his debts, and he died in poverty of "chronic diarrhoea" at Brooklyn City Hospital, on Raymond Street (now Ashland Place), next to the jail he'd once helped get built.

[13] This building, now 8 Old Fulton Street, is still at corner of Furman. It was landmarked in 1973.

[14] An 1887 map labels a structure at the waterfront, just about in line with Fulton Street, "P. R.R. Annex."

[15] The Everit family operated a slaughterhouse/butcher shop at the corner of Fulton and what's now Everit Street, named for them.

[16] The Collector was once a powerful federal officer responsible for collecting the tariffs on goods coming into New York City. In the 1820s,

It is possible that the building used as a stable by the Jewell flour mill firm is that very identical structure, though in the opinion of the octogenarians of Brooklyn Mr. Thompson's place was higher up the street. Both of these structures are, of course, on the east side[17], for they were built when Furman Street was an open strand and when the merry, rippling waters of the bay formed the west side. The stables in question are an old brick structure, low but long, built of smallest bricks, and with a rain-drip cornice that showed some taste in the designer. The building runs back to Columbia Heights, which here is supported by a straggling stone retaining wall. Between these two old structures are a number of iron shops, one of which is maintained by the patriarch of the place, whose forges were in operation before the warehouses on the west side shut out the sunlight and the sea. Beyond what I have surmised to be the Thompson warehouse come huge buildings, which serve also as a retaining wall for the slope, and which are used for different purposes very difficult to guess at. The atmosphere, moral and physical, of the place overcomes them, and they all have a look of prisons that have been used as warehouses, and of warehouses that are being temporarily used as prisons[18]. One of them is a factory where

---

the post was held by Jonathan Thompson; in the 1830s, by the corrupt Samuel Swartwout. E.R.G. may have mixed up the two. Neither seems to have had a son who died in 1886.

[17] The Jewell Milling Company used buildings on both sides of the street. In the front of the old Brooklyn City Railway Company building were offices and grain storage; in the back, "Feed Mill Eng.," connected by a grain spout across Furman Street to buildings at No. 2–6 Furman (also 2–6 [Old] Fulton), where the actual milling seems to have been performed. The railway company had moved down the block, to a three-story brick building at 24 (Old) Fulton Street, which was torn down in the early twentieth century.

[18] Along Furman and Columbia Heights, from Doughty Street to just past Poplar, were several irregularly angled, mostly brick buildings that appear foreboding on a map, let alone in person. There was a foundry, an iron works, a sarsaparilla factory, a tinware factory, and so on.

coffee is polished[19]. This is the height of modern refinement, and even Boston cannot quite come up to such culture. I have heard that Boston dusts her teas, but we in Brooklyn polish our coffee. Think of that and weep, ye modern Athenians[20]!

On Columbia Heights there is a long row of houses known familiarly as Quaker Row[21]. Beneath it on Furman Street is a great barrack-like structure, acting as a retaining wall with the most extraordinary windows, which seem as if invented by a young architect who ate pork chops until he had the nightmare and in his most fearful throes devised a new kind of Gothic. The three lower stories cannot possibly have any windows in rear, and the windows of the fourth story appear to be on a level with the long, frowsy, melancholy grasses of the slope[22]. Farther on we come to buildings

---

[19] Coffee polishing, the process of removing skin and impurities from green coffee beans, was done at Nos. 63 and 65 Furman Street. The buildings were used for storage by the E.R. Squibb and Sons Pharmaceutical Company in 1932 when they caught fire. Today the site is an empty lot, just north of Squibb Park, which was built in the 1940s.

[20] An allusion to the memoirs of John Bacon, Esq.: "Ye modern Athenians, devoted, like the ancients, to your idols, while HE, who should be the object of your supreme regard, seems an UNKNOWN GOD."

[21] These were houses on the west side, between Cranberry and Orange, wiped out by the B.Q.E. and replaced with a park called the Fruit Street Sitting Area. No. 106, the Field mansion, had been built in 1845. Field's grandson, artist Hamilton Easter Field, bought a few more on the row and opened a gay-friendly art gallery and commune called the Ardsley School. In the early twentieth century, residents included John de los Passos and Hart Crane; the latter stayed at No. 110, in the same room from which a bed-ridden Washington Roebling had monitored construction of the Brooklyn Bridge, Crane's *idée fixe*.

[22] Nos. 95–119 Furman were directly below Quaker Row, but they were three stories; he means Nos. 123–137, south of Orange above, which variously housed a barracks, lodging house, oil kettle, cooperages and more—all wiped out by the BQE. Like many buildings on Furman Street, all had gardens on the roofs for the homes on Columbia Heights.

that have no windows at all in the rear, and whose roofs form the gardens of the aristocracy on the Heights. On one of these there is an astronomical observatory, with one of those domes that betoken the possession of a telescope[23]. It would be hard to find a better locality for one-half of a celestial world, but the sweep of that telescope to the north or to the east must be exceedingly limited. It also commands a splendid view of the Statue of Liberty[24], and if the poor creature does but wink or try to wipe a copper tear from her eye the observer knows of it and can expose her to the rude comments of the public. Then we come to the retaining walls[25], which are not utilized in any way and are simply brave ramparts of great stones looking like part of a fortification. Some of the blocks of gneiss are not so closely set together, but that grasses have found lodgment between them and there wave in a sad suicidal way when the wind stirs them, as if they mourned the unforgotten past, when the trees grew upon the slope and the cedar birds slunk around and about the stringy trunks looking like small telegraph poles, or hid themselves in the brambles that flurry out their flower-laden sprays under the protecting shadow of the locusts.

When we come to Pierrepont Street, there is a marked change; better building and a more scientific angle of inclination. The stone wall is carried up about seventeen feet, and there is a light brick wall of a perpendicular character, upon which one can discern the clinging branches of some creeper, perhaps a grape vine, perhaps a wisteria. This is the beginning of the bad part of the old Shore road, for the cliffs bulged forward here so that the track had to go out toward the water. When it was decided to open Furman Street all the way to Joralemon's, Mr. Henry E. Pierrepont looked very blank, for he had to remove the cliff for a length of 800

---

[23] No. 211–13 Furman Street, just north of Pierrepont.
[24] It had opened to the public just six weeks earlier.
[25] A fifty-foot retaining wall ran from about Clark Street (with a break for the observatory and for Montague) almost to Joralemon Street.

feet along the shore, and this, done even in the most economical fashion, necessitated an expense of fifty thousand dollars to build a bulkhead to hold the surplus earth, and to erect a retaining wall. Perhaps when he first studied the work, he may have regretted his father's predilection for the Heights; for even that farseeing, comprehensive mind could not have foretold the future of Furman Street. But he went bravely to work, set over a hundred men to digging and filled the shallow waters in front of him with his excavated earth, gaining five acres of most valuable waterfront land. Here he created the Pierrepont Stores in 1853, making them 200 feet long by 70 feet wide[26]. John A. Prentice, whose stores are on the south side of the Wall Street Ferry, declared that Pierrepont was overdoing it, and he divided up his land between smaller warehouses and a long row of houses, some of brick and some wooden[27]. This row stretches to Joralemon Street, and two of the houses are on the site of the ferry that plied between the Livingstone distillery and the Old Slip in New York. Experience has proved that the big stores were not too big and that the houses can only be occupied by tenants who pay small rents. Consequently, all the other warehouses on the west side of the street were built of the same gigantic dimensions as the Pierrepont structures, giving to Furman Street a most unique character and appearance[28]. On the

---

[26] North of Montague Street, Nos. 220–52, the Pierrepont Stores were leased to another company in 1888, the year Henry E. Pierrepont died, and sold seven years later, though a 1929 map still refers to them as "Pierrepont Stores." Today their former site is occupied by a seemingly abandoned NYC Transit building, some parking spaces and sand dunes.
[27] Between Montague and Joralemon there were a dozen brick homes and thirty-three brick-lined wooden houses that backed up onto almost a dozen water-facing storehouses. The homes were replaced by commercial and industrial buildings in the early twentieth century.
[28] From about Doughty to State streets, the west side of Furman was lined with an unbroken row of storehouses. The trend continued on the waterfront south of Atlantic Avenue, too, into Red Hook.

one hand it is a row of prison-like warehouses of colossal dimensions. On the other it is a series of massive retaining walls topped with beautiful gardens or of hideous structures that serve the same purpose.

It is to be doubted if there is such another street in the world. In Genoa, the slope would have been terraced from top to bottom in shallow strips not more than five feet broad, upon which would have been planted flowering bushes, pomegranates, figs and olives. There would have been upon the summit stone houses of heavy architecture, and at the base tall structures whose ground floors would have been groceries, and the rest of the building elegant dwelling apartments. There would have been at every cross street a stone stairway upon which beggars would have clustered, clawing at the coats of passersby and demanding charity with execrations and outcries. Girls would have tripped up and down in utter unconsciousness of their display of rounded limbs and trim ankles. Fat middle-aged men would have ascended halfway up and groaned and taken out their handkerchiefs to wipe the drops of perspiration from their bald heads. Donkeys loaded with manure or paniers of fruit would have gone up and down in a dogged fashion, stopping sometimes in a belligerent way as if determined to allow nobody to pass. It would have been very pleasant, no doubt, but on the whole I find Furman Street picturesque enough as it is and am not sorry that it was not modeled upon Italian lines. I do, however, cordially regret that anyone ever built houses to act as retaining walls for the slope and honestly believe that they are neither safe as structures nor healthy as dwelling houses.

E. R. G.

POSTSCRIPT

Furman Street had already changed drastically by E.R.G.'s time, and it would continue to do so. Today, from Old Fulton to what would be about Cranberry, only one or two buildings remain from the nineteenth century; the rest were replaced. In the 1920s, Squibb Pharmaceuticals built a factory, the back of which faces Furman, on Columbia Heights, from Doughty to Middagh. It was sold in the 1960s to the Jehovah's Witnesses, who stuck their WATCHTOWER sign on the top. They sold it in the 2010s, and it became part of the luxury workspace campus now known as Panorama. Most of the next several blocks have similarly been replaced by modern luxury housing and hotels.

For the remainder of Furman Street, the buildings on the east side of the street were torn down in the 1940s, replaced by a monstrously ironic, twentieth-century perversion of E.R.G.'s fantasy Genovese terrace—the cantilevered lanes of the Brooklyn–Queens Expressway. It opened in 1950, stacked up from the street to the Heights the way the old homes and retaining walls used to, complete with gardens on top—the Brooklyn Heights Promenade. The piers and warehouses on the west side of the street have in recent years been replaced by the various modules of Brooklyn Bridge Park, helping to spark all that luxury development, which resumes briefly at Furman Street's southwestern end.

Furman presently embodies, in parts, the essence of postmodern Brooklyn, with its unaffordable housing and waterfront reclamation, as well as the worst excesses of modernist superdevelopment, in the streetlife-killing highway. What it has completely lost are the traces of its nineteenth-century variety and color, so vividly described by E.R.G. —Ed.

9

Clinton Street

DOWN CLINTON STREET.

A Highway of Promenade, Homes and Boarding Houses.

Brooklyn Beauty and Its Contrast With New York Plainness—How the Favorite Thoroughfare Was Made and Saved—Historic Notes.

Sunday, December 26, 1886

There is a pretty little poem (by Leigh Hunt, if I remember rightly)[1] in which an incident is related of Haroun Alrashid. The mighty Khalif of Baghdad had for his friend, favorite and confidant Jaffar, a Barmecide prince of the old fire worshipers, and beheaded him, according to the usual fate of Oriental favorites, and had forbidden even his name to be mentioned. But his spies informed him that there was a man of Baghdad who never ceased praising the memory of Yahyeh and his son Jaffar, both in the bazar and the coffee house, and the Khalif, wearing the red robe of anger, sent for that man and bade him stand before his musnud and exculpate himself if he could. The man said that he personally owed everything in life to the dead favorite and that he preferred impalement to ingratitude of spirit, though he who was gone could not be affected now by praise or censure. Haroun Alrashid had a heart, and it was touched by this fidelity of soul, and he heaped gifts upon the man and commendations for

---

[1] He does—"Jaffár" (1850), by James Henry Leigh Hunt.

his nobility of mind. He thanked the Khalif for his generosity, and (in the words of the poet),

> Then looking upward as if toward his star,
> Said, "This, too, I owe thee, Jaffar."

In promenading up and down Clinton Street, which I do very often, I am continually reminded of the fact that we of Brooklyn owe, too, this splendid thoroughfare to Hezekiah Beers Pierrepont. It is for walking purposes the best street in Brooklyn, and its very limitations of length enhance its value as a promenade. There is in every city some particular street where the dandies walk and the pretty girls show their bright eyes and brilliant toilets, and Clinton Street fills this highly honored place in the fair City of Brooklyn. The discreet and intelligent lounger who uses his eyes will see more beauty in five minutes' walk upon the flagstones of Clinton Street than in the promenade from Madison Square to Central Park along Fifth Avenue. Beauty in Brooklyn is universal and is divided with extraordinary evenness among the poor, the well-to-do and the rich. In the New York promenade the prettiest girls noticed by the observer will certainly be carrying bandboxes or queerly shaped bundles of some kind and may be set down infallibly as being shopgirls of some description. If one were to do so improper a thing as follow them it would be found that they lived in the poor quarter, either on the East Side or the extreme West Side. The further one mounts up in the *beau monde* of New York the more depressingly homely do the girls become until one is tempted to believe that millions have a bad effect upon the blood and nervous system. Were it not for the continual recruits arriving in Gotham from other cities and from the State, nearly all of whom have special attractions and come to make the most of them in the matrimonial market, New York would speedily acquire the reputation of being a city of ugly women. But in Brooklyn, there is a marked preponderance of agreeable and charming faces, and there is no quarter where this can be better ascertained than Clinton Street, and from the constant promenades upon this charming street I have come to the conclusion that the blonde beauties are still the majority here, whereas in New York, as is well known, the brunettes now outnumber their blue-eyed sisters in the proportion of five to three.

"This, too, we owe to thee, Jaffar." Had it not been for the extraordinary prevision of the first Pierrepont, Clinton Street would have been a very short street indeed. For after it had been opened partially, in 1830, the great marine chandlers, the Schermerhorns[2], purchased property on the Heights and were going to create a ropewalk, which would have reached to Court Street and would have ended the career of the fashionable promenade. But Mr. Pierrepont, divining their intentions from their purchases of land, contrived to head them off by carrying through the council of the village trustees a plan for the opening of a street, a short one of only one block, right in the center of the contemplated rope walk. The Schermerhorns then relinquished their nefarious intentions of ruining the future of the Heights in general and Clinton Street in particular and established their ropewalk in a far more suitable location[3]. This was an exceedingly good thing for them, for they not only prospered with their ropewalk, but the lands which they had purchased on the Heights became in time very valuable. So Clinton

---

[2] Abraham Schermerhorn (1783–1850) inherited in 1826 almost 160 acres of farmland near Gowanus Bay that his father and uncle had used as a summer estate. Abraham sold it in 1835, and it became the core of Green-Wood Cemetery. His daughter Caroline married William Astor and became The Mrs. Astor, the legendary New York socialite.

[3] Abraham and his brother Peter (1781–1852) operated a shipping business on Water Street in New York. The built a ropewalk in Brooklyn, in the vicinity of what became Schermerhorn Street, which they used for their shipping business until the ropewalk burned down in 1841. Schermerhorn Street ends at Clinton Street.

Street was saved, and its fair proportions were uncurtailed, and in time it reached out to Hamilton Avenue, where it may be said to end, for though the street beyond that avenue that goes to Gowanus Bay may be called by the same name, yet it is not of the same nature, but is given up to wharfage and marine pursuits[4], and dust and dirt and things objectionable to those who walk for the pleasure of seeing the social world of this city. The two end blocks of Clinton Street proper partake very much, it may be observed, of the local color of their surroundings. The north end being close to Fulton Street[5] is influenced by Fulton Street and has grand stores of a high character; the south end being close to Hamilton Avenue, which is a poor neighborhood of an inchoate condition, has stores of the description that might be expected. Between these two ends, Clinton Street is a long succession of fine dwelling houses and conspicuous churches. And the houses have the peculiarity of being very distinctive for the most part, as if they had been built in little batches of one or two or three at a time, not like the blocks of today which are run up on speculation and have a distressing monotony of appearance[6].

Clinton Street was opened more than fifty years ago, and as its growth covers that long length of time it cannot be a matter of surprise that the houses have a physiognomy of their own. Nowhere in America, throughout the whole range of its scores of first-class cities, can one find a street where the houses proclaim so plainly to the observant eye that they are the property of those who dwell in them as Clinton Street. Where a city is in that stage that its best street is lined with villas standing in their own gardens, there is no danger that

---

[4] Today, this end of Clinton Street passes a few industrial buildings, as well as the Red Hook Houses, built in 1938–39, and Red Hook Park, land for which was acquired 1934–47.
[5] Now Cadman Plaza West.
[6] He contrasts unique houses built by individual owners with those built by developers according to homogenous blueprints.

there will be a painful uniformity, because such houses have opportunities of displaying variations of construction which are denied to the close-ranked phalanxes of an older street. When the houses stand shoulder to shoulder there would seem to be little variation possible, save what may be obtained by greater or less frontage. In the blocks built by speculation, of course, all have the same frontage necessarily, but even in the old times it was so customary to divide up the land into twenty-five feet front lots that in many parts of Clinton Street you will not see a house either more or less. But ownership shows itself in the throwing out of a bay window on the second floor, on the first floor, or in the case of a corner house on the side street, or it may display itself in supplementary buildings, conservatories or picture galleries, or in the stained glass of the hall door, or in many little differences showing the power of the inhabitant to do as he will with his own and spend what money he likes upon his home. Delightful word! The paradise of the poor old bachelor's dreams, the nirvana never to be attained, the water and the fruit that tormented the starving Tantalus[7]! Clinton Street is lined with houses that are unquestionably homes. One sees the carriages rolling up to the sidewalks and discharging freights of female loveliness and matronly dignity and the gray hairs of honorable age at the doors of houses that seem redolent of all the comforts and delights of home. Rosy-cheeked, bright-eyed schoolgirls with packages of books under one arm demean themselves by molding snowballs with the disengaged hand and pelting each other, and muscular young boys shovel off the sidewalks as if it was the best fun imaginable—to the great disgust of the poor boys who con-

---

[7] Tantalus was punished for trying to steal ambrosia from Olympus (and then trying to feed his dismembered son to the gods in penance) by standing in a pool of water he could never drink, under a tree whose fruit he could never reach. This is the first time E.R.G. suggests in these columns that he's a bachelor.

sider that they have vested rights in snow time in that same work, which the rich men's sons have no business to infringe.

If Clinton Street be a street of homes, it is also a street of boarding houses. It is becoming the practice for many men who do business in New York to take a room or suite of rooms on some cross street leading into Clinton, eat breakfast and dinner there and skirmish for a free lunch in some of the downtown barrooms of Gotham. Fortunately for the comfort of the Brooklynites and for the strangers living within their gates, the vast preponderance of homes in this city has its effect upon the boarding houses, which are homelike. Because in some cities in America, and especially one not very far from Brooklyn, it is the homes that are like boarding houses, and the boarding houses are like hotels. There is promiscuity without friendliness in the latter, and in the former the family meet at the table at mealtimes and separate immediately afterward. The ladies retire to their bedrooms, or to the room of the lady of the house, and the men go to their clubs or to the billiard room to indulge in caroms and cigarettes, with occasional libations. In Brooklyn boarding houses, I am given to understand, there is much friendly intimacy among the various families, and the men remain at home as husbands and fathers should, and play a sociable game of whist, or take a hand at the delightful mystery known as freezeout poker. Nowhere does the boarding house appear in a more favorable light than in Clinton Street, Brooklyn, and since civilization appears to make home an impossibility, a dream never to be realized for hundreds and thousands, why we may console ourselves with the thought that the wind is tempered to the shorn lamb[8] and that we live in a city where the boarding-house plan is at its best and highest. But I have learned from looking constantly upon the

---

[8] A French proverb popularized in English ("God tempers the wind to the shorn lamb") by Laurence Sterne's 1768 novel, *A Sentimental Journey*.

face of Nature to appreciate the dignity of isolation. Men are not bees, nor is the human race more than partially gregarious. I like the humor of the bears, which jump with my own. They have powwows when all the bears meet, but in their domestic relations they prefer that there should be a good stretch of forest between the caves or the hollow trees, where each pair of bears dwells in harmony. Mankind loses originality of character and power of intellectuality by living too gregariously, and few indeed can preserve nobility of purpose and pure singleness of heart when dwelling in a herd.

I cannot believe that Hezekiah Beers Pierrepont could have been the great man he was had he lived in a human beehive. Great he unquestionably was, but his talent—that of civism or the comprehension of growth of a city—has not been reckoned among the sciences or useful arts, and yet it is one of the grandest. To us who inherit not only the benefits of what he planned and did, but the way of understanding things which he originated, there is a great difficulty in appreciating him, because it seems to us so inevitable that everything should be as he made it. But if we could go back to his time and generation, many of the very men who swear by Brooklyn and rightly think it the finest city in the Western world would have been his fiercest opponents. He swam all his life against the current of popular opinion, but he had the power to convince his brother trustees not only by his arguments but by the influence that the true gentleman and the man of integrity always exert upon their fellow men. A man may be a gentleman and yet not a mirror of honesty, but he will have his influence. A man may have a heart as true as a spar of Georgia pine and be externally as rough as a bear, and yet he will have his influence. But the union of the two qualities is irresistible. They were united in Hezekiah Pierrepont, and that alone enabled him to overcome the vehement antagonism that the project of opening Clinton Street aroused among his fellow citizens. Old Joralemon in particular fought the project tooth and nail and declared that it should never pass through his land[9]. He had a general objection to streets going through the Livingston property, which he had purchased, and he successfully blockaded Hicks Street, which stopped at his line until he died, when the heirs were glad enough to open the way. But Clinton Street was particularly obnoxious to him because Mr. Pierrepont had named it after a governor who was hateful in his eyes[10], and set his heart upon preventing it from being carried through his land. Nothing could resist the firm persuasive dignity and foresight combined of Mr. Pierrepont, and the street was carried through Joralemon's land in spite of him.

At that time, the Pierrepont cross streets, the heart of the Heights, all ended at Clinton. Not one of them was carried through to Fulton or Court streets until subsequently, when the work was finished by Mr. Henry Pierrepont. It must then have been a queer-looking place, for where Pierrepont and Clinton meet now were the remains of old Fort Sterling, erected by the British after the Battle of Long Island[11]. When the cruel war was over and the English had taken themselves off and dismissed their Hessians and their red-skinned allies, the Americans whose possessions were in the vicinity of the fort and who had suffered not a little from the neighborhood of the red coats, considered they had a good right to what had been abandoned by the foe and accordingly began to strip and dismantle the barracks in the central square. In this

---

[9] South of modern Joralemon Street.

[10] DeWitt Clinton is best remembered for his terms as governor of New York, 1817–22 and 1825–28, though he was also a mayor and senator. Most famously, he spearheaded construction of the Erie Canal. He also ran against James Madison for president in 1812.

[11] It was built in fact by American rebels and captured by the British. New York State and the parks department both put the site of Fort Sterling, sometimes spelled Stirling, several blocks away, at Columbia Heights and Clark Street. At Pierrepont and Henry, closer to E.R.G.'s site, the British built Fort Brooklyn in 1780.

way many objects whose origin has been a matter of curiosity were disseminated over Long Island, particularly iron grates with the royal arms of England on them, which came, no doubt, from fireplaces in the officers' quarters. The provisional Government of the United States made some attempt to claim ownership at Fort Sterling, but there was a flaw in their title; nor could this be made good by any post facto formation of a constitutional government, and the claim was abandoned. This fact has been overlooked in the proceedings with regard to the search for the lost treasures of the British frigate, the Hussar, which struck on the Pot rock in the Hell Gate passage and filled and floundered, taking with her much treasure which was being taken to Newport for the military chest[12]. The United States has not the shadow of a right to a single guinea in the entire hoard, should it ever be recovered. After the Remsens and others had taken away all they cared for, the place had a woefully disconsolate and dreary aspect, and if the Gowanus darkies thought the neighborhood haunted they had some excuse for their fears. Both the Livingston mansion and the Cornell–Pierrepont villa[13] were utilized as hospitals, and there were blood marks upon the floor where the red heart's blood had dripped slowly down in thick crimson gouts that sank into the wood and made stains that could not be removed. The dead were buried all along the ledge of the Heights, and when the rains washed away the earth the bones protruded in a ghastly and terrifying way. But the skeleton that was found just outside the ditch of the old fort, with a drawn sword held by the bones of the right hand, died neither in the Battle of Long

---

[12] The H.M.S. Hussar hit rocks in Hell Gate, a dangerous strait between Queens and Randall's Island, in November 1780 and sank. A story quickly spread that it had been full of gold to pay soldiers, which became legend, even though the British denied it and the ship did not ordinarily carry gold. It persists to the present-day—that a fortune is sitting at the bottom of the East River, waiting to be claimed.
[13] See Chapter 6.

Island nor in the mansions used as hospitals for the wounded. He was an officer, as the sword showed, and he was buried just outside the ditch of the fort, and it is my conjecture that thereby hangs a tale.

The remains were discovered when Clinton Street was being opened, and the workmen did not pay any particular attention to the rotting fragments of cloth or to anything save the sword, which came away easily enough because all the bones of the hand had become separated. It was surmised, as a matter of course, that he was a victim of the war and no more was thought about the matter. But the fact that he was buried just outside of the ditch of the fort, with his naked sword in his hand, without any scabbard, at a point remote from any fighting in the disastrous Battle of Long Island, which was fought mainly upon Prospect Heights[14] and the clear ground in the vicinity of the north side of Gowanus Swamp, makes me impressed with the idea that he was run through the heart in a duel with a brother officer. Such little disagreements were common enough in those days, both at home and on foreign service, and the usual practice was to fight in the ditch of a fort if practicable, because that was under military jurisdiction and the civil authorities either had no control or thought they had none. In India to this day such things happen, and if there is a fatal result it is reported that the dead officer died suddenly of cholera or of black-vomit fever [15]—two maladies that carry off a perfectly healthy man in a few hours. The sword is in the possession of Mr. Henry E. Pierrepont, and the part called the foible is badly bent, as if from a vehement contact with the forte of another sword in parry. He was probably fighting in his shirt sleeves when he fell, and the muscular contraction that followed the fatal sword thrust in the heart prevented him from relinquishing his hold upon his own weapon. He was there-

---

[14] He refers to a large swath of high land in and around Prospect Park.
[15] More commonly called yellow fever.

fore buried with it, and his brother officers said a muttered prayer over him and left him, little thinking that not far from the spot would one day rise one of the finest churches in Brooklyn—Holy Trinity[16]. But the subject of the churches on Clinton Street is so important that it deserves an article devoted to itself alone.

E.R.G.

---

[16] The Gothic-revival masterpiece on the corner of Montague Street, built 1844–47. (The tower was completed in 1869.) The Episcopal congregation disbanded in 1957, and in 1969 another Episcopal congergation, St. Ann's, moved into the building. It's now called St. Ann and the Holy Trinity Church.

10

Clinton Street, Part II

A HIGHWAY OF CHURCHES.

Clinton Street Ecclesiastically Considered.

Good and Bad Architecture—First Baptist, Holy Trinity, Remsen Presbyterian, St. Ann's, Pacific Methodist, St. Matthew's Lutheran, Second Unitarian, Christ Episcopal, St. Paul's and Tabernacle.

Sunday, January 2, 1887

It certainly must be confessed that there is an imposing array of ecclesiastical architecture upon Clinton Street. From Pierrepont Street to Third Place, eligible corners are occupied by churches belonging to the many denominations into which Christianity is divided. A shallow thinker once characterized America as a country where there was but one sauce and innumerable religions[1], and the tendency of the nineteenth century is rather to increase the number than to diminish them. Nor would a man of healthy moral nature and of strong religious convictions have it otherwise. It is as necessary for the welfare of the world that men's religious impressions should be permitted to crystallize freely as that political aspirations should have the freedom of illimitable expression. From the moment that men are willing to accept a formula, no matter how liberal that formula may be, there

---

[1] An oft-quoted joke about European faith and food, attributed to Voltaire, goes, "England had sixty religions but only once sauce, France one religion but innumerable sauces."

is, there must be, a cessation of interest in the subject, and the soul sinks into the torpor of indifference. We have seen something akin to this in the history of the pictorial arts of Europe, where the acceptance of the so-called classical standard developed a conventionality not only of treatment but of conception. Trained not to go beyond the models of excellence established by all the academies, the young students who had imagination and the fire of genius suppressed these most noble faculties and poured the whole of their energies into the one admissible groove of technical skill. Invention and observation were dwarfed, and he was the best painter who was the most servile copyist of the accepted standards.

Were there but one faith, however, there would be fewer churches, and there would be none of the impressive grandeur that all feel who enter into a medieval cathedral. Coleridge said that Westminster Abbey was a petrified religion[2], meaning thereby that the architect had been so penetrated with the awe with which humanity regards Omnipotence that he had been able to imbue the cold and senseless stones with his own feelings. Such is, indeed, the gift of genius throughout the ages, finding at one time art, at another time architecture, at another the forum and at another the printing press as the most fitting channel of expression. It is not that we have not the genius of our forefathers, nor is it that we lean less assuredly upon those high hopes that Christianity gives, but it is that the genius of this century does not express itself architecturally. If it did, how soon should we see all the leading denominations building cathedrals common to all the members of their faith within the city? There would be the local church and there would be the city church, presided over by the most gifted minister of the denomin-

---

[2] In *Nature*, Ralph Waldo Emerson writes, "'A Gothic church,' said Coleridge, 'is a petrified religion,'" but I could not find that sentence in Samuel Taylor Coleridge's writings.

ation. Here the strangers would come, and here, too, would resort those whose religious impressions had ceased to be in unison with their own sect, and upon high days here also would come many from the local churches. But it is useless to speculate in that direction, because nothing can be more obvious than the fact that up to the present hour American genius has not expressed itself in religious architecture. In other branches of the art something has been done here and there that shows that even in building we are not mere slaves of conventionality. But the architect of a church is confined between the two horns of a dilemma. He is expected to retain the form of medieval architecture, for all admit that it bears the impress of deep religious feeling, and he is expected to meet all the requirements of modern ideas. Under such circumstances his work is always a compromise and often a failure. Added to these conditions is a third—a limited money supply, with which he must rival, at least externally, those glorified structures whose cost was never counted and that took centuries to build. Taking these things into consideration, it is marvelous that we have done what we have done.

The first church that the peripatetic critic and philosopher will encounter in his travels upon Clinton Street is the First Baptist Church, at the corner of Pierrepont[3]. It is of red brick bonded with sandstone, both the local brownstone and the finer-grained variety from Ohio. There was consider-

---

[3] The northeast corner, part of the present site of 1 Pierrepont Plaza. The building E.R.G. describes was built in 1880, on the site of a humbler church, when the congregation merged with another that had been on Nassau Street, between Fulton and Washington. Their church was torn down the same year. The "edifice will be missed by the residents of the neighborhood," the *Eagle* reported, "as it was quite an old and characteristic building," first established in the 1820s. It was replaced by a six-story printing press. The church on Pierrepont was sold ca. 1891 to the Brooklyn Savings Bank. "The residence section of Brooklyn has changed rapidly since the … church was built," the *Eagle* reported in 1891; many of the congregants had moved to Park Slope and New Lots.

able ingenuity in its construction, for it had to be exceedingly compact, as the ground upon which it was erected is decidedly limited. It may roughly be described as consisting externally of gable ends arranged in the form of an imperfect Greek cross, with a small and somewhat insignificant belfry at the point of union. The material is one that our architects handle very successfully, and the bonding is done with taste and skill. It certainly is not a failure as a building, but at the same time it must be confessed that it has not the ecclesiastical air, nor would anyone be surprised at hearing that it was a school or an insurance building. This fault cannot be ascribed to Holy Trinity, which is on the next block, at the corner of Montague, for this is deeply clerical, and has the same sense of awesomeness which seems inseparable from pure Gothic architecture. The human mind who leans instinctively to hero worship must busy itself at the sight of this church, with some thoughts of the man to whom we are indebted for this exquisite style of architecture. No man knows him. At the beginning of the thirteenth century, Gothic was developed simultaneously in France and England. Amiens, St. Owens[4] and Salisbury cathedrals were all erected so nearly at the same time that their plans must have been worked out by the same man at the same hours[5]. The only clue we have is the fact that they were built by an association known as the Free Masons, and every stone has the sign of the mason and the counter sign of the master out in the reverse side. Three marks are visible in the towers and crypts. No Tolfee teocalli[6], no Hellenic Parthenon, no Egyptian pyramid, no Etruscan mausoleum, no Roman aqueduct, can so impress the mind as the soaring spire of Holy Trinity.

---

[4] In French, Saint-Ouen, in Rouen.
[5] Construction on the Amiens and Salisbury cathedrals began in 1220, but their architects were not the same men. Construction at Saint-Ouen did not begin for almost another hundred years.
[6] A teocalli is an Aztec temple. He may have believed the Tolfee to be a Native people, though I can find no record beyond a hill in Michigan.

Whether we stand in front of it on Clinton Street and look up at it with craning neck or see it afar off from the promenade of the bridge or the plaza of Prospect Park[7], it is an exquisite creation and a fitting symbol of the religion that aspires to the infinite beauty, holiness and love of heaven. Internally, however, Trinity Church, Brooklyn, is not so satisfactory. It is of the variety of Gothic known as flamboyant, but this demands more money than we have[8] and better stonemasons and better glass windows. Flamboyant was the ecstasy of triumph in medieval art in its means and capacities. The columns were slender and the capitals huge, to show how perfectly the architect was master of his materials and how thoroughly he could calculate thrusts and powers of resistance. But the masons and stone carvers of that time were almost equal to the sculptors of today, and their rounded masses of foliated work priceless and altogether beyond the power of modern imitation. They are imitated in Trinity, however, by plaster moldings painted to simulate the color of stone, and this piece of trickery, so out of keeping with the noble exterior, gives one a thrill and a sense of pain akin to the discovery that some party leader beloved and honored above his fellows was a paltry palterer of his word and influence and a hoarder of ill-gotten millions. The stained glass, too, is not satisfactory. The great west window of the chancel is fine in the upper part, but below it is too much under the influence of English art as it developed itself under William and Mary, the figures of the apostles and saints being decidedly conventional in conception and mediocre in color. It is conceded now that the earliest stained windows of the Gothic were the best, for these mere ambitious efforts that introduce subjects and personages were seldom handled with due regard to the limitations of a transparent medium that neces-

---

[7] Development in Brooklyn was so low that the spire was visible not only from the Brooklyn Bridge but also what became Grand Army Plaza.
[8] Edward Rowland Greene was a member of this church, and his father was a vestryman.

sarily forbids the introduction of perspective and luminous background distances. There are conditions under which a story can be told in the stained glass of a window, but as a rule it is better to regard it as simply a mosaic of the most brilliant transparent colors. The lower part of the interior of Trinity seems dull and wants the accentuation of light reflecting brass work. Before the introduction of gas there was abundant opportunity for giving this, but with the present system of illuminating, the architect finds himself put to sore straits so long as he is compelled to retain a semblance of medievalism in his interiors. There is a Presbyterian church on the next block, on the corner of Remsen and Clinton streets[9], about which it is difficult to say anything complimentary. It shows, however, that it is possible to develop a variety of Gothic ecclesiastical architecture that is without a single impressive or pleasing feature.

The next church on Clinton is St. Ann's, between Joralemon and Livingston streets[10]. This is the new structure that takes the place of the old St. Ann's, on Sands Street, the first Episcopalian church erected in Brooklyn, and very dear to all the old habitants of Ihpetonga, but which was torn down for the bridge entrance[11]. Externally, it presents a great main gable and two side gables decorated with perforated pinnacles. The material is brownstone banded with Ohio stone, and this, combined with the finials and crockets and pilasters, gives a very ornate appearance, something like, if I may be

---

[9] On the southeast corner. It's still there, but the church closed in 1974, and by 1979 plans had been drawn to convert it into co-ops.

[10] It was built in the 1860s. A century later, when the St. Ann's congregation moved into the old Holy Trinity building on Montague, it sold the landmarked Livingston church to the Packer Collegiate Institute, which had been housed around the corner since the 1850s. The old church housed an auditorium and later classrooms, dining halls and a lounge. Packer no longer uses it, however, and paperwork was filed in 2020 to convert it into condos.

[11] See Chapter 4.

permitted the simile, a pretty girl with too many ribbons. Had it not been for this, the grand conception of the main gable and the high-soaring peaked roof would have produced a strong impression, but these advantages are frittered away or concealed by meretriciousness of decoration. The use of bond courses for color effects does not belong to pure Gothic but preceded it. We find it first in those Byzantine ecclesiastical towers which are popularly called Carlovingian, though the successors of Charlemagne had nothing to do with them. The material employed for bonding was obsidian, or volcanic, glass, and had it not been for these churches in the south of France and the north of Spain there would have been no proof that there had been a volcanic eruption in Auvergne under the second dynasty. From these regions the custom spread to Italy and was maintained there and only there during the best periods of Gothic architecture. He must indeed be a prejudiced man who could assert that the exterior of St. Ann's had the same religious aspect as that of Holy Trinity. But inside the advantage is all with the former, for there is clear evidence that the architect was endeavoring to originate an interior that should not be a poor, tricky imitation of medieval splendor but in strict conformity with modern requirements and ideas. The columns are slender shafts of iron with iron capitals, painted indeed but not disguised; and these not only bear up the galleries over the aisles but also support the arching, which appears to be the support of the clerestory walls. But these wooden arches are, I think, dummies, the whole weight being carried by the beams, either iron or wooden, which rest upon the capitals and go up to the clerestory. If this is so, it would have been better to have carried the iron shafts right up to the clerestory and have supported it upon broader capitals of a decoration in harmony with the metal employed. The use of iron in modern architecture is a factor of the utmost importance, but it has its own constructional laws, and its decorative features should spring out of them and in its own inherent quality.

Boldly hammered iron capitals would have been a magnificent feature and would be in keeping with the immense breadth of the nave of this church and the stupendous sweep of the chancel arch. The ridge of the ceiling is one hundred feet from the flooring, so that the reader can appreciate what the chancel is. So justly proportioned is this noble church that its decorations need not be considered, because time will teach the parishioners what is most suitable and in harmony with the place. The main features, the lofty clerestory, the well-arranged windows, the broad nave and the thrice noble arch of the chancel will be appreciated in the course of years, and everything else can be, and no doubt will be, changed until the adornments are in the same spirit and imbued with the same loftiness.

I must not omit mention that when the congregation migrated from old St. Ann's they brought with them the memorial tablet of white marble commemorating Joshua Sands. It is thus inscribed:

```
          To
Commemorate their respect
For the character and benefactions of
       JOSHUA SANDS,
Long a warden of this Parish. This
tablet is erected by the Vestry of St.
Ann's Church.
  Oct. 77,           Ob. A. D. 1835.
```

The church also boasts a noble lectern and pulpit of brass work—memorials of Dr. Schenck, the late rector, who was one of the best beloved men of Brooklyn[12]. The pulpit is a highly artistic object, giving in bold and skillful repoussé upon its sides the emblems of the evangelists, and on its center panel the form of the Good Shepherd, himself the lamb of God. These objects show in a striking manner how much brass decoration is needed in church interiors and how excellently it fills the void so conspicuous below. There is also a memorial brass tablet upon the flooring of the nave. One feels at once that here is a church with the true essentials of beauty, one that is bound to grow into something of which all Brooklyn will one day be proud.

At the center of Pacific Street, we meet with a Methodist Episcopal Church, built of brick with brownstone front[13]. The eastern window is of the style called rayonnant, or cartwheel, and the side windows are what may be called Deacon's Renaissance. Though nothing could well be homelier than the façade, one catches a glimpse of a cornice upon the side, which is of the most artistic brick work. This makes one suspect that once the front was of brick also, at which time, no doubt, the building possessed some attractive features. The Baptist Church on the corner of Pierrepont Street is proof that good brick work was done in Brooklyn even before the erection of the Long Island Historical Society's splendid structure[14]. The English Lutheran Church on the corner of

---

[12] Dr. Noah Hunt Schenck (1825–1885) helped free St. Ann's from debt. "St. Ann's, under his direction, was raised from a comparatively poor and struggling parish to one of the most prosperous in Long Island," *Frank Leslie's Sunday Magazine* reported when he died, "and the congregation increased so that at times the church was unable to hold it." He's buried in Green-Wood.

[13] It was on the northwest corner, occupying the same lot today as the apartment buildings at 214 Clinton Street and 147 Pacific Street. Church construction finished in 1851, and it was demolished in 1892.

[14] Later called the Brooklyn Historical Society, now the Center for Brooklyn History, 128 Pierrepont Street was once catercorner to the First Baptist Church.

Clinton and Amity streets is a proof that bad brick work was the rule when it was erected[15]. There can be no doubt that inside it is convenient, well lighted and well arranged, but its exterior is something to marvel at. There is one style for which brick is most unsuitable, and that is the classic, which has been adopted here. A square, squat brick tower breaks through the upper cornice of the pediment, but the architect was not going to lose the splendiferous effect of a brick pediment for such a little thing as the foundation of his tower, so underneath it is another pediment, shrunk and contracted as it were by the weight of the bricks resting on it. Upon this short tower has been reared a wooden octagonal tower, upon that a wooden hexagon with a Queen Anne pediment on each face, upon that is a round construction with six windows, and from that aspires a wooden spire[16] shaped like a candle extinguisher in a country house where there is no gas. Oh! what a difference there is between this and the noble spire of Trinity.

Leaving St. Matthews' behind us, we advance toward the corner of Congress. The gladsome message carved in stone, "The truth shall make you free," is the legend on the little church, one block from Amity, which the profane call the Holy Turtleback, but which in sober earnest is the Second Unitarian Church[17]. It is a low structure in the form of a

---

[15] On the northeast corner, St. Matthew's English Lutheran Church was one of several homes for this congregation. The church sold the land on Clinton in 1894, at first to the board of education, for a schoolhouse, but then to neighbors who objected to the schoolhouse and pooled their money. The church moved to Park Slope, where many of its parishioners had moved, to 306 Sixth Avenue, at the corner of 2nd Street, where its 1895 structure remains.

[16] This spire was entirely removed in February 1894, as the wood "had become so decayed as to become dangerous," the *Eagle* reported.

[17] It opened on the southwest corner ca. 1858. The Unitarians abandoned it in 1924, but it remained standing until 1962. The land formed part of a site a developer wanted to turn into a supermarket, but an

shortened Latin cross, and at the western end is a campanile tower, not quite so imposing as that of Pisa. The walls are of mortar, and will in time be covered with creeping plants, and if the windows had been made with lanceolated heads it would have been as charming as it is sensible and unpretentious. Then there is a gap, and no church is in sight until we come abreast of the square Gothic Norman tower of Christ Church[18], at the corner of Harrison Street[19]. This edifice is somewhat conventional as regards the exterior, but inside it is a good example of the best type of a plain early English parochial church of small size. The window of the chancel is one of the finest specimens I ever saw and is one of those rare exceptions where it is possible to obtain perspective in stained glass. The subject is the great stairway that Jacob saw in his dream, upon which angels were ascending and descending. Here the fact that the supernal stairs will not go back simply intensifies the idea that the patriarch's dream seems intended to convey, that there is constant communication between earth and heaven. We don't want those beloved stairs to fade away in the distance, but we are prepared to accept the invisibility of the uppermost steps. Not only is the subject within the exceedingly narrow limitations of stained-window art, but the treatment is absolutely original, and the angels are depicted in a happy medium between realism and conventionality. Some conventionality is necessarily unavoidable in such a subject as for instance in the wings, which modern criticism seems to eliminate from angelic forms upon the plea that science forbids arms and wings to the same beings. For my part, I want my angels with

---

organized community fought instead for a park and won—the city bought the land, and Cobble Hill Park was dedicated in 1965.
[18] Built in 1841–42, it still stands, though in disrepair. In 2012, the bell tower was hit by lightning, knocking stones loose and killing a pedestrian.
[19] Harrison Street was renamed Kane Street in 1928, in honor of election commissioner James Kane (1842–1926), a one-time alderman (like a modern city councilmember) and local Democratic-party bigwig.

wings, nor do I see any other way in which an artist can express the angelic character. The interior is very plain. The pillars have no artistic capitals, and the lanceolated arches are exceedingly simple. The walls are painted unpretentiously, with the vine, recalling Christ's words to his disciples[20], and the roof of the aisles in somber semi tones.

St. Paul's, on the corner of Carroll Place, is the fourth Episcopalian church on Clinton Street[21]. Built with roughly squared stones of volcanic basalt and trimmed with red sandstone, this church strikes the eye at once from its massiveness. Its southern tower is particularly solid, though the architect need not have furnished it with crenelations for musketry as it is not likely that it will be what church towers once were, a refuge and fortress against invading enemies—the blockhouse of feudal times. In spite of the crenelations, this structure makes the observer feel that it is the work of a man of genius in his profession, with immense enthusiasm for Gothic architecture. …[22] It is filled with the mysticism of arrangement in which medieval architects delighted. There is an apse facing to the eastward, with five lanceolated windows forming the folds of the sacred hood, which must be three, five or seven. Then it has real transepts, although there are no entrances through them, and these have windows, consisting of a rose window above and two lanceolated windows below, forming an irregular trefoil. The nave is broad and airy, and as there are transepts there is of necessity a crux, an imposing feature in ecclesiastical architecture, and in St. Paul's distinguished by a very fine roof, with splendid arched

---

[20] In John, Chapter 15, Jesus tells the disciples he's "the true vine" and they're fruit-bearing branches.

[21] The building, opened in 1869, is still an active church.

[22] I have omitted a sentence here, because it is not entirely legible, thanks to a small tear, as well as poor printing and scanning.
"Thoroughly [missing] in [missing], it is yet the only one of the forms that is intensely ecclesiastic, and this [missing] enormous study of the subject."

ribbing. The pillars of the nave are of red sandstone, and the capitals are fine specimens of foliation. The walls of the clerestory are diapered, and those of the aisles painted a dark turkey red, those of the chancel being similarly décorated but more elaborately. It is beautiful to see with what preciseness and enthusiasm the architect has used the faculty of constructional decoration afforded by pure Gothic. This is in strong contrast with the Presbyterian Church, at the corner of First Place[23], which never could have been designed by an architect but must be a specimen of the combined artistic powers of the ruling elders and some builder and contractor. It is presumably Byzantine in style, though that is doubtful, and its heavy blocks of brownstone have no real affinity with any known formulas.

Far different is the Tabernacle Baptist Church, at the corner of Clinton and Third Place[24]. The ashlars are of rubble, and these reveal the important secret that our coarse brownstone does not look so well when squared and dressed as when used roughly in irregular masses. The style of the Tabernacle is that of a small English country parish church built with exceedingly limited funds, for the clerestory disappears in a great peaked roof from which dormer windows would peep out. The façade faces the south, and over the main entrance there is what appears to be a new style of rose window. I thought at first that the Baptists were half ashamed of the artistic character of their church and had withstood the architect's prayerful plea for a rose window and had filled up the circle with stones bearing the inscription, "Baptist Tabernacle Church." But it appears that this surmise was

---

[23] It was built in 1867. Sixty years later, the congregation moved and sold the building to the Norwegian Seamen's Church, which occupied it until moving to Manhattan in 1983. The building still stands, having been converted into apartments, probably in the 1990s.

[24] Built in 1875 on the northwest corner, it was sold to the Syrian Orthodox in 1927. The lot was subdivided in 1968, and the modern Nos. 488–498 Clinton Street were built the same year.

erroneous and that the congregation were in reality very fond of their pretty church and had a great pride in their stained-glass rose window. No doubt the sterner of the brethren felt that it was a judgment upon the others who had departed from the primitive ugliness of denominational architecture when the wicked boys from the Flats and from Gowanus Canal pelted the window with bits of coal and reduced its vain beauty to fragments of glittering glass. The boys who had obtained some knowledge of the interior arrangements were aware that the organ pipes were immediately beneath this window, and their desire was twofold, not only to break the window but to do it so adroitly that the pieces of coal and fragments of glass should fall down the organ pipes. They had the satisfaction of accomplishing this dual feat, and the congregation blocked up the window. Then they tried their hand at missionary work and endeavored to convert the heathen of Brooklyn Flats[25], bringing their tormentors into their Sunday School, but without much success. Between the educated, the refined and the Christian women of Clinton Street and the outcasts of Brooklyn Flats and the daredevil young desperados of the canal, there is a gulf which requires incessant bridging and is daily growing broader. Nor will the George nostrum[26] have much effect upon it. E.R.G.

---

[25] Likely a reference to the Red Hook waterfront, off which are shallow waters, or "flats." There are also Gowanus and Bay Ridge Flats.

[26] The populist economist Henry George (1839–1897) was a celebrity following publication of his seminal 1879 study *Progress and Poverty*. His primary principle was a single tax, on land value rather than labor. Because "land is a fixed resource, the economic rent is a product of the growth of the economy and not of individual effort," *Britannica* explains.

11

Columbia Heights and Columbia Street

CONTRASTS OF A HIGHWAY.

The Heights and the Street Called Columbia.

Glories of the One and Squalor of the Other. Yet Perhaps as Much Happiness in the Latter as in the Former—Artistic Houses and a Magnificent Panorama—The Quarter from Atlantic to Hamilton Avenue—Among the Squatters of Shantytown—Hogs, Dogs, Goats and Cinder Pickers.

Sunday, January 16, 1887

Many a budding poet in the wicked City of Chicago has tried his flutterings in an ode to the Illinois River, which, born amid the sweetness and purity of the prairie, becomes, before its existence ends in the lake, a thing so foul, so loathsome, that the imagination even of a Chicago poet recoils from it. The Illinoisian bard has in its two existences magnificent opportunities for discipline. He pictures first the chain of pools far out upon the expanse of the corn-laden prairie, the children playing along the sedgy banks, the flowers nestling among the tall tufts of last year's graves and peeping out as shyly beautiful as oreads, the bathers in the heats of Summer, the cows standing knee deep in the cool waters in sequestered nooks where the sunlight shoots through the thick bushes and the foliage of the trees in pencils of golden hue. Then the scene changes, and there are factories, and the masts of schooners, and then more factories and great ships and steamers, and the river is no longer pure and wholesome and sweet to look upon but a hideous black sewer receiving every abomination, hateful in appearance, odious in smell, filthy and polluting to the touch, a horror in the center of the city, threatening plague and pestilence, a black nightmare on men's souls. Many a human existence, continues our friend the Bard of Chicago, has been a sad parallel to that river, and has become as foul and fearful with sin ere it reached the lake of that unknown region to which all human life is hastening. I have often thought that Columbia Street, in our own native City of Brooklyn, had some points in common with the river of Chicago. There are contrasts in its long stretch, which are instructive enough, though not so violent as those suggested above.

Columbia Heights rises from Fulton Street at a rapidly increasing grade calculated to make horses pant, and as soon as it is fairly above the level of the tops of the houses on Furman Street it begins to be aristocratic. The houses belong to that class that is popularly known as swell. They are for the most part owned by the inhabitants, and many of them were built by the owners. Here one sees the domestic architecture that is most fashionable, the terra cotta decorations and the superb stained-glass doors of the halls. There is mosaic on the flooring; there are magnificent hanging lamps in the corridor, of which glimpses are caught by the observers when the door of the hall is opened; there are bay windows and side windows; there are massive door plates of hammered brass; there are curtains of rich damask looped up artistically with watteauish[1] ribbons of the popular yellow. Between the folds of these, one sees magnificent vases from China or Japan standing upon quaintly carved teak tables, or self-assertive bowls from the Five Churches factory[2] holding rare flow-

---

[1] Jean-Antoine Watteau was a French Rococo painter noted for his use of color and light in depictions of the theater and commedia dell'arte.

[2] Vilmós "Wilhelm" Zsolnay of Pécs, Hungary, opened a small ceramics company in the nineteenth century that grew into an international concern. The factory in Fünfkirchen (or Five Churches, the city's German name) was especially known for its glazes and lusters. "Zsolnay

ers blooming amid the snows of Winter. From time to time some lovely feminine head, the hair of a golden silkiness and with a natural wave like the head of Clytie[3], makes its appearance, bending down toward the happy blossoms in the bowl, half caressingly and half in the enjoyment of perfume. Then a rapid glance is given at the street, with no apparent consciousness of the deep admiration of some passerby, and the vision of loveliness disappears with just sufficient slowness to permit one to observe the artistic nature of the morning wrapper. There are carriages on Columbia Heights, but as the street is narrow they do not come prancing and dancing along, as they might do in the park. And there are many pedestrians, too, but they have a reserved air, as if conscious that Columbia Heights is a dignified location, with the burden of great wealth upon it. When Columbia Heights is, so to speak, merged in Pierrepont Place, the air, far from being dignified, rises to palatial, and this atmosphere is maintained through Montague Place[4].

And what a charming entourage there is on every side! Every house is a good house, neighbored by good houses. Behind them are the famous gardens of the Heights, located upon the roofs of the tall storehouses and factories of Furman Street. Here individual culture makes itself apparent, for no two men have the same idea of a garden, except professional gardeners. One man loves to see everything rising from grass. Grass is the groundwork, and he has plots of bright-colored flowers like nemophilas and eschscholzias, which are to the green of the turf what precious stones are to the setting. Another man likes preciseness, well-graveled walks and a rustic Summer house covered with wisteria at the end, or perhaps

---

pottery has a well-known reputation and ... was excellent in quality," the American Ceramic Society reported in 1906.

[3] A water nymph in Greek mythology.

[4] Columbia Heights ends at Pierrepont Street, but its path continues, after a slight curve to the east, for two blocks to Remsen, as Pierrepont Place and Montague Terrace.

an observatory with a refracting telescope. And beyond the garden there is always Nature, not, indeed, in her grandest, but in a very sweet and lovely aspect. The inhabitants of the Heights are compelled to see the sky, which so few men ever look at. Here it is constantly before them, with all the changes of cloud forms, and the exquisite chiaroscuro of sunlight and shadow upon the great masses of cumuli, and the fretwork and fairy penciling of faint cirri, and the great bars, crimson and gold, of stratocumulus. These variations have for their background the almost infinite gradations of blue of the sky. Below all this is the bay and the rivers that run and the puffing tugs and the great gliding steamers and the white-sailed ships and the wondrous towers and tracery of the bridge and the point of Manhattan Island, with its campanile spires and tower-like buildings, and the darkened ridge of Staten Island and the enigmatical statue on Bedloe's Island[5] and the far-off indigo-blue mass of Orange Mountains in the foreign land of Jersey.

So much for Columbia Street upon the Heights. Columbia Street south of Atlantic Avenue is another matter[6]. It begins like any other ordinary poor street, where people live to be close to their work in factories or bonded stores or along shore. Columbia Street is at first only one block from the water, and hence there are buildings contiguous to it which have the appearance of being colossal, bonded warehouses. With these are mingled many structures of the same appearance, whose tall chimneys, however, reveal the fact that they are factories. Upon Columbia Street itself there are few of these buildings, and it is given up to small houses and small stores. Conscious apparently of the limited accommodation within, the enterprising dry-goods merchants hang much of

---

[5] The Statue of Liberty. Congress renamed Bedloe's Island Liberty Island in 1956.
[6] Today, Columbia Place (south of Joralemon) and Columbia Street (south of Atlantic) are separated by the BQE and Adam Yauch Park, but then they flowed into each other uninterrupted.

their stock upon the outside, so that the traveler walks under an awning of dress goods and blankets. This gives the street a gay and effective air, quite in keeping with the theatrical bill posters that adorn the fences and the dead walls. There is a great schoolhouse not twenty years old, but somehow it has the air of being a most venerable and ancient structure, which is partly due to the fact that the municipal Solons who erected it thought it unnecessary to make it a thing of beauty and went to the opposite extreme[7]. Anything more depressing to the juvenile heart than the windows of this establishment architecture has not succeeded in developing in any age or clime. And this is saying a good deal, for the hearts are stout in this part of Brooklyn, which is considered a perfect nursery of pugilists and truckmen. The trucks of the latter, when not in use, line the curbstones on both sides in a homelike fashion. As for the pugilism, there are knots of five and six men and young fellows at every corner where there is a saloon, and the talk is mostly upon "scrapping" matters. I affected to be arranging the buckle of an Arctic overshoe in a neighboring hallway and gathered the following gems of conversation. "I seen it all. Long Petey led for his nose wid his right." "Ah! stay there, you mickey, wot yer giving us? Wasn't I dere meself? Petey feinted wid his left, and when Bill Simmons tried to counter wid his right, Petey cross countered him under de jaw, and put him to sleep real beautiful." I was pained at losing the rest of this scientific discourse, but the thermometer was not at a point where lingering was a luxury, so I passed on. Beyond the casual fact that there seemed to be an unusual number of candy stores, I

---

[7] The old P.S. 29, on the southeast corner of Columbia and Amity Street, named "the worst school building in Brooklyn" by the *Eagle* in 1915. Its classrooms were low, cramped, badly lit and poorly ventilated, and its wooden stairways were narrow. As early as 1884, local officials were looking to replace it, but the school did not move to its present site, on Henry between Baltic and Kane, until 1921. The school's original location is now roughly the tennis courts at Van Voorhees Park.

observed nothing specially remarkable until I crossed Hamilton Avenue.

Then there came another change in the existence of Columbia Street quite as marked as the first. I had passed into Shantytown. Novelists, more especially Thackeray, have asserted that outside of every important city in Ireland is a suburb of shanties where primitive pigs wander in primeval association with man and share his humble home[8]. How far this is true I can't say, since when I traveled in Ireland I was always on the lookout for beautiful scenery and interesting architecture and took no note of the squalor. I have no doubt it is there, though Thackeray is a very biased witness. Throughout his rambles in Ireland he seemed to have detested his fellow countrymen the English for being snobbish and cold hearted and cruel and prim in dress, conversation and bearing. But he also seems to have detested the Irish for being the opposite, for being warm hearted, natural, ragged, poor and dirty. And he found little to praise, save the fish and the poultry. But now that Columbia Street has opened its wealth of interesting facts to my astounded gaze, I am free to confess that I think shanty towns must prevail very largely in communities where there is a formidable percentage of Irish population. The shanties were built on Columbia Street with the permission of the owners of the land, who receive a small ground rent from the shantyists, so that they are not squatters[9], like those who established themselves on the West Side

---

[8] William Makepeace Thackeray published a chronicle of his four months traveling in Ireland, *The Irish Sketch Book*, in 1842. In it, he describes the poor families in County Cork on a market day. "As the weather is fine, they were sitting outside their cabins, with the pig ... We saw ... the family pig almost everywhere: you might see him browsing and poking along the hedges, his fore and hind leg attached with a wisp of hay to check his propensity to roaming."

[9] A map from 1886 indicates the west side of Columbia Street, from roughly Mill to Lorraine streets, was "occupied by squatters," failing to adopt E.R.G.'s nuanced distinction. Today this land is occupied by the

between New York and Harlem. They are constructed out of varied materials, in which iron roofing and coarse planking are most prominent, and at first glance they seem exceedingly miserable. Everything tends to deepen the impression of squalor, the rusty stovepipe wandering in uncertain elbows around the ramshackle structure; the multitudinous materials of the roof, held in their place by a choice assortment of cobblestones; the absence of windows facing toward Columbia Street; the peculiar arrangements for catching the rainwater, and the tumbledown appearance of the outer porch or hallway. Add to these things the inequality of level of the different shanties, and the ice and frozen snow around them, and the natural squalor of an unfinished street, and one may be pardoned for thinking the inhabitants very miserable. The mise-en-scène, too, is forlorn beyond description, for Columbia Street is here a long waste stretch, with great gaps snow laden between the crossing streets, which alone have the level of Hamilton Avenue, and there is hardly a comfortable structure within sight. Far off in the distance there is shipping and to the right there are the houses and structures of Red Hook, and to the left the spires and houses of Brooklyn. But here is all snow, ice, filth, cold, confusion and apparent anguish.

These appearances are intensified by the aspect of the dumping ground, where there are ragged women and frowsy men working away in company with hogs, dogs, goats, cats and poultry. Two goats, when I approached, were rending from each other a mass of paper which seemed specially palatable and luscious, and perhaps was a theatrical poster of a Hyde & Behman company[10]. A fat, fierce sow that had survived her offspring was in an ecstasy of delight over a heap

---

western part of the Red Hook Houses. There was a smaller site of "squatters" at Halleck Street, in the gap between where Columbia Street splits off, roughly the site today of Todd Triangle.

[10] Richard Hyde and Louis Behman were a prominent pair of vaudeville impresarios with their own theaters in Brooklyn and elsewhere.

of rotten oranges but seemed inclined to dally with a black-looking compound from an oil refinery, which smelled good to her precise nostrils but did not taste so satisfactory. Cats with sore eyes and pieces torn out of their fur slunk about with a curious mixture of apprehension and fierceness. The fowls would have shared in the oranges if the old sow would have let them, but she drove them away with tremendous savageness, and then the dogs chased them. Women and children were sifting cinders, picking out microscopic pieces of fuel that were still capable of combustion. Nearby a man was burning up tin cans in a great pile, using for fuel the oily lampblack from the refineries, which so tempted the old sow. This was for the sake of the tin, which, exposed to so fierce a heat, melted and collected in a little precious pool, whereas the iron plates were quite invulnerable to it, for tin melts at 700 degrees and iron requires something over 2,500. The children did not gather round the fire and apparently were insensible to the cold. There was one girl who left her bag under the care of her little brother while she went to recreate herself with a little diversion at sliding. Her arms were bare above the elbow, she wore a thin calico gown and the underclothing must have been very scanty, and her feet were incased in the most ragged shoes I ever beheld. She was about 14, redheaded and freckle faced, but with intensely blue eyes, with slender, well-shaped limbs and with a slight symmetrical body, and she did not seem to be aware the mercury was down to 8 degrees above zero, 24 degrees below freezing. She slid up and down the ice-covered ground below the dump with great agility and enjoyment, looking around her with a triumphant glance, as if asking, "Cud any of yez beat dat, now?" and then resumed her cinder picking with the businesslike air of a clerk who has been out to lunch and resumes his seat at his desk in the office.

But I somehow doubt the misery of the people who live in these shanties. One of them, nearly at the termination of Columbia Street, a little before one comes to the huts that have signs about them, "Boats to let[11]," is a shanty no better looking than any of the others, with an L attachment made principally of bamboo poles and the matting that covers Oriental packages and chests. The owner must be connecting with the India dock, or some one of the docks or stores where Oriental goods are to be found. From the peculiar sounds that came from the wing of Honest Mike's villa I know that there were hogs in the calm enjoyment of their litter and their swill. Every hog I saw along the line of Columbia Street, including the heroine of the ranges, was of a superior breed. They were either Chinese hogs or Berkshires or a cross breed between the two. The goats were of the true Harlem breed, the Capra Harlemensis[12], and the nonchalance with which they regarded the approach of human beings showed that they controlled the situation and were regarded in the highest esteem. The ducks that waddled on the ice in the road, or quacked vehemently under the shadow of a shanty wall at the sea end of Columbia Street, were not common ducks, but of the genuine Muscovy variety. The dogs were sporting dogs, not curs, and had every appearance of being well supplied with bones. If the cinder pickers were masses of rags, I saw emerge from various shanties several comely, well clad young women of fine appearance. I remarked that very many of the shanties had their outhouses so arranged as to protect them from the elements, and in some of these I noticed plentiful supplies of coal. I doubt the misery; the dirt, however, was undeniable.

Before all things let us be just and hold the balance with an even hand. The point is to be correct rather than to do

---

[11] On the east side of Columbia, between Grinnell and Bay streets, were three boathouses, on the edge of an inlet of the Gowanus Bay, later filled in. Grinnell was renamed "Creamer Street" in 1891, after prominent physician Joseph Creamer, a police surgeon and coroner.

[12] The mostly undeveloped Upper West Side, up to Harlem, was at the time known for its squatters and goats. Capra is the genus for goats, but the species seems to be a joke.

effective writing. It would be fine no doubt to pile on the agony and picture the cinder pickers in miserable homes, feeding a worn-out and battered old stove with their scanty gleanings from the dump. It would not be difficult to depict a fever-burned man in the agonies of ague, lying uneasily upon a heap of filthy rags shared with an old sow who had just brought a squealing litter into existence. The pinch of poverty, the anguish of cold and hunger and illness, the isolation of the shanty outcasts from the comforts and consolation of the doctor and the divine might be handled with much effect. But I doubt it, and heaven forgive me if I am wrong. I believe that the citizens of Shantytown, barring the dirt, are living more natural, honest and comfortable existences than if each family had three rooms in a lofty tenement of the finest brick and terra cotta. Are we not too much in the habit of concealing our dirt and making believe that it has been removed? Do we not in effect throw it under the table, where the cloth hides it? Is our sewage system an undoubted success, so that we can afford to look down at Paddy in Shantytown, who lives in the unleveled region where there are no sewers? I was once the enviable occupant of a third-story front room in a handsome house in a good quarter in Brooklyn. It had a brownstone front, with window and door caps neatly carved, and supported by handsome brackets. There were double doors to the hall, and the flooring between them was of black and white marble in checquers. The hall lamp was a fine specimen of brass repoussé; and there was a hall mat with Salve on it[13], which alone was sufficient to swell with satisfaction every honest heart. But there was a stationary washstand in my room, with hot- and cold-water attachment, as my estimable landlady said, and from it arose odors, especially in the small hours of the morning, when I

---

[13] Once a common doormat expression, it's Latin for "hello."

do my heaviest thinking about silver[14] and the Bartholdi statue[15] and others subjects of like gravity, which would have sickened a Mongolian mule. After mature deliberation I came to the conclusion that the cowardly careless brute of a builder had brought the waste pipe of the water system into the cesspool, either ignorant or careless of the obvious fact that gases will rise by the same channel down which water falls. Our civilization is in many things unreal; we conceal much that we cannot destroy, and we hide with perfumes odorous secrets that will betray themselves. Is Paddy to be despised? He and his family live apart in decent isolation—so much more respectable than the promiscuity of a tenement house. He has no rent to pay, which is something of a consideration, especially if the money saved is invested in savings banks and not in whisky for himself and finery for his women. He has all the salt grass he likes to cut from the end of the street for fodder and litter for his animals, whose society is dear to him, for he has no equal as a raiser of livestock and a trainer of dogs and horses, and the secret of his success is that he loves the brutes, who repay him by answering love. Just look at the eyes of Irish deer hounds and red setters and see if there is not a wealth of affection for humanity in their beautiful orbs. There is dirt in Shantytown, there is sluttishness[16], but I am satisfied there is much material comfort and some undoubted superiority of moral feeling.

E.R.G.

---

[14] Likely a reference to the debate in economics at the time between the gold standard and free silver.

[15] The Statue of Liberty again, designed by Frédéric Auguste Bartholdi.

[16] Or filthiness. "Slut" originally meant a woman who was literally dirty.

12

Red Hook Lane

HISTORIC RED HOOK LANE[1].

What is Left of a Once Celebrated Thoroughfare.

The Indian Trail to a Corn Field—Ihpetonga as Iroquois Garrison Village—The Underhill House—Mrs. Melmoth, the Actress, and Her Mansion—Reminiscences of Stuart, the Painter—The Fate of Boerum, a Bad Man of Brooklyn.

Sunday, January 23, 1887

The change from the baby in the cradle to the strapping young man leading a blushing bride to the hymeneal altar is not greater than from the hamlet of Brooklands to the proud City of Brooklyn. There are undoubtedly certain quarters that time has passed by either too disdainfully or too reverentially to affect much alteration, as for example the Navy Yard, whose enclosures guard some of the aboriginal swampland of the Wallabout. But there are others that have been metamorphosed completely, and in none has the change been

---

[1] Red Hook Lane was a prominent road in Colonial and Revolutionary Brooklyn, connecting Brooklyn and Red Hook. It "was originally twenty-five feet wide," the New York *Times* reported in 1894, "and ran from Boerum Place diagonally across Atlantic Avenue, between Court Street and Boerum Place ... Then, turning, it cut the southeast corner of Pacific Street and Court Street. From there is passed along to Tompkins Place, and then to Henry Street." Today, only a fragment remains, connecting Fulton Street and Boerum Place in Downtown Brooklyn. Ten street signs were put up in 2008 in Red Hook to mark the lane's former locations, together forming the Red Hook Lane Heritage Trail.

more thorough or more stupendous than at the Red Hook. In the endeavor to reconstruct the past by the aid of imagination, a horrid suspicion has beset me to the effect that Ihpetonga was not the name of the Heights, as is universally believed, but of a village of aborigines situated where the present municipal buildings now stand, and that the hamlet of Breuckelen was constructed cheek by jowl with this village. Furthermore, I am convinced that this village of Ihpetonga was a sort of garrison of Iroquois detached partly to watch the proceedings of the white men and partly to overawe the aboriginal Algonquins, to whom Long Island really belonged, but who had been reduced to a condition of dependence by the warlike Kono Shioni, or Confederation of the Long House[2]. This confederation had long arms, and from the council fires in Central New York arranged the affairs of tribes in Virginia. The Iroquois were maize eaters, and there was a large patch of maize belonging to Ihpetonga that stretched from the foot of Clover Hill as far as Court Street, and Red Hook Lane was undoubtedly an Indian trail leading from the Village of Ihpetonga to that field. Then it extended to the Red Hook, which was a fishing place of some fame in these days. Whether there were silent oysters and happy clams in the drowned meadows around the Hook I do not know, but I should think it highly probable. No doubt the Algonquins had frequented the spot long before the arrival of an Iroquois garrison, and they were notorious consumers of bivalves of every form and flavor, and were, indeed, ingenious inventors of clam bakes. But the Iroquois would probably disdain such food and would restrict themselves to fish and corn.

Ihpetonga is Iroquois, and nothing but Iroquois, and means District of sons of Noble Ongs—Ong being the true

---

[2] See Chapter 7. E.R.G.'s Native history is marked by nineteenth-century stereotype and inaccuracy; it should be considered skeptically, if at all.

name of the Iroquois. All the Algonquin general names of localities terminate in sett, setts or settas, whereas the Iroquois terminate in *ga*, which by a peculiar, awkward, painful and most improper coincidence, has precisely the same force as the Anglo, or more properly Ongle word *ga*, a shire or county, and this is identical with the word *gau*, and this with the Hindu word *ganw*, pronounced *gum*. There is every reason for believing that the Hollanders and Englishmen from New England who settled in Long Island were viewed with a most friendly eye by the Iroquois garrison, who received them as brothers. History shows that the Iroquois had a marked preference for the English and Dutch and a haughty disdain for the French, and had it not been that the Iroquois tomahawk was thrown into the scale against the French, it is exceedingly doubtful if Quebec would have been conquered, in which case there would have been no United States[3]. Here and there one gleans strange facts that throw some light upon the state of things in the [western] end of Long Island under the Dutch Governors. A man petitioned one of them for this Indian maize field whenever the Indians should abandon it, and he received a patent for it and entered into possession at the time of the first Indian war, which was entirely with Algonquin tribes. We may therefore conclude that the Iroquois, after informing their white brothers of the Algonquin conspiracy, withdrew the garrison Ihpetonga and gave up their maize field to the people of Breuckelen, although the greedy foresight of one man enabled him to get the whole benefit for himself. I trust that the time will come when there will be a public acknowledgement of what this country owes to the friendship of the Iroquois. Fenimore Cooper, in all his Indian romances, has made blunder upon blunder, has confounded the Hurons with the Iroquois, although the latter detested them, both on their own account and because they were al-

---

[3] The British conquered Québec in 1759 during the French and Indian War, inspiring the French later to support the American Revolution.

lies of the French, and has made the Algonquins enemies of the Hurons, who were actually their champions and protectors against the terrible Iroquois. The disappearance of the Hurons and the Algonquins is in fact due in a great measure to the Iroquois, who nearly exterminated them.

Red Hook was then what Sandy Hook is now, only that the point was much more elevated. But, like Sandy Hook, it was a pleasant wilderness of trees, principally cedar, to which some of the original Dutch inhabitants added locust trees. Old Van Twiller[4], when he was governor and director for the Dutch Company[5], went round picking up islands and points of land, and in this way he bagged Governor's Island and Red Hook, giving himself patents for them in the most generous way. But the home governing body would not certify these patents, pointing out that there was no likelihood that he would improve[6] them and that improvement was the only condition upon which patents could be granted, and Governor Stuyvesant[7] presented the patent for Red Hook to the hamlet of Breuckelen, but that short-sighted community, instead of holding onto it with hooks of steel, sold it for some miserably inadequate sum to Colonel Van Cortlandt[8], who profited by the kills that surrounded it and put up two tide mills[9], where the grist was ground that came from the Indian maize field. At that time, even before it passed into the ownership of the Van Dykes[10], there was a succession of small

---

[4] Wouter van Twiller, the fifth director of New Netherland, who governed from 1633 to 1638, when he was replaced by Willem Kieft.
[5] The Dutch West India Company, which controlled New Netherland.
[6] Or develop.
[7] Peter Stuyvesant, the seventh and last director of New Netherland, who governed from 1647 to 1664.
[8] Stephanus van Cortlandt (1643–1700), two-time mayor of New York City.
[9] These were at the corner of Dikeman and Van Brunt streets.
[10] Van Cortlandt's heirs sold the land in 1712 to Matthias van Dyke.

farms in what is now South Brooklyn[11], stretching all the way from Clover Hill and from the hamlet of Breuckelen to the creek that separated the hook from the mainland[12]. These ran down to the Buttermilk Channel, and the farmhouses fronted on the lane, so that Red Hook Lane at that early time was a bustling thoroughfare. All the corn went to Van Cortlandt mills to be ground, except the Flatbush and Amersfoort[13] corn, and that was handled by the tide mill on the Gowanus Creek, which at that time had not risen to the dignity of a navigable stream, so that the mill dams were not considered obstructions. Happy, happy days, when there was no Gowanus Canal and no Congress to make yearly appropriations for the improvement of navigable mudholes[14]. While New York was a nest of traders, producing nothing and desiring nothing save to make money by the fur trade, the western end of Long Island was a flourishing farming community, free from all danger of Indian wars and having no enemy save the greedy municipal government of New York.

It is not possible now to retrace the windings of Red Hook Lane[15], but we know that it not only went to the mill dam bridge erected by Colonel Stephanus Van Cortlandt but that it also sheered to the right and ended in the famous graving ground where ships were caulked and cleaned pretty much on the site of the west end of the present Atlantic

---

[11] Now roughly Carroll Gardens and Cobble Hill.
[12] The Gowanus, before it was canalized in the 1860s.
[13] The Dutch name for Flatlands.
[14] The Supreme Court established, in the 1824 decision Gibbons v. Ogden, that the federal government had the authority to oversee interstate commerce, including by river. The Rivers and Harbors Acts were semiregular legislative bills to improve such bodies of water, including the Gowanus, overseen by the Army Corps of Engineers.
[15] You couldn't literally walk along Red Hook Lane, because the street grid annihilated it, but at least one map from E.R.G.'s time includes the street grid superimposed atop the path of the old lane.

Dock[16]. Of that famous lane, which occupies so large and conspicuous a place in the history and the reminiscences of Brooklyn, but one feeble trace remains, in the block leading out of Fulton Street. Here fifty years ago Colonel Underhill, a noted builder, erected a villa to be the cynosure of every eye, and the proudest mansion of the lane, and this by the whirling of time has become the offices of the Department of Education[17]. It stands back some distance from the sidewalk, and there are trees and grass and iron railings in front of a structure that was an unhappy mingling of the classic, the Egyptian and the Palladian or neoclassic. The caps of the columns in front of the colonnade are by no means inelegant modernizations of the lotus leaf decoration of the Egyptians, and one may trace in many a wooden villa of Brooklyn the cunning of this eclectic hand. Inside, less changes have been wrought than might be supposed possible, for the Commissioners, as they succeed each other in office according to the ebb and flow of popular politics, have dealt very tenderly with the place, and the neo-Egyptian doorways and the amazing scroll work in wood to imitate stucco decoration remain in all their pristine integrity. With the exception of that house there is not a structure from Fulton Street to the Hook that can boast of the least antiquity, and with the exception of

---

[16] A major commercial enterprise with a deep-water basin, docks and warehouses for unloading and storing maritime trade, built in Red Hook in the 1840s, where Atlantic Basin is today. The managing company was liquidated in 1922.

[17] James E. Underhill was a noted developer in Brooklyn who ca. 1830 built a splendid house for himself at the intersection of Fulton and Red Hook Lane, then one of the busiest intersections in Brooklyn, as Fulton led to the village center and the Lane led to farms and mills in South Brooklyn and Red Hook. Around 1850 the house was taken over by the Board of Education for its offices; in 1888, it was replaced by a new brick building with an entrance on Livingston Street, and in 1891 additional lots were purchased to create the modern 131 Livingston Street, still used by the now "Department" of Education. Underhill died in 1866 and is buried in Green-Wood.

that block there is no Red Hook Lane. It can be traced at a gentle angle across what is now South Brooklyn, and it has been wiped out by the rectangular blocks of the streets and places of that splendid quarter. Nothing has been spared—nothing.

And yet there were things worth sparing. There was the house where Mrs. Melmoth, the famous actress, passed the last twelve years of her life[18]. She eked out a scanty maintenance by keeping boarders, and among them was the famous native artist Gilbert Stuart. A half-length portrait by him of Judge Egbert Benson was painted there and is today in the possession of the Long Island Historical Society[19]. It is in fine condition and is painted with considerable care, but, like all his half lengths, the lower part is enveloped in an artistic gloom which prevents details from being visible. Contrary to the system of painting exhibited in the well-known head of Washington, this head of Judge Benson shows no sign of impasto. It is painted in a thin coat of opaque pigment upon the canvas and wants the vivid color sense and strong feeling of vitality which marks his masterpiece[20]. Yet at the same time it is painted with remarkable delicacy and was no doubt a fine likeness, for the eyes are pregnant with sentiment and the features of the face full of refinement and amiability. As a portrait it must be regarded as second to nothing that Gilbert Stuart wrought. As a work of art it shows clearly enough that the artist who paints for immortality and expects his pictures to live after him must adopt either the impasto method or some modification of it. By this means alone can he hope

---

[18] Charlotte Melmoth retired from the stage and bought a cottage, where she lived with a friend and her two slaves. She died in 1823.

[19] Now the Center for Brooklyn History, it lists no portrait of Benson among its holdings, but the New-York Historical Society has a painting of the judge by Stuart. Benson was, among other things, a member of the Continental Congress and the first United States Congress.

[20] Stuart's famous unfinished painting of George Washington, known as the Athenæum Portrait.

to defy the blurring, obliterating hand which Time cruelly passes over works of art. A question arises whether Stuart did not paint the replica of the full-length portrait of Washington, which has become the National portrait, now in the possession of Mr. Henry E. Pierrepont, while he resided in Brooklyn. Mr. Pierrepont's impression is that the original and the replica were painted at the time, at Washington, and no doubt he has good reasons for his belief. But this is so contrary to the practice and to the characteristic disposition of artists that I doubt it, and I prefer to believe that this replica was painted in Brooklyn itself. Mr. Pierrepont has avowed his intention of willing this most valuable painting to some public society, and I sincerely trust that the society chosen will be the Long Island Historical Society[21], which is doing the most faithful work and is an active factor in the education of the citizens of Brooklyn in local history and sound patriotic feeling. The casket in which the jewel would be kept would be worthy of it, for no building in America excels in its artistic beauty.

A curious legend has been woven around the Melmoth mansion, which it is supposed was situated somewhere near Baltic Street[22]. After its amiable mistress died, the place became a tavern and was a haunt for profligates of the wildest type. One of them, named Boerum[23], having boasted that he feared neither dog nor devil, was twitted into going to the Livingston distillery[24] for some gin at the witching hour of midnight. His road led through what had been the Indian

---

[21] This copy of the portrait, one of several, is probably the one now owned by the Brooklyn Museum.
[22] Henry Stiles, in his *History of the City of Brooklyn Vol. II*, puts it on what's now Carroll Street, between Clinton and Henry.
[23] There were many men in generations of the Boerum family, which around the turn of the eighteenth century owned most of the land that would one day be named Boerum Hill.
[24] At the foot of Joralemon Street, ca. 1769–1819.

cornfield and a bogle[25] of some sort was supposed to hover around an eminence in the center called the Cobble Hill[26]. Popularly styled a ghost, this supernatural being was not a real ghost—a common, respectable wraith, as the Scotch say—but an evil presence, a holy terror of unknown character. Boerum did not return, and his companions found him at daybreak, when they ventured to the spot, lying face downward, insensible, with the empty bottle in his hand. He breathed faintly and was carried to the tavern that he had quitted some hours before and restoratives were applied. But nothing could rouse him from the paralysis of terror that had invaded his whole corporeal system, and he died on the second day at the full of the ebb tide, without regaining consciousness[27]. The negroes, who in that day were the chief repositories of that occult lore that has been poetically termed the right side of nature, explained that the being that hovered around the Cobble Hill was a serpent spirit which had been adored by the Indians in their religious festivals at the formation of the maize ears and again at the gathering of the harvest, and this may be accepted as another proof that Ihpetonga was really an Iroquois garrison village, since the Iroquois called themselves children of the serpent[28], and their religious ritual contained so much that is akin to the Aztec ritual that their relationship to the Mexicans has been conceded by all ethnologists[29]. The Cobble Hill was probably a

---

[25] A Scots word for a supernatural being, such as a ghost.

[26] Roughly, the block bounded by Atlantic, Pacific, Clinton and Court.

[27] Stiles writes that not far from Cobble Hill "was a ghost-haunted spot, about which dreadful stories were whispered." Gabriel Furman writes that in the 1790s, it was reported that a spot one hundred feet northeast of Atlantic and Court was "haunted by the spirit of a murdered man."

[28] One nineteenth-century theory was that the etymology of "Iroquois" came from words meaning "true snake," but many, many other theories exist.

[29] If ever true, it isn't anymore.

mound, perhaps even a sacrificial mound reddened by blood more crimson than flows in the veins of any animal, but it was leveled without any scrutiny, and the evil spirit that made his lair there has long disappeared.

The commercial activity that once belonged to Red Hook Lane in the days of the Van Dyke mills was to that which now exists along the Hook and Van Brunt Street as a puddle in the Atlantic Ocean. It gives a man new ideas of Brooklyn to walk along the line of the docks and see the foreign steamers and great ships and the enormous buildings used as bonded storehouses. Having seen Furman Street one might be pardoned for thinking that there was enough to justify a Custom House in Brooklyn[30]. But as one walks on and on and on and sees no end of the storehouses and the docks and the steamers and the ships, the thought involuntarily arises whether it is right and proper under our form of government that we, the independent citizens of a free city, should be virtually considered as a part of New York. The history of the two cities shows the utmost hostility on the part of New York toward Brooklyn, and there is nothing in the annals of nations more tyrannical, more heathen than the seizure of the whole water line from the Wallabout to the Hook. The right to all land between high and low water mark means simply the right of wharfage. There is not an owner of such property who has not paid or is not now paying rent to the municipality of New York. There is and there always has been in the municipality of Brooklyn a faint heartedness, a sort of apology for existing independently of New York, which has been the ruin of the community and has given courage to unscrupulous men to do things contrary to public interest and to municipal right. The state of things would be ended forever if there were a Custom House for

---

[30] Until the creation of a federal income tax in 1913, most of the nation's revenue came from tariffs, the majority of which were collected in New York, so control of the Customs House was a vital concern. It's now mostly irrelevant.

Brooklyn. If there must be only one Custom House let it be given to the city that has the greater foreign commerce. Which is the dog and which is the tail? From all outward appearances the foreign commerce of Brooklyn and New York is in these proportions—Brooklyn two-thirds and New York one-third. New York is the tail and wags the dog. New York's greediness and want of convenient dockage facilities with stores combined lost her the coffee trade, which went partly to Brooklyn, partly to Baltimore. New York never possessed the china trade, which always belonged to Brooklyn, which also has the sugar trade[31]. The time has come when Brooklynites of every age must shout to the United States Government, "Give us a Custom House or give us death."

E. R. G.

---

[31] The majority of the country's coffee came from Brooklyn at the turn of the twentieth century, mostly from John Arbuckle, who in 1871 began importing beans from Brazil to modern DUMBO, where he'd roast, grind and package them before shipping them west. (Before this, coffee beans would typically be sold raw, to be roasted and ground at home.) His counterparts in sugar were the Havemeyer family, who moved their company to Williamsburg in 1855, eventually becoming Domino. At one point they refined more than half of the country's supply, importing the raw stuff from the Caribbean and Pacific.

13

Myrtle Avenue

AN OLD INDIAN TRAIL.

Now Lined With Shops and Thronged by Buyers.

The Great Saturday Night Market of Brooklyn. Scenes on Myrtle Avenue—Stylish Houses Where Clinton and His Hessians Crept—Mistakes of the Battle of Long Island.

Sunday, January 30, 1887

Myrtle Avenue is possibly another of those great thoroughfares that Brooklyn owes to Indian trails, nor have I much hesitation in affirming that these trails were made by the famous Iroquois[1]. From the moment that the hypothesis is adopted that the Ihpetonga was a garrison village of the Six Nations located where the City Hall now stands, the various trails have a meaning, and one can see that in its origin our glorious city followed certain well-defined lines of growth based upon these trails. New York was a trading post established upon a sand bank with a back country of lava beds, and the Indians, the mythic Manhattas, either did not exist at all or confined themselves to the region of the Harlem River[2]. But in Long Island the circumstances were entirely different, nor can we believe that the Six Nations, who were so well acquainted with all that passed from the St. Lawrence to the James River, were indifferent and supine spectators of

---

[1] Again, E.R.G.'s history of Native Americans should be disregarded.
[2] There was some thinking, especially in the late nineteenth century, that Manhattan had been a hunting ground, not a residence, for various Natives who lived to the north and east.

the settlements of New Amsterdam and on Long Island. The fur trade of which Albany was the outlying depot could not have existed for a moment without their permission. New York was but the station for the reception of the peltries and their transmission to Europe. The furs themselves came from regions over whose inhabitants the Iroquois exerted sovereign sway. When the Lenni Lenapi, the Delawares, sold lands, the Iroquois broke the compact at once. They said through their ambassadors: "You cannot sell land, for we have made squaws of you. Attend to your hunting and fishing and leave the affairs of men to us." It is like a Roman sentence out of Livy[3]. The Algonquin settlement near Brooklyn was Mareckiawig, and it will be seen at once that the canoes of the Iroquois at Red Hook could have intercepted all communication between New Amsterdam and the Algonquin towns had the garrison deemed it necessary to have recourse to violence. But there is every reason for believing that the Iroquois had the most friendly intentions toward the white men and were at Ihpetonga as a measure of precaution, and also to warn the Dutch to be careful about how they distributed firearms to tribes so treacherous and so unbalanced as those of the Algonquins. It is certain that the French won the lasting and terrible enmity of the Iroquois by arming the Hurons and the Algonquins, who would have driven back the Six Nations had not they been armed by the English and the Dutch. Then they exterminated their red enemies, carried Montreal by storm, filled the French frontier with shrieking and desolation and contributed in no small measure to the discomfiture of the subjects of King Louis.

Mareckiawig is supposed by Stiles to have been the shore of Wallabout Bay, and he defines its etymology thus: *Me* or *ma*, definite article; *reckwa*, sand; *ich*, locality. But it is doubtful

---

[3] Livy was an ancient Roman historian known for his epic *Ab Urbe Condita Libri*, 142 books covering about five centuries, from Aeneas to Drusus.

if this is correct, for after the settlement of the Walloons at the Wallabout[4] and after Jansen de Rapalie's purchase of the Rennigackonk tract[5] and after Governor Kieft's purchase of the tract from Rapalie's land to Newton Creek, the whole front of the Wallabout, to the mouth of the creek, was in the possession of the white men. And yet Mareckiawig was still in existence, as we learn from the petition of the Wallabout settlers to be allowed to make war upon the Indians. The postscript to this petition says, "We cannot at present resolve to attack the Indians at Mareckawick, as they have not hitherto given us any provocation." But the settlers were harassed by continual alarms, and knew that the Indians meant war, having probably regular information through the Iroquois garrison at Ihpetonga. The wording of the petition is more consistent with the hypothesis of an Iroquois garrison than any other. It says: "Whereas a short time ago the scum of this place (which we may with justice call our fatherland) hath revolted against the righteous side, our common friends; and whereas, we see their preparation for hostilities tending to the ruin and destruction, etc. etc." This language seems to imply clearly enough that the Algonquins of Long Island had thrown off their allegiance to the Iroquois, the common friends of the English and the Hollanders. We may therefore suppose that Mareckiawig was situated not where Stiles supposed, but somewhere in the present Eighteenth Ward[6], and then Myrtle Avenue becomes obviously the Indian trail from it to Ihpetonga. The following etymology of Mareckiawig is based upon the resemblance of the word Reikiairek, the

---

[4] It is generally accepted today that the name Wallabout derives from *Waal bocht*, Dutch for "Walloon bend," as the original colonists were from the Wallonia region of Belgium.
[5] Joris Jansen Rapelje, a Dutch West India Company man, bought in 1637 a 335-acre farm on Wallabout Bay, along a stream the Natives called Rennigackonk.
[6] Modern East Williamsburg, bordered roughly by Meeker, Bushwick and Flushing avenues, and Newtown Creek.

Capital of Iceland[7], a region in whose nomenclature there is an obvious mingling of Saxon and Lap words to a greater extent even than in Kymric[8] or any thiotisc[9] language. *Ma* or *me*, great; *reckia*, royal or governing; *wick* or *wig*, town. The belief that *wick*, meaning town, is Aryan, is devoid of the least foundation; though it is found in English nomenclature, it must be ascribed to the Laps or Quins of Scandinavia, whose names offer a series of striking coincidences with Algonquin. In pure Aryan there is no word, not one, which implies royalty or any difference of rank, and the attempt to explain away the force of *ric* in Scandinavian names as meaning only rich is too ridiculous for anything save Homeric laughter[10] and could only have originated in the brain of someone profoundly ignorant of the Middle Ages, when the present nationalities were being forged by an Omnipotent hand upon the anvil of destiny.

Myrtle Avenue was graded and paved from the City Hall to Nostrand Avenue in 1835, and then only upon one side. But long before that time, prior to the Revolutionary War, it had done active service as a road to Bushwick, connecting the settlements of that locality with the ferry, and also with the Jamaica Road[11], the Kings Highway. It must have been a road of considerable importance, because when the patriots drew their lines of fortification for the defense of Brooklyn, the chief redoubt (armed with five guns) was Fort Putnam, now Fort Greene Park, commanding directly this road and indirectly protecting Fulton Street, then the Jamaica pike. The intrenchments stretched from the head of the Wallabout marsh to Fort Putnam, and from the fort to the head of the Gowanus marshes, thus protecting the ferry, the hamlet of

---

[7] Now commonly spelled Reykjavik.
[8] Referring to Welsh and similar languages.
[9] Referring to Germanic languages.
[10] Boisterous laughter, after Homer's descriptions of the gods' laughter.
[11] Myrtle Avenue and Jamaica Avenue intersect in Richmond Hill, Queens.

Breuckelen, the Wallabout settlement and the Gowanus settlement. The battle of Long Island was fought outside these lines and was a series of blunders and disasters. It is inconceivable that the patriot leaders should have insisted on fighting regular troops in their own way, thus playing the game of their enemies and negativing their own advantages. Had 5,000 Americans occupied the wooded heights from Prospect Hill[12] to Myrtle Avenue in the region of that fashionable quarter, the Hill[13], five times the force of Sir Henry Clinton[14] could not have dislodged them, and had he attacked the lines of intrenchments with the patriot riflemen in his rear they would have decimated him and perhaps taken every man of his army prisoners. These unrivaled marksmen, not a few of whom could hit a squirrel's eye with a rifle ball at the top of the tallest tree, were advanced in a solid body and marched and countermarched and thoroughly demoralized, falling victims to the Hessians, whom they could have annihilated had they been in the woods. In spite of Washington's experience with General Braddock's force, he ignored the strong points that nature had prepared for the defense of Brooklyn[15], nor during the whole war, though he always threw up breastworks, did he ever seem to realize the superior cover of the woods. In our last war[16] both sides took to the woods instinctively, and often weak detachments by cutting down trees made chevaux de frise, which were practically impregnable. Now these old Brooklyn woods have disappeared and

---

[12] He refers to the highlands in and around Prospect Park.
[13] Fort Greene and Clinton Hill.
[14] The British officer found and exploited a weak spot in the American defenses at the Jamaica Pass.
[15] British soldier Edward Braddock led the colonial army in the French and Indian War, with a young George Washington as an aide. His men were trounced at the Battle of the Monongahela in 1755 by the Natives and French, who exploited the surrounding woods to remain unseen. E.R.G.'s saying Washington should have known better.
[16] The American Civil War.

there are lines upon lines of fashionable houses in the latest architectural style in the very quarter where Sir Henry Clinton and his Hessians crept through the trees and secured the vantage ground of Prospect Heights that won them the battle.

In 1835, according to the testimony of an old clergyman, there was hardly a house on Myrtle Avenue, nor was it much more populous than before the energy of American enterprise startled the sleepy headed Dutch of Bushwick and founded Williamsburgh[17]. Then, indeed, Myrtle Avenue began to pick up and to become a place of active commercial importance. Yet, if one examines this thoroughfare critically from its beginning at the City Hall trapezium to Fort Greene Park[18], surprise will be felt at the ramshackle, miserable character of many of the buildings. In this section of the avenue the impression is forcibly conveyed that the customers who deal in those stores are entirely of the poorer classes, and that much outlay would not be warranted by the returns. There are not a few stores which are low, wooden structures, apparently one story in height, and there are many others that tempt purchasers by a liberal display of their goods on the sidewalk, which fortunately has a commendable breadth. Stoves, furniture, crockery and vegetables, dry goods and ready-made clothing form arcades, in the true Baxter Street

---

[17] The Town of Williamsburgh seceded from the Town of Bushwick in 1840.

[18] Myrtle Avenue once reached as far west as Fulton Street (now Cadman Plaza West). From Fulton to Adams, it was swallowed up by Cadman Plaza and the Brooklyn Supreme Courthouse in the 1950s. From Adams to Flatbush Avenue Extension, it was subsumed by the Metrotech redevelopment of the 1990s. From there to St. Edwards Street, where Fort Greene Park begins, Myrtle Avenue is now lined mostly with public housing (built in the 1940s) and luxury apartment complexes. In 1888, a year after this column ran, the first leg of the Myrtle Avenue elevated train opened, and it remained in service to Downtown Brooklyn until 1969.

and Chatham Street[19] style. And this is inevitable when one glances inside some of the stores and sees how little calculated they are for a favorable display of goods.

Even in these that are well built and have every advantage and resource found in first-class stores in other thoroughfares, there is a tendency to the same illegal practice, which may there be considered as a necessity of local traffic. There is also a readiness to enter into colloquial praise of their goods, which is highly embarrassing to a philosophic lounger and observer of men and manners. What can be more awkward for a lorn, lone bachelor who has incautiously stopped to admire a huge turkey than to be seized by the button by an enterprising salesman and adjured to take it home to his lady[20]. The ruffian still holding on to the button of the overcoat winds up with "gentleman, let me weigh it for you; Jim, weigh that turk—dirt cheap at sixteen cents a pound, gentleman. You can't do better along the avenoo."

On Saturday nights the pressure is terrible. About 8 o'clock the procession of buyers commences, composed entirely of people who must have things cheap and who will not buy unless allured by cheapness. On such occasions the objects on the sidewalk are largely reinforced. The shoemakers spread before their eyes large assortments of arctic overshoes and of those caoutchouc compounds[21] that the Boston girls musically term gums. These are at divers rates, some 35 cents, some 44, some 99. The dealer knows the fascination that the large label "99 cents" has upon his customers. It seems to say the living price, the bedrock rate, is $1, but, because times are hard, he will throw off a cent and sacrifice himself rather than not make a sale. This convinces them, this piteous spectacle of Abraham offering up his shoes at a sacrificial rate, and he has twenty customers at 99 cents, whereas he might

---

[19] Busy, bazaar-like commercial streets in Manhattan, the first now Park Row, near City Hall, the other once in the notorious Five Points district.
[20] He describes himself.
[21] Natural rubber.

only have had two at a dollar. Great is thy power O Humbug! Side by side with the shoe tables are other merchants, who make appeal to the same passion for cheapness. At one will be an old, white-bearded man, who, sweeping his hand over a collection of tin whistles and imitation jet brooches and hair combs, repeats incessantly in a monotonous voice, "Any toy or any jewel on this table, 5 cents." At another will be an orangeman crying out with the voice of a stentor, "Ten for 6 cents." Further on will be a huckster of bananas, shrieking, "Ripe banannies, the whole bunch for a quarter." Then there will be magnificent displays by a fishmonger, who by opening his window establishes communication between the fish within and the fish without. Clams appear to be the favorite dainty, and these are displayed on plates and sold by the plateful, and one can see feminine customers counting to see which plate has been favored by fortune. Beside the clams there are piles of lobsters, just boiled and steaming, surrounded by a perfect cloud of savoriness. Then there are small crabs, not very inviting, and baskets of oysters. The groceries are in full blast, giving away a chromo[22] and a package of sugar to everyone who buys tea and coffee, which is all ready for the buyer in paper packages. In front of every grocery store is a small stand where a young girl is grating horse radish and selling it by the teacup. I watched one whose hands were blue with cold, but business was brisk and she seemed happy, and continued rubbing away upon the grater, which must have been about the temperature of a block of ice, for metals have the happy power of distributing both heat and cold. Then there were the truck wagons from Flatbush or Bushwick selling heads of cabbage, and potatoes and onions. The various dry goods stores on the "avenoo" were crowded with customers and blazing with gas lights, and the even electricity lent its potent aid to charm the senses of the customers. It was a sort of carnival, the prevalent

---

[22] Short for chromolithograph, a colored print.

thought being, "you working people have your wages in your pocket; come in and spend the last cent." There were saloons with unlicensed minstrel performances "for to-night" being marked conspicuously and also "admittance free." Even the Bower of Pugilism of Mr. Pendergast[23] once of Williamsburgh, and supposed at one time to be the coming man, has its special entertainment on Saturday night when Young Mike and Steevey Cole and other good uns put on the mittens and paste each other on the cheek and kissing trap, rattling each other's ivories, and distilling the ruby[24] to the great contentment of the beholders.

The procession itself is more interesting than the displays of the stores. There is no one in the crowd who is not either a worker or the mother or wife of a worker. The latter, the wives and mothers of workers, have a business air about them and seem determined to get the value of the hard-earned money in their fists, setting their native wit against the seductive wiles of the salesman. But the mere fact that they are buying certain articles on Myrtle Avenue shows that they are not a match for their antagonists. It may be asserted that neither tea nor coffee can be sold cheap, and that the adulteration of these two articles that enter so largely into the diet of modern times is at the bottom of half the diseases that prevent people from making old bones. The adulteration of beer and alcoholic drinks presents the same melancholy results, so that the prohibitionists and the drinker are poisoned by the honest tradesman with the same unscrupulous readiness and conscienceless greed[25]. But the stout, determined

---

[23] Joe Pendergast, a popular local boxer in the 1880s.
[24] Old boxing slang, possibly meaning to produce blood from the eyes.
[25] It was not uncommon in the nineteenth century for tea to be mixed with leaves from other plants, or for coffee to be combined with peas, beans, rye or chicory, beet or carrot roots. Lead could be added to brandy, and watered-down gin could be masked with turpentine, wood vinegar or wood or coal naphtha. Wine might also be watered down,

women who take the wages of their sons and husbands never dream of this, nor would they, if they knew it, grind their own coffee and buy expensive teas at the high-price stores. They like the bustle and excitement of Saturday night trading, and it pleases them to be addressed as lady by attentive salesmen. When they purchase vegetables and meat they are on their native heath and no butcher or truckman can get the best of them, and they delight in the contest over these articles. The husband or the son slouches along, smoking his pipe and leaving everything to the old woman. These, however, are the domestic ones. There are hosts of young people who make the rounds just for the fun of the thing, without any intention of buying anything save shoes and stockings or perhaps some sham jewelry. These are principally girls, filled with the delight of the coming rest on Sunday, whose elastic spirits bound up immediately that the pressure of daily toil is removed from them. They are as pretty as peaches, with bright eyes sparkling with joyousness, red cheeks, red lips that show pearly teeth within, soft, smooth skins and glossy black hair. They are mostly brunettes, and they giggle from the time they enter Myrtle Avenue until they leave it. There are no bounds to their happiness when they capture some stalwart young worker and make him walk between a pair of them and pay for oyster stews. And above the laughter and the cries of the tradesmen and the tramping upon the hardened snow, and above the gaslights and the electric lights, right over the parapets and terraces of Washington Park[26], the kindly stars look down and the giant Orion blazes with belt and sword, and the Dog star flares and the beloved star Capella sheds soft influences upon her human children below.

E. R. G.

---

mixed with brandy, colored with beet root, elderberry or sloes, or deacidified by carbonates of calcium, potassium or sodium.

[26] The original name of Fort Greene Park, officially renamed in 1897.

14

Court Street

WITHOUT A NUMBER ONE.

Court Street a Civil Service Examination Puzzle.

Origin and Characteristics of the Thoroughfare—A Stroke of Municipal Enterprise—The Struggle of Two Kinds of Business—A Commercial Rival.

Sunday, February 6, 1887

Court and Clinton are my favorite streets, *par nobile fratrum*. It is therefore with unfeigned sorrow that I chronicle the painful fact that there is no number one to the former[1]. It is one of those unfortunate streets used by the Civil Service examiners for the confusion and mental torment of candidates for the position of postman or park policemen—a shocking example, as one may say. This Board of Inquisitors ask which is the longest street in Brooklyn, which is the shortest, which street first crosses Fulton Street, and having surmounted these perils the neophyte is next requested to locate No. 1 Court Street. "Point out on the map," says the inquisitor with the silkiest voice, "as near as you can the location of No. 1 Court Street." Bubbles of agony rise upon the forehead of

---

[1] In 1887, the first building on Court Street—on the west side, at the intersection with Fulton (now Cadman Plaza West)—was No. 2. Across the street was the plaza in front of City Hall (now Borough Hall); odd-numbered buildings didn't begin for a few more blocks, at the southeast corner of Joralemon, the first of which was No. 45–55, to correspond with No. 46 on the other side of Court Street. So there was—and is—no building with the address 1 Court Street.

the doomed man, who immediately remembers that there is something abnormally wrong about the numbering of Court Street. Some of the candidates pick out number two, which is joined in the strictest bonds of brotherly union with the number three hundred and something or other on Fulton Street[2], and some of them go for Hopper's undertaking establishment at the corner of Joralemon Street, which is actually No. 55, but which would be No. 1 or No. 2, if someone had not blundered in the days of auld lang syne. It is a singular fact that when Brooklyn was a village its affairs were managed with a foresight and discrimination amounting to actual genius. But no sooner did it receive its charter as a city than politicians usurped the place of men who had shown statecraft, and who, in a larger field, would have been statesmen, and the former proceeded to make a shocking mess of their first work of importance. This was the building of a City Hall[3], and the opening of Court Street, which was a corollary of the former undertaking as its name implies.

It is obvious to anyone who will calmly consider the fact that Court Street really and truly begins at the south side of Joralemon Street, and that the long strip of magnificent structures on the west side thence to the angle on Fulton Street has all the air of an appendix, or a list of errata at the end of a book[4]. This is said entirely without prejudice, and

---

[2] 340 Fulton Street, replaced (along with several other buildings here) by what's now known as 211 Montague Street, a bank built in 1962.

[3] Now Borough Hall, opened in 1848.

[4] The west side of Court Street, from Fulton to Joralemon, featured a series of handsome Victorian office buildings, including the Continental Building (1874–1926), the Phenix [sic] Building (1876–1926), the Garfield Building (1881–1925) and the Hamilton Building (ca. 1861–99). The first two were insurance companies; Garfield was a patent-medicine firm. The Hamilton was built by A. A. Low. "It is safe to say that there are few lawyers or benevolent, dramatic or social organizations that have not at one time or other occupied offices or rooms in the old building," the *Eagle* reported in 1899, including the

the writer utterly disclaims any intention of lowering the value of the Dime Saving Bank[5], or the towering edifice of brick and terra cotta which is so conspicuous an object to the visitor to Brooklyn when he first enters the square[6], or more properly the trapezium in front of that imposing municipal edifice the City Hall[7]. But truth is truth. The fact is that the municipal council of Brooklyn in the first transports of governing a city were attacked to some extent with the disease long known under the name of swelled head, but first classified and described by Charles A. Dana scientifically under the title of megalomania[8]. They planned an edifice that was to cost at a minimum estimate some $750,000, and if any gentle reader of the EAGLE has built himself a house, and knows the ratio between a minimum estimate and the subsequent total expended, he is in a position to state with some accuracy what the cost to the rising City of Brooklyn would

---

Long Island Historical Society. It was replaced by the still-standing Temple Bar Building.

[5] The Dime Savings Bank of Brooklyn, chartered in 1859, built in 1883–84 a headquarters on the southwest corner of Remsen and Court, which the *Eagle* in 1885 called "remarkable for the variety of its architecture and the wealth of its ornament." In 1908, the bank moved to a new, now-landmarked home on Fulton Street.

[6] Likely the Garfield Building, on the northwest corner of Remsen, which the *Eagle* in 1885 called "a truly remarkable building ... It shows what can be done with brick and terra cotta, even in the way of ornament, there not being a stone in it above the second story. The tower forms an effective feature, and the long slope of the roof with its double row of windows has a quaint effect."

[7] There was no blocks-long park in front of Borough Hall back then, just a small triangular plaza bordered by Court Street and an extension of Fulton Street on the east side of the building, where today there is a footpath.

[8] Charles Anderson Dana was one of the most notable nineteenth-century American journalists. He, and/or his paper, the New York *Sun*, was often reported to have coined the word "megalomania," though he may have just popularized it, as in an 1886 column published a few months before this one.

have actually been. The municipal solons did not take this into consideration, but they proceeded to acquire two blocks of real estate, one upon which the city buildings now stand[9], and the other a long narrow strip running at right angles to the first and parallel with Fulton Street. If I am not grievously mistaken it was the intention of those wise men of Ihpetonga to lay out a long narrow park in front of their structure in rivalry of that park which then stretched in all its pristine beauty before the palladian edifice of New York's municipality. But when the property had been obtained, and when the foundations had been laid, someone called a halt, and pointed out that there were no adequate means for continuing the project, which immediately dropped dead upon the hands of the projectors.

Court Street was obviously the street to the courts of law and judicature, which were to be held in that superb building that never rose above its foundations, for without some such opening the lawyers and their victims would have been forced to make a long detour or circumbendibus down Clinton Street to Fulton Street, and then up again to the scene of legal oyster opening and distribution of shells to clients. Had there been no scheme of a City Hall and park in the air I am convinced that so wise and thoroughgoing a man as Hezekiah Beers Pierrepont would have run his cross streets to Fulton Street, but his halting at Clinton[10] shows clearly enough that all citizens were agreed as to the necessity of a municipal building and the advantage of having a park in front of it, and that the locality was a settled thing in advance of any municipal action. The ultimate fate of that long parallel strip of land that the municipality acquired with horticultural intentions is not known to me definitely, but I suspect that the buildings on Court Street, from the elbow on

---

[9] Behind City Hall, heading east down Joralemon/Fulton, were the Municipal Building, the County Court House and the Hall of Records.
[10] Montague (then Constable) and Remsen streets did not originally extend to Court; they stopped at Clinton. See Chapter 6.

Fulton Street to the southwest corner of Joralemon, were erected upon part of it. If that be so, if the municipality had power to dispose of property that had been taken by the right of eminent domain for purposes other than those specified in the act of condemnation[11], what is the flaw in the title to the park lands north and south of the reservoir[12]? Lawyers contended in that instance that the lands having been condemned for park purposes could not be sold for building purposes, and that the city would not give a satisfactory title to the purchasers. And, therefore, those persons who had invested in these lots refused to take them or pay for them. And so far all the courts have maintained this view, although the question has not yet been passed upon the court of last resort. But if the final settlement should be in accordance with this view, what effect, if any, will it have upon that part of Court Street that appears to have been built upon park land, or land, at any rate, condemned for municipal purposes? I trust that it will have none, for whatever may be the law about the matter (and it is evidently a sound one and meant to prevent an abuse of the power to condemn property) the equity of the thing would clearly allow the city to correct a previously false step. The city erred in taking the east side park lands, and no doubt the city erred in taking up this strip upon which Court Street structures have been built, but common sense and equity both concur in the disposition that (as I suppose)

---

[11] An old-fashioned way of saying acquisition by eminent domain.

[12] The original site for Prospect Park was bifurcated by Flatbush Avenue. When the present site was chosen instead, the land the city had acquired east of Flatbush became known as the "East Side Lands," and the city was unsure for years what to do with it. One idea was to sell it, though some questioned the legality of this. Instead, it was gradually developed as the Central Library, Mount Prospect Park (former site of the reservoir), the Brooklyn Museum and the Brooklyn Botanic Garden.

was made of the latter. And this is why Court Street—poor, distressed Court Street—has no number one[13].

Court Street was the first thoroughfare due to municipal skill and energy. Some streets were created upon the lines faintly traced by Indian trails, others were due to individual action and genius, and others have been the result of Aldermanic acumen. But in this instance there were germs of street life already in existence. It was declared officially open in 1834, and was graded and paved in 1836, but before that time there had been a street known as George Street, which ran through the Patchen property[14] and was opened by Mr. Patchen[15] and named after George Patchen, who was a full nephew of the famous Leatherbreeches, one of the characters of Old Brooklyn, who has been saved from oblivion by both pen and pencil[16]. George Street ran from 100 feet north of State Street to Pacific Street, where it met with the old Red Hook Lane, which had angled its way from Fulton Street and then ran due north and south as far as Harrison Street[17], where it once more deviated into a diagonal course and meandered through meadows and gardens on its southwestward tack to the Hook. So that when the municipality opened Court Street, there was a street already in lively operation from State to Harrison, and beyond doubt the wagons going to the grist mills made this primitive bit of Court Street lively and bustling. South of Harrison stretched the

---

[13] He believes the buildings addressed Nos. 2–44, from Fulton to Joralemon, should not have been built, and if No. 46 then instead had been No. 2, then No. 45–55 across the street would've been No. 1.
[14] One-hundred-and-fifty acres, from roughly State to Amity streets, the waterfront to Court Street.
[15] Ralph Patchen, a distiller after whom Ralph Avenue was named.
[16] A nickname for Jacob Patchen, bestowed by Alden Spooner, publisher of the Brooklyn *Star*. Jacob was colorfully cantankerous, fighting with city officials over building or paving roads on his land.
[17] Now Kane Street.

lands of the Bergen and Cole farms[18], and this part was not opened until much later. So that all the municipality really did in the matter was to open the section between State and Joralemon, not a very great feat. It has always seemed to me that the Patchens were badly used in the matter of naming the street, and that it should have retained its name of George. Who knows with what motives the property of this family on Court Street between Atlantic Avenue and Pacific Street has been left in precisely the condition it was when the street opened? Those who are curious to know what old Brooklyn was like can get a better idea by visiting this block than by porting over old drawings in old books. There they are, the wooden hovels of those Brooklynites whose means were not ample[19]. Everyone did not live in these days in such a villa as the Pierrepont mansion[20] or the Livingston house[21], and there were many respectable and good citizens, whose opinions were valued, and whose counsel was sought in municipal affairs, who lived in just such quarters.

The Wyckoff House, now the Quartet Club House[22], is on that part of Court Street that was the old Red Hook Lane

---

[18] Jacob Hansen Bergen inherited about two hundred acres of eastern Red Hook, between about Court or Clinton streets and the Gowanus, in the seventeenth century from his father-in-law, Frederic Lubbertsen, who lived at the intersection of Hoyt and Warren. Descendants sold it in 1750, and in the 1780s or '90s most of it had been bought by Jacob Bergen (likely a descendant) and, south of about Fourth Place (or, west of Henry Street, Coles Street) Jordan Coles, Esq., a prominent mill owner, amid other interests. Coles died ca. 1835., and Bergen in 1847.
[19] Especially on the west side of Court, there were several one-story wooden residences, as well as a coal yard and marble works.
[20] The Four Chimneys. See Chapter 6.
[21] Philip Livingston's magnificently large colonial country house, located approximately at today's 277 Hicks Street.
[22] On the west side of Court Street, in line with Wyckoff Street, next door to St. Paul's, separated from the street by a row of low wooden buildings. Behind the clubhouse in 1886, on a lot as long as the church's, were a beer garden and bowling alley.

and was in its day the finest structure on the lane, with perhaps an exception in favor of the Underhill villa, now occupied by the Department of Education[23]. This is not saying much for it, for the villas of that time were not to be compared with those that had been built prior to the Revolutionary War. A great change has come over the spirit of Brooklyn since the days when Court Street was opened—a change lamentably for the worse, and I do not hesitate to say that much of the municipal folly of which men complain with perfect justice can be traced to it. There was then a hearty respect paid to wealth and superior attainments, but there was no special class arrogating the latter to themselves because they possessed the former. The man in the wooden one-story structure was an associate and friend of the men who lived in the villas of the Red Hook Lane and the delightful heights of Clover Hill. Their sons are now separated. Politics had not fallen as an appanage to the brewers and distillers and saloon keepers and tobacco men who now try to own the public to whose weaknesses (if not vices) they minister but was the occupation of every man because he felt his power of citizenship. The most important men in the history of old Brooklyn were of humble occupations, but that was a matter of no significance then. One man was a milkman, another a butcher, another kept the ferry, and so on, and by their natural shrewdness and good, hard sense they did much good service in building up this great city. Nowadays the fluent, pert lawyer, who can hardly pass an examination in any branch of literature or science outside of his professional information, presses into the front to speak volubly on subjects that he has not studied and whose importance he cannot comprehend. Thinking has become a lost art, and he only wins and wears the palm who is quick and ready and superficial. Well, well. We have not improved the men, but we have decidedly improved the architecture, for those wooden

---

[23] At the intersection of Fulton and Red Hook Lane. See Chapter 12.

houses between Atlantic Avenue and Pacific Street must be fiendishly cold in Winter and unpleasantly warm in Summer. And yet men were happy in them and lived and loved more ardently, more thoroughly than the young fellows of this blasé, beer-drinking, cigarette-smoking generation.

Court Street is, in my fancy, something like a thawing day in Winter, when the streets are filled with a slush that is neither ice nor water. Court Street is a business street, but the storekeepers apparently have not made up their minds whether their customers are aristocrats from Clinton and Henry streets and the places[24] or poor people from the vicinity of the raging canal and Hamilton Avenue. They had better decide pretty quickly, for the storemen on Smith Street are developing great energy in pushing for the trade of the poor classes. Court Street commerce is something like the creature with long ears who was born between two bundles of hay, and who was attracted by each so powerfully that he could not make up his mind which to tackle, and so died of irresolution and starvation combined[25]. Of course, the aristocratic element must win, because Smith Street is eating the other bale of hay very fast, and whether they like it or not our retail merchants must cater for the other section. I see the signs of the coming revolution, and in a little while Court Street will be to South Brooklyn what Flatbush Avenue is to that section that stretches from Fulton Street to the plaza of Prospect Park. I am very fond of looking in the store windows and am afraid that there is a conspiracy on the part of some of the storekeepers to present objects of fictitious interest for the purpose of deceiving this humble correspondent of the EAGLE. A rumor was flying about South Brooklyn that soon-

---

[24] Probably a reference to First through Fourth places, many of whose houses have the large front gardens for which Carroll Gardens is named.

[25] A variation on the paradox of Buridan's ass. Equally hungry and thirsty, and equidistant between hay and water, it dies because it can't decide which to get first.

er or later Court Street was to be written up[26], and I fear in consequence of this report certain things have found their ways into store windows that should not be there. I suspect that to use a mining expression, there has been a salting[27] of archœological treasures. Otherwise, how am I to account for a pair of very remarkable leather shoes in one window said to have been found in the ark on Mount Ararat and supposed to belong to Ham or, as the name ought to be written, Kham[28]? There is also the metallic teapot, cut from the lava mud of Herculaneum[29]. The objects are interesting, but I cannot believe that the account given of them is correct. My own shoes are made by an Irishman of supreme ability in the manipulation of leather, whose only fault is that he spells his name with more y's than is decent or commendable. I took counsel with him, and he took pains to ascertain the facts. They were these: A worthy agriculturist of Bay Ridge found them in his garret, and being much troubled about the birds attacking his fruit trees, manufactured a scarecrow of the most lifelike appearance and put these shoes on its feet. An inebriate from the asylum of that place[30], whose hat and boots had been locked up at his own request, broke away and helped himself to the hat and shoes of the scarecrow. He walked into Brooklyn and suddenly appeared at a shop where he was well known. Here he obtained all the assistance

---

[26] This suggests E.R.G.'s project was attracting attention.

[27] A scam in which precious metals or stones are added to samples to increase the value of a mine.

[28] According to Genesis 8:4, Noah's ark "rested ... upon the mountains of Ararat" in Turkey after the flood. Ham was one of Noah's sons, whose son Canaan is cursed to become "a servant of servants" because Ham saw his drunken father naked. This curse was twisted for centuries to justify racism and slavery.

[29] Like Pompeii, an ancient city in modern Italy blanketed and preserved by volcanic ash after the eruption of Mount Vesuvius in 79 CE.

[30] The Kings County Inebriates Asylum opened near Fort Hamilton ca. 1869, on the site of what's (for now) the Visitation monastery and school. See Chapter 26.

and liquor he needed, leaving the shoes behind him as a memento, and the dealer gave them to the present owner. They are curious, being probably more than 200 years old. The teapot is of Britannia metal and has every appearance of having been one of the spoils of Fort Sterling when the English evacuated Brooklyn[31].

I cannot omit notice of the fact that Court Street is honored by two important Catholic churches and their dependent schools and institutions. In the long perspective of this thoroughfare from the City Hall to Hamilton Avenue there are three tall spires, the first of which is St. Paul's Catholic Church[32], the second is the Second Congregational Church, opposite Carroll Park[33], and the third is St. Mary's Catholic Church[34]. They are all of brick, and of solid, substantial structure, but I cannot award them the palm that is due to more recent ecclesiastical buildings in brick, some of which show a real comprehension of the beauty that lies in this material if properly handled. One of these is a Catholic church on Sackett Street, which I have already noticed[35], but the finest bit of ecclesiastical brick work is on Grand Avenue, where this material is raised to the dignity of structures in Zaragoza and Bologna[36]. St. Paul's Church on Court Street has behind it an enormous brick building that extends all the way to Clinton Street and that is of a naked ugliness that

---

[31] See Chapters 6 and 9.
[32] Still on the southwest corner of Congress Street, it was founded at least as far back as the 1830s.
[33] Catercorner to the park, on the northwest corner of President Street, it was built in the 1850s and converted to condominiums in 1983.
[34] Still between Luquer and Nelson streets, it's now known as St. Mary Star of the Sea. It opened in 1855.
[35] St. Agnes, now sister church to St. Paul's. See Chapter 1.
[36] Likely a reference to the handsome Universalist church at 457 Grand Avenue, in Clinton Hill, built in 1882 and taken over by Seventh-day Adventists in the 1930s.

surpasses belief[37]. But the parish is erecting, close by, a school building to be known as the St. Paul's Catholic school, which will when finished [be] one of the ornaments of the city, well worthy of careful, painstaking scrutiny and enthusiastic comment[38]. St. Mary's schools are in a dingy part of Court Street and correspond with the locality. The Second Congregational Church is opposite to our little Court Street park[39] and is in itself a most beautiful park when the wisteria vines that cover the whole façade are in bloom. These vines shelter innumerable nests of sparrows, which keep up a constant twittering and chattering as if they were very much at home in the order of sanctity. I do not love the sparrow, but it is a pleasant sight to see those little things sheltering themselves in the church, just as man may if he chooses flee from all oppression of earthly cares and shelter himself within the folds of the garment of infinite love. How utterly false was the much-admired conception of Goethe concerning that garment in "Faust.[40]"

E. R. G.

---

[37] The St. Paul's Orphan Asylum, possibly torn down in the 1940s, now the site of 200–220 Congress Street, built in 1949–50.

[38] 205 Warren Street (now also called 199 Warren Street) was built in 1887. It's still worthy of painstaking scrutiny and enthusiastic comment, but it was converted to condos in 1984.

[39] Carroll Park was a private garden in the 1840s but became a public park in 1853. It was renovated in the 1870s, 1890s, 1930s, 1960s and 1990s.

[40] An allusion to the poet's famous metaphor of the Living Garment of God, which posits nature as a piece of clothing god wears to reveal himself to us. A spirit tells Faust, in Part I, "In floods of life, in storms of action / I walk up and down / Weave to and fro! / Birth and grave, / An eternal sea / An alternating weaving, / A glowing life / That's how I create on the whizzing loom of time, / And work living garments on the deity."

15

Washington Street

ONCE THE VILLAGE PRIDE.

Washington Street in Its Earlier and Its Later Estate.

Merchant Treadwell's House Still Extant—The Methodist Episcopal Church and the Brooklyn Institute—Coming Glories of Architecture—The Italian Ragpickers at the Lower End of the Street—Will American Institutions Civilize Them?

Sunday, February 13, 1887

It may be questioned whether Washington Street was not more fashionable than either Sands or Front in the good old days, when the clustering homes about the ferry constituted the village and the farmhouses in the region of the City Hall the Town of Brooklyn. It seems difficult for us to realize a division between parts now so thoroughly united, but the union was at one time most unpopular. All the local celebrations were held apart, and it is possible that for a short period the town doubted the patriotism of the village and hesitated to believe that there was any earnestness in their Fourth of July festivities. And this feeling existed because the New York Ferry Company inflicted upon the unhappy village a ferry-master who was an undoubted Tory and who was lampooned as such by the poetical Colonel Spooner, journalist and publisher of the Brooklyn Directory, first issued in 1822[1].

---

[1] Alden Spooner, a colonel in the state militia, among other things, published a poem in his Long Island *Star* in 1811 about delays in ferry

We learn from Furman's manuscript notes[2] that in the following year on the Fourth of July there was a grand procession consisting of the Brooklyn Artillery and Village Guards, the clergymen of the village, the firemen, all the Revolutionary soldiers, the citizens and the Sunday school scholars. The procession marched through Fulton, Nassau, Washington, Sands, Main and Front to Cranberry Street to the First Presbyterian Church, erected the year before and probably the largest building in the village[3]. In spite of its size, the record says that it was densely crowded. After the devotional and oratorical exercises many of the citizens flocked to the Steamboat Hotel[4], which was in connection with the Ferry House, where a plentiful American repast was served, and no doubt there was a hearty consumption of cider laced with Jamaica rum and punch, to say nothing of good humming ale of October brewing[5]. The evening was spent by very many ladies and gentlemen at Duflon's Military Garden[6],

---

service that ends with the implication that the new ferryman is a tory, "then used in a politically reproachful sense," writes Henry Stiles. E.R.G. may be mistaken in believing this incident indicated the ferryman opposed the American Revolution. The previous ferryman, Burdet Stryker, was part of the committee that raised the funds for the vault that houses the remains of the prison ship martyrs in Fort Greene Park.
[2] See Chapter 8.
[3] The congregation is still active, but it moved to Henry Street in the 1840s. The property, between Hicks and Henry, was sold to Plymouth Church and became the site of its historic home.
[4] At 1–5 Fulton Street (now Old Fulton Street) from 1822–35, when the street was widened and at least part of the building was razed. It had a ballroom on the second floor and was operated by Gerardus C. Langdon, who later got into the coal business.
[5] "Humming," according to Anchor Brewing, "is an ancient beer term, found everywhere from Robin Hood to Herman Melville, historically used to describe a strong, effervescent ale with a lot of character or just in praise of a truly good beer."
[6] It sat behind Borough Hall, where today Court and Joralemon intersect, on the grounds of the present Municipal Building. It was a

where there was a grand display of fireworks. I have no doubt that they enjoyed themselves much more than we do, and am quite sure that it was better to look at good fireworks exploded by experienced hands than our present practice, which results in so many deaths and disastrous accidents. But what is chiefly remarkable in this account is the restricted area of the procession and the inference necessarily drawn from it that the town had its celebration apart from the village.

At that time, however, Washington Street did not debouch into Fulton[7], nor did it extend beyond the rope walks which Joshua Sands laid out between Concord and Tillary streets. But there were good houses on it even then, and there certainly were discriminating souls who preferred it to the famous Sands Street, for it has been recorded that Dr. Charles Ball[8] moved his house from Sands Street to Washington, thereby showing his good sense, for it would have been difficult to find a site for a house affording lovelier views than did Washington Street in early days. Adam Treadwell, a wealthy New York merchant, of the firm Treadwell & Shaw, built himself a large frame house on one of the corners of Washington and Concord streets[9], the very year of the Fourth of July procession noted by Mr. Furman, impelled to

---

theater, where the second performance ever in Brooklyn was given, by the African American Shakespearean actor John Hewlett, who later left the racism of New York for England. Later, it was also a beer garden with a bowling alley and shooting gallery. Behind it was an old and dilapidated Potter's Field, lost when construction began on the Kings County Courthouse in 1861.

[7] Today Washington Street becomes Cadman Plaza East and then terminates at Johnson Street, but in E.R.G.'s day it continued another block to the small, fountained plaza outside the City Hall, at the intersection of Fulton (now Cadman Plaza West), Court, Myrtle and Montague.

[8] He opened an office on Fulton and Sands ca. 1806 with his partner Dr. Mathew Wendell.

[9] The northeast corner, now within Walt Whitman Park.

do so by the purer air and the exquisite scenery from what was at that time one of the highest spots in the village. But he became disgusted in after years at the manner in which people who had the same appreciation as himself for pure air and a glorious outlook began to build around him, so he sold his house and went back to New York[10]. I believe that it was purchased by the father of Alderman Charles Fowler[11] and that it is still extant and is No. 199[12], an old frame house of the superior class and of large size, standing in its own extensive grounds, with tall trees that probably will wave poetically when the Springtime comes around, but which at present writing are as still as a coating of ice over every branch, limb and twig can make them. Sparrows, with the feathers puffed out so as to make them resemble little fluffy balls, are painfully conspicuous in their uneasy roosts in the ice laden trees of No. 199 but are safe from the hunger of the cats that prowl about the garden under the numerous lines laden with multitudinous towels that adorn it. Certainly, the old house must now be a boarding house, and very lucky indeed are the boarders who inhabit the large, comfortable rooms of one of Brooklyn's early aristocrats.

I think that possibly the Episcopal Church of St. Ann's, on Sands Street[13], gave a splendor to it which it really did not deserve, for Washington Street, topographically, must have been superior to it. The houses faced the north and south and consequently were benefited by the cool breezes of the hot season that came from the south and were sheltered from the ice-laden winds of the Winter that are from the west. One can observe in sauntering down this street that

---

[10] Treadwell, a furrier, is better remembered today for the small Treadwell Farm Historic District on the Upper East Side.
[11] A Whig elected in 1854, and a minor figure.
[12] The house was likely torn down a few years later and replaced with modern commercial buildings, later themselves torn down for Cadman Plaza.
[13] See Chapter 4.

there was a remarkable clinging on the part of many individuals to their homes here. No. 199 is neither the only nor the oldest specimen of other days. No. 165[14], for instance, is a beautiful specimen of the oldest fashion of houses in America, for I remember seeing in St. Louis a log hut built precisely in the same way, which was so comfortable that it was preserved. By a fortuitous combination of circumstances, it was exactly in line with the other houses, so that though odd looking it was not out of place. No. 165 is covered with cedar shingles and is low and two stories in height. The door is precisely in the center, and there are two windows on each side of it and five windows in a fine row on the upper floor. At the gable ends there are two stout chimneys, and no doubt there were open fireplaces for a long time. Whether there are now I cannot say, but I doubt it, for in the windows are samples of a certain universal remedy, and I have noticed that a fondness for patent medicines and a persistence in stoves and heaters and other unhealthy and sinful habits are frequently conjoined[15]. Next door to this bit of old America, which survives with poetical fitness in Brooklyn, an intensely American city, is No. 161[16], also an old house and of the Sands regime too, dating back to the days when the white-haired century was in her blushing teens. This house is like other old houses in Brooklyn, having gorgeously carved woodwork about the door posts and the transom, and no doubt it was comfortable and convenient, but it does not go to the heart like its neighbor. The practice of building long, narrow houses, with the gable end fronting on the street, which is now universal all over civilization, is derived from Holland and is not to be charged either against the Puritans of New England

---

[14] On the east side of the street, just south of High Street.
[15] The building is marked as "Bottling Medicine" on an 1887 map, suggesting it was used for commercial or manufacturing purposes. An ad appears for the address in *Brooklyn Life* in 1901 for Lia Rand's Skin Tonic, which "positively cures acne and blackheads" for $1 a bottle.
[16] On the southeast corner with High Street.

or the cavaliers of High Virginia. It cannot be commended, for it offends the laws of ventilation and light. Neither is it an economy of space, at least to my unskilled vision, for it seems to me that 50x50 is practically the same as 25x100. And it has led to the abuse of architecture visible in No. 149[17], which is a huge structure, towering to the skies upon a small frontage and robbing its neighbors of their fair share of sunlight, or, in legal parlance, their easement.

In 1832 the Washington Street Methodist Episcopal Church was erected[18], and about the same time, the Brooklyn Institute[19]. No one can doubt that at that time Washington Street was the most important place in Brooklyn, for the choice of the site for the Institute proves it. How much, how very much this city owes to the intelligent philanthropy of John Graham, who may be termed the father of the Institute[20], and whose foundation for a course of lectures yearly

---

[17] A five-story structure that was "being built," on the 1887 map, between High and Sands streets.

[18] On the west side of the street, No. 240–246, just north of Tillary, now part of Cadman Plaza Park, across from the federal courthouse.

[19] Near the southwest corner with Concord Street, also now part of Cadman Plaza Park, it was founded in 1823 as the Brooklyn Apprentices' Library Association, the first free library in Brooklyn. Two years later work began on a building on Cranberry Street, on the corner of Henry; the Marquis de Lafayette laid the cornerstone, witnessed by a seven-year-old Walt Whitman, which he later described as "the dearest of my boyish memories." It outgrew that home, and the Washington Street building opened in 1843—rebranded as the Brooklyn Institute. The building was destroyed by fire in 1890, but the organization continued to grow, becoming the Brooklyn Institute of Arts and Sciences, at one time an umbrella organization for the Brooklyn Museum, the Brooklyn Children's Museum, the Brooklyn Botanic Garden, the Brooklyn Academy of Music and other institutions.

[20] John and his brother Augustus, Scottish immigrants who made a fortune in white lead, funded the library, as well as the city's first hospital and the Graham Home for Old Ladies, in Clinton Hill. See Chapter 19.

upon the subjects revealing the goodness of God through nature is one of the noblest that ever sprung from the human heart. It is only through nature that we can ever learn to love and to comprehend Infinite Love; nor is there any better tonic for the dreamy introspection that is the curse of modern literature and art than the Graham lectures. Deeply as I admire the work of John Graham's tender heart and comprehensive brain, I am not precisely in love with the architecture of the Institute, which is a frowning, forbidding mass of gray granite, with a recessed entrance guarded by Ionic pillars, from which an incompetent designer has contrived to take all force, beauty and symmetry. Above the flat and unclassical substitute for a pediment peeps a low mansard roof, which possibly was an afterthought. In the *tout ensemble* there is an ignorant seeking after [of] effects by the jumbling of Green and Egyptian styles, which was special to that eminent builder, Colonel Underhill[21]; nor have I any doubt that he was in some way mixed up with the Institute's architecture. It was, however, a bad period for public buildings, and it is difficult to find one that is entirely satisfactory. Perhaps the very best is the sub Treasury building in New York[22], where there was the most precise rendering not only of the forms of classic architecture but of the exact proportions. If anyone wishes to get a faithful idea of classic art he need not go to Athens, for he will find it at the head of Broad Street, upon the corner of Nassau and Wall, but he will assuredly not see it at the Brooklyn Institute on Washington Street.

It seems fated that Brooklyn's first departures in architecture should be made in this street. In the block between Tillary and Johnson two structures are being reared nearly side by side, which cannot fail to have the most important bearing upon public buildings in this city. One is the new Post Office,

---

[21] See Chapter 12.
[22] Now known as Federal Hall, on Wall Street, it was completed in 1842.

the other the great dry goods building[23]. The Post Office is a mingling of Byzantine and Renaissance, which is a permissible miscegenation, easily defended from critical censure. The former arose from the necessity of making Roman architecture conform to structures demanded by a new civilization. It was not in the power of Roman architecture to build a temple in Rome, even in its palmiest days, and therefore Roman temples were Hellenic absolutely. Roman architecture displayed itself in the forum, in the aqueduct, in the amphitheater and in fortifications. Christianity demanded either a new architecture or a modification of the old, and Byzantine churches were a modification of the stately Roman basilica for religious purposes pending the evolution of Gothic, the new architecture that the heart of Christianity panted for. Renaissance was the first turn of the tide back from the Gothic to the old Roman stately horizontal line made by a succession of arches and cornices. What killed Gothic was the inability of the architects to obtain skilled stone carvers at the wages of ordinary stone cutters, and it is precisely the same thing which has prevented the permanence of the Gothic revival. Gothic architecture is only possible when every man from the President to the bootblack thinks more of God's glory than his own comfort. The architecture that is coming derives majesty from the powerful continuity of its lines but is without the infinite tenderness of the Gothic. It is most suitable for public buildings, however, for that very reason, nor can anyone look at the massive gray walls of the new Post Office without being impressed by a sense of solidity and firmness akin to majesty. I must say, however, that I think the bartizan towers ought not to have been on a street so narrow as Johnson and should rather have been upon the Washington Street façade.

---

[23] The former was built on Johnson, the latter on Tillary. The dry goods building was replaced in the 1930s by a new addition to the old post office and federal courthouse, which had opened in 1892.

The dry goods building is much more Byzantine in spirit than the Post Office, and hence affords more opportunity for decoration. I understand that this structure is to be exceedingly lofty, but that it is purposed to build only the ground story and then open it as a dry goods store, and to continue the construction subsequently, as may be deemed most advantageous. The ground floor façade is a series of arches of Ohio gray sandstone, resting upon pillars of red syenitic granite, highly polished. The arches of the Post Office are more Roman than Byzantine, and therefore cold and stern; nor do the cosettes carved on the *voussoirs* mitigate this impression to any great extent. In the dry goods building the architect has introduced in the arches the cable decoration, one of the most effective ever devised. The shafts of red granite are huge monoliths about seven and one-half feet high, surmounted by capitals six and one-half feet across. One meets frequently in the north of Spain with Byzantine architecture in which one huge capital rests upon four shafts. Here the monolith is partly divided, so that in a perspective view the shafts would appear to be double. The effect is very striking and will reproduce to a certain extent the idea of an Eastern bazaar, for the building is 135 feet by 235 feet, and these low ponderous shafts and immense arches and quaint carvings of interlacings will carry the imaginative in fancy to the huge bazaars of Constantinople, some of which are domiciled in the structures of the old Byzantine municipalities. But there is no strict adherence to Byzantine forms, for the bases upon which the shafts rest are of unpolished red granite decorated with very bold scroll work, whereas in Byzantine the decoration invariably consists of the head of an animal on one side of the shaft and the tail on the other, presenting the effect of crushing something obnoxious under the pillars of the church. This, which arose from the venomous hatred of the Byzantine for all whom they deemed heterodox, was never departed from and will be found in pillars which were supplied by contract to the Moors in the south of Spain and along the east coast, and in a modified form it will be discovered in the transition architecture preceding pure Gothic, which only commenced with the beginning of the thirteenth century.

I have avoided all mention of Washington Street below a certain point[24]. It neither belongs to the old and the picturesque days of the village of Brooklyn nor to the new and gorgeous perspective opened out by these splendid buildings. The approaches to the bridge cannot be said to have killed the lower part[25], for it was dead already, and this union of the Brooklyn Elevated Railroad with the bridge railway was a consummation devoutly to be wished[26]. Toward the outer side there are factories of white lead[27] and of linseed oil[28], which are where they ought to be, and it is a pity that some tobacco factories and oil companies in South Brooklyn cannot be transported by some kindly genii to the same locality. Add there are shanties or rather wooden houses in the last stage of dilapidation around these factories, which shelter a vast number of Italians. Sometimes a door swings open and lets out a vile, pestiferous odor, partly from the rags that the Calabrians are shifting and sorting, partly from the Calabrians themselves. They appear to be very degraded citizens indeed and are more animal and less rational than is safe in a republican country. On Sundays one may hear from these hovels a perfect series of what one supposes to be violent threats, in staccato accents; but it is nothing of the kind, only

---

[24] He refers to what we now call DUMBO, north of York Street.
[25] The entrance to the recently completed Brooklyn Bridge began at Washington and Sands.
[26] The elevated train station at York Street was connected to the trains going over the bridge at Prospect by a covered passage along Washington Street.
[27] The Brooklyn White Lead Works occupied a city block bordered by York and Front streets, Washington and Adams.
[28] Cambell & Thayer Linseed Oil Works occupied most of a city block bordered by Front and Water streets, Main and Washington.

two ragpickers playing the national game of morra, which consists in throwing into the air so many fingers and guessing how many there are upraised in the four grimy hands. They are wonderfully expert and yell out the numbers with lightning-like rapidity, but the one that loses is generally tempted to settle accounts with his sheath knife—perfectly proper in the Basilicata or in the Calabrian Mountains but not exactly the thing in Brooklyn. It is one of the canons of American faith that our institutions can civilize anybody, but Italians, from the heel of the boot to the top of the hat, are a tough crowd. The civilization of Magna Græcia with the culture of Sybaris and Cortona and the philosophy of Pythagoras swept over these men and left them as it found them. Rome with her municipal laws succeeded to the Hellenic cities but was powerless to change these Italian Kelts. Then came the Ostrogoth and the Lombard, and affected them no jot nor tittle; then the power of the Church, but they were constant to their degradation, and then the Bourbon, who became like unto them. No higher compliment can be paid to the Amadæi dynasty than the fact that their efforts to civilize in Southern Italy have induced some of this stubborn race to migrate. Perhaps the Brooklyn Institute will succeed where so many have failed, but we shall see.

E. R. G.

16

Smith Street

A MARKET THOROUGHFARE.

Hiring Shops at a Low Rent and Drumming the City.

Busy Scenes Along Smith Street—Saturday Night Basket Time—The Lair of the Kings County Republicans.

Sunday, February 20, 1887

Smith Street[1] is one of those thoroughfares that in Brooklyn do duty for markets, and it may be that it is in itself an argument in favor of such establishments. For when the observer gets down to what may be termed the bottom facts in the case, it is very clear that Smith Street does much more than a local trade. With some exceptions, the cross streets that run from Court Street toward the Hill region and Prospect Heights[2] are inhabited on this side of the Gowanus Canal by poor people—a necessary consequence of the canal itself, for the better class, or rather the richer class, have gone away from a neighborhood supposed with good reason to be unhealthy. But an examination of the numerous stores, the groceries, the druggists, the butcher shops, etc., etc., is sufficient to convince anyone that they contained articles that poor people do not buy. Those who are in a frenzy of rage at the audacity of men who combine for the purpose of ob-

---

[1] Named for Samuel Smith, who came to Brooklyn from Huntington to farm ca. 1806, eventually acquiring a large piece of land centered on present-day Smith and Livingston streets. He held many local political positions and was elected mayor in 1850.
[2] Fort Greene and Clinton Hill, as well as Park Slope.

taining decent renumeration for their labor, the Mugwumpian chief caricaturist of *Puck*[3], are in the habit of believing that the poor squander their wages in the silliest way. But if such men would spend an hour or two upon Smith Street from 8 to 10 o'clock on Saturday nights, they would be convinced that though the poor like hearty, nourishing food, such as porterhouse steaks, they do not purchase young chickens for broiling nor domestic ducks nor squab pigeons, all of which will be found hanging from hooks in front of stores on Smith Street. The truth is that many of the butchers and grocers upon this thoroughfare keep wagons with lively-going horses, in which they solicit custom on Clinton Street, Henry Street, the places and even the Hill. They have been tempted by the low rents to establish themselves in a poor neighborhood, and they had had the energy and enterprise to extend their trade by going to look for it. They drum for customers. Many charming ladies provide what the French call *comestibles* for their households, including delicacies that will tickle the palates of husbands and render them pliant and amenable to reason on the great bonnet question[4], without ever entering the stores that supply them, without anything but the haziest idea of even the location of Smith Street.

Low rents enable these purveyors of marketing to deal with their customers with surprising liberality. Not only are the goods cheap, but they are of excellent quality, and it is this latter fact that enables them to drum so successfully in the aristocratic parts of South Brooklyn and the region east-

---

[3] *Puck* was an illustrated, weekly political-humor magazine (1871–1918), among other things opposed to political corruption, as were the nonpartisan Mugwumps, a political movement in nineteenth-century America.

[4] According to an 1857 article in *Punch*, the satirical London publication, The Great Bonnet Question was whether a lady could wear the same hat to church that she wears on the street. E.R.G. more broadly seems to joke about keeping a husband happy so he'll agree to purchase more hats.

ward. A lady has no trouble whatsoever. Mr. Honorius Candidianus of Smith Street drives up in his wagon with his fast-trotting horse, and the neat maid makes her appearance in the parlor and says, "Oh! if you please ma'am, here's the butcher, and he says, ma'am, that you can have a pair of canvas-back ducks very cheap ma'am, and that he has some nice Spring chickens from Philadelphia and some wild swans from Canada, ma'am." Who on earth would eat a wild swan I cannot imagine, but it is a fact that they are sent into the market, which would not be the case unless someone ate them. The obliging butcher not only takes the order for the poultry or game, as the case may be, or the meat, supplying it at once from a wagon, but he at the same time receives orders for vegetables, which are sent in later. At present this is an admirable system, because the purveyors put their judgment of the articles at the service of their customers, choosing for them the best the market affords. But in this way ladies lose the opportunity of learning how to choose for themselves, which public markets made necessary, and are entirely at the mercy of their butchers and grocerymen, which is not just to their husbands. Wives by the marital vow take upon themselves obligations that are scrupulously observed among the poor but that are evaded or entirely neglected among those who are better off. At present it is the interest of the purveyors of Smith Street to deal not only fairly but generously with those who rely so implicitly upon them. This halcyon state of things may not continue, and the households will suffer because the wives of the Nineteenth Century have souls above fulfilling their marriage vows and believe they were born for nobler things than choosing good meat and seeing that it is properly cooked. What those noble employments are has not yet been satisfactorily settled, but hitherto the economy of time gained by the neglect of household duties has mainly been spent in reading frivolous literature and gossiping with other women as selfishly indifferent to their duties as themselves. For this reason, if no other, there ought to be public markets, but from the *argumentum ad bursam*, the money point of view, they are even more logical, since the rents would be even lower than those of Smith Street and would at the same time give the city some revenue.

The market character of this thoroughfare is not maintained throughout, neither does it begin at the beginning of Smith Street by any means. In fact, it is not obvious until one arrives at Atlantic Avenue, where, on the corner[5], there is vast emporium of meats of every description, salted, smoked and fresh, from which the retail dealers draw their supplies. From Fulton Street to this point Smith Street seems to wish to evade its manifest destiny of being a place for marketing and struggles hard to maintain the character of a street of quiet, respectable, even genteel dwelling houses, which it received from Jay Street, of which it is the lawful continuation[6]. This fact is clear enough on the first block south of Fulton, for here the stores are few and far between, and these few are of a retiring and quiet nature and of a superior order. The houses are for the most part of brownstone, and one of them of large size was the home of one of these semi-religious institutions which owe their being to the firm conviction of the New Englander that he is better than other men and has a patent right to take them under his guidance and teach them how to live and especially how to vote[7]. This society

---

[5] The northwest corner, No. 82–88 Smith Street, now part of the Brooklyn Detention Complex, opened in 1956.

[6] South of Fulton, Smith Street is just Jay Street by another name.

[7] No. 16, directly behind the Board of Education offices discussed in Chapter 12, was the home of eponym Samuel Smith. He died in 1872, and his house was sold the following year. The Union for Christian Work, founded in 1866 as the Liberal Christian Union, an umbrella organization for several churches that accepted modern science and ethics, moved in around 1880. It used the building for offices and its free library, which held about 9,000 books in 1881, as well as an employment office, chess and checkers tables, a washroom, a sewing school for girls and night school for boys, "free to the well behaved." Local Republicans met there as early as 1882, as did various lodges. It

has now moved away, and Smith Street though bereaved is not in mourning—at least not much, neither would it show any marked anguish if the office in the basement of the aforementioned building were closed also. For here the Kings County Republican organization has its lair, where, in the opinions of all good Democrats, things are devised which are neither for the benefit of Brooklyn in particular nor of the poor man in general. Rightly or wrongly, there is a belief current on Smith Street and on Court Street, too, that this particular organization represents the thoughts, feelings and sympathies of the rich, especially rich manufacturers and employers of labor. And it is playing upon this chord with great adroitness and persistency that politicians of the most selfish aims and corrupt morality have been enabled to take so firm a grip on this city[8]. In old times, in Europe, those who lived upon a street were bound by the strongest ties, and if any marauder or insolent follower of a noble misconducted himself, out they all flocked, clubs and broad swords in their hands, ready to defend their street, like so many bees attacking an intruder upon their hive. This feeling has probably passed away, but it is certain that Smith Street, south of Atlantic Avenue, cares nothing for Smith Street between Fulton Street and Atlantic Avenue. They belong to different worlds.

---

was taken over in 1887 by the New York and New Jersey Telephone Company. The building was about where the delivery entrance is today of 380 Fulton Street, which opened in 1916 with the high-end fur shop Balch, Price & Co. It was given an Art Deco facelift in 1935.

[8] The year before, Republican reformer Seth Low had declined to run again for mayor, and intraparty fighting helped the Democrats (and their corrupt political machine) take back City Hall. Daniel D. Whitney, a grocer at 20 Fulton Street, served one term. As mayor, he was a "dull, plodding, but honest man of Long Island traditions and sympathies," the *Eagle* reported in his 1914 obituary.

When once the traveler passes across the broad avenue for which Austin Corbin is going to do so much[9], he is struck by the fact that though the houses are manifestly poor and though the people and the children playing about belong to the working classes, there is an almost uninterrupted continuity of stores lasting for many blocks, as high up as Union Street. Butcher shops succeed to grocers, grocers succeed to sausage and delicatessen stores apparently without end. Sandwiched in between are dry-goods stores, evidently not of the same character, but appealing to a lower class of customers; and the stationers and the lamp and crockery stores belong to the same category as the dry-good establishments. The fish stores are of both orders, some of them being on the upper plane, some on the lower. There is not an unusual number of saloons in the place, and these are eminently respectable in appearance and conduct. The young men who have congregated at the corners since the strike[10] do not choose those corners where there are saloons, but rather where there are groceries, for, possibly, they have been connected with the coal and lumber traffic on the Gowanus Canal.

The corner grocery is a standing joke for the humorous paragrapher all over the country, but the proprietors, who are for the most part Irish and Germans, are generous and warm hearted to a fault, and if it were not for the credit they

---

[9] Corbin, head of the Long Island Rail Road, was already planning what became the Atlantic Avenue terminal. See Chapter 2.

[10] In January 1887, coal workers in New Jersey went on strike, demanding higher pay. The major coal companies had conspired together to limit supply, boosting their profits. By February, the strike had spread to Brooklyn. The newspapers were generally sympathetic to the workers, though the strike caused great inconvenience, making coal scarce; at the time, it was widely used for cooking and heating. The strike sent the poor, especially, scrambling for wood. It was settled by mid February, before this column went to print, but E.R.G. probably reported it earlier.

give, many a poor man and his family would have neither coal nor food. Here in Smith Street the groceries and the bakeries have not only the custom of the poor of the neighborhood but, like the butchers, have their wagons, with which they supply customers in the quarters of the well to do. This enables them to give long credits to the working men, and I have no doubt whatever that the strikers reckoned pretty confidently upon their assistance. In fact, without their tacit or avowed consent to a strike it would be a moral impossibility, since under the present conditions of labor very few men in certain lines of employment are able to put a dollar in a savings bank.

Saturday night is basket time on Smith Street, and here one sees the great army of labor preparing for the blessed holiday of Sunday. The immense changes that a few years have wrought in the civilization of this country have been profitable in the highest degree to these working people, who minister to the tastes that fashion and refinement have introduced among us. Thrice fortunate is the young girl who works for one of those dealers in gentlemen's outfitting, where there are no cheap articles, where everything is of the very best material and made in the very best way. Whether she is a shirt maker or a maker of cravats, or of underwear, she can earn, without great hardship or straining of energies, from $11 to $17 a week. With such an amount coming in weekly and with economy she can save enough to buy a lot and to lay the nucleus for her own home in a place like Brooklyn, where homes are cheap and where communication with New York and its workshops is rapid enough now. But what is the condition of the young girl whose hard fate has connected her with one of those horrible barrack factories where shirts and underwear are turned out by the ton at the cheapest possible rates, to be used in cutting down prices for the destruction of a rival house? Let her work as hard as she may, she cannot, even with fourteen hours' hard labor, day in and day out, earn more than from $4 to $7. No slave driver of a gang picking cotton under the old regime ever made his shivering victims toil as these poor creatures. With their shining needles they keep at bay the monsters want and sin, pressing upon them to devour them, as knights in the old time combated dragons with their lances. Here they come to do their marketing upon Saturday night, and Smith Street knows no brighter nor pleasanter faces. They live partly upon hope, partly upon the inherited energies of well-fed ancestors, and for the rest they make out as well as they can with their bitterly insufficient pittances. Two girls have a room between them, for which they pay 75 cents a piece by the week, and they have an oil stove upon which they do their cooking, make their coffee and fry their little messes. They cannot, they must not, spend more than a certain sum, for if they do, they must go without a meal or two on the last day before payday. They never buy the good meat, because they cannot afford it, but select the trimmings—the block ornaments, as they are derisively termed in the butchers' shops—and the scrap rashers of the hams and shoulders in the grocers' stores. They cannot put in practice the thousand and one receipts[11] upon which one can live so pleasantly on small means according to theorists, because they know nothing of cookery, as how should they? Oatmeal fried with scrapple may be an agreeable and nourishing food, but it is not for them, because they have neither the time nor the knowledge necessary for its preparation. Amid all the darkness of their situation, amid the gloom that frightens labor as an expiring sun would frighten our unhappy planet, these flowers bloom brightly, smile sweetly, laugh gayly and dress neatly. But how they do it is an enigma, a miracle.

So it is also with the men. Some men are fortunate, others unfortunate. "A is happy, B unhappy, yet B is worthy I

---

[11] An archaic term for recipes.

dare say," as Mr. Gilbert sweetly sings[12]. Two brothers start out in life, one becomes a machinist, works in a large factory and is a member of a union that turns out whenever the destines decree that there shall be a strike. The other gets employment in a silversmith's and becomes a chaser. Henceforward his lines are cast in pleasant places, he receives very high wages and has employment so fascinating in its nature that there are many rich gentlemen who work at it as amateurs. His hours are such that he can have a lovely home in South Brooklyn (his own property) and go and return to his work by the dummy and car combined[13]. In his industrial niche he is sheltered from all the storms of labor troubles. Day by day he sits at his work, picking out silver with his little chisels and translating the design of the draughtsman into leaves and flowers and ferns of silver that seemed to have bloomed in the metal palace of the Kobold king[14]. The car brings him and his good wife to Smith Street on Saturday nights, and they buy the best and juiciest and the dearest. They eat of the fat and drink of the strong. "I've got what'll just suit you, Mr. Chiseler," says the butcher, and displays a delicate hind quarter of lamb. "I saved it for you on purpose." It goes into the big basket, which contains young rhubarb grown in Georgia and sent up by the steamer. Spring lamb and rhubarb! Why, Lucullus[15] could not fare any better. But he well deserves it, and much good may it do his honest heart! Yet, poor B, poor, unhappy B, the machinist, also deserves

---

[12] A reference to "See How the Fates Their Gifts Allot," from W.S. Gilbert and Arthur Sullivan's *The Mikado* (1885).
[13] That is, taking a steam-powered dummy train and a horse car, requiring two fares but less walking.
[14] Kobolds were goblinlike creatures of German folklore, some of which were said to live in mines and be expert metalworkers. The word "cobalt" is derived from their name.
[15] A Roman general who retired wealthy and was known for hosting lavish banquets. "Lucullan" means extremely luxurious, in reference to food and feasts.

good fare, but he does not get it, for Mrs. B is forced to whisper in the butcher's ear for five minutes before their basket gets its load of chuck steak. The machinists are on strike, you see[16], and B must live on credit. But on Smith Street B and his kind can get credit, for whatever *Puck* may think about it, the purveyors with whom B and his class deal are as much convinced as they themselves of the justice of B's cause.

E. R. G.

---

[16] This seems to be hypothetical; I found no record of machinists' striking in Brooklyn in early 1887, though some did at Pioneer Iron Works in Red Hook in May 1886, others in Williamsburg that August. May 1886 was a big time for labor strikes in the New York metropolitan region, as everyone from piano makers and pattern makers to marble cutters and machinists fought for eight- or nine-hour workdays.

17

Fifth Avenue

ANOTHER MARKET STREET.

The Wonderful Development of Fifth Avenue.

How Commercial Eddies Form in Great Cities. Rapid Disappearance of the Long Lines of Villas—The Crowds Upon Saturday Nights. A Peep Into the Future—A Glance at the Past—Solution of the Gowanus Mystery.

Sunday, February 27, 1887

Many of the streets whose salient features I have attempted to describe have said their last word for many a day. Change will come to them no more. They are what they are, and 'tis highly improbable that they will be anything else. But such will not be the fortune of the great throughfare that I am now to consider. For Fifth Avenue falls under the category of eddies, one of the phenomena of cities after they have attained a certain size and degree of populousness. When a city becomes great, the different localities begin to develop a peculiar feeling of indifference to the whole and of pride in themselves. If we consider New York, it is sufficiently obvious that the central part of the island and the parallel sides have no uniformity of feeling and are not one in population until we reach Harlem, where there is a general blending into thorough harmony[1]. That the East Side contained a strong eddy of reaction against the centralization of commercial

---

[1] The large estates uptown had by this time begun to be chopped up into lots for rowhouses, though the area had not yet become the center of Black culture it would in the twentieth century.

and financial interests in New York was always apparent, but this was ascribed to the Dutchiness of the inhabitants, not to the working out of any law in cities. When, however, [all of] a sudden Eighth Avenue developed precisely the same characteristics, had its local banks and insurance companies, its great dry-goods stores, its popular shoe stores and its grand groceries, its local markets, its own theaters and concert rooms, and was plainly becoming sufficient for itself in all the varied branches of a high civilization, it was absurd to explain this by referring to the nationality of the inhabitants. That argument had been possible in the case of the Bowery and its continuation, Third Avenue, but it was ridiculous when applied to Eighth Avenue. The truth was then apparent that from an instructive appreciation of the loss of time and inconvenience from overcrowding in rushing to Wall Street for financial matters, and to Broadway for theatrical amusements, the people of Eighth Avenue had shaken off all dependence upon other localities and had determined to be all in all to themselves. This generated in time a feeling of strong local pride, and though to the United States and the world at large, "a promenade on the avenue" may mean a walk on Fifth Avenue, yet upon the West Side it is well known that it refers solely to Eighth Avenue, their pride, their glory, their city. Singular as it may seem, Fifth Avenue in Brooklyn is destined in a few years to be an eddy of a very high character indeed[2].

It is at present inchoate in places, not because it was out in the wilderness and people preferred living nearer to the center of things, but because it was one of these long lines of beautiful villas set in fine gardens for which Brooklyn was

---

[2] The construction of Fifth Avenue, from Flatbush Avenue to Green-Wood Cemetery, began in 1846. "Without doubt, hundreds of those who are now alive among us will live to see the day when this section of Brooklyn will be as thickly populated as many parts of the downtown wards—strangely as such an assertion may sound to one who walks over the ground now," the *Eagle* reported that year.

once so famous. The old order of living lingered here longer than elsewhere, for we cannot disguise from ourselves the fact that the rich as a class have no longer the love of gardens and shrubberies and hothouses that prevailed when Fifth Avenue and its environs were dotted with the fine mansions of the Coopers[3] and the Tuckers[4] and the Pooles[5] and the Polhemuses[6] and Cortyelous[7]. Here and there one finds a millionaire who is fond of horticulture, but he is generally of opinion that he can gratify his fondness better by having a place in the country independent of his townhouse than by trying to combine the two by creating at vast expense a *rus in urbe*[8]. Long Island has not a few gentlemen of this way of thinking, notably at Glen Cove and Babylon, and there are some noble villas upon the Hudson, though not so many as there were, because this love of country life is no longer the

---

[3] W.B. Cooper owned most of the land between Carroll and 1st streets, Fifth and Sixth avenues.

[4] Major Fanning Cobham Tucker (1782–1856) was a prominent resident of the Heights and at one time president of the village of Brooklyn. He founded a ropewalk in what's now Downtown Brooklyn that survived into the twentieth century, thanks to his descendants, albeit with more sophisticated methods of producing rope. See Chapter 4.

[5] Thomas Poole owned a house "at some distance from" Fifth Avenue, Stiles writes, around present-day Dean and Bergen streets, as well as a surrounding farm, in the mid nineteenth century.

[6] A prominent Brooklyn family descended from Rev. Johannes Theodorus Polhemus (1598–1676), Brooklyn's first permanent minister. Descendant Theodore Polhemus owned several farm tracts along the primitive road that became Fifth Avenue and farther east, on the border with Flatbush.

[7] Jaques and Adrian Cortelyou, descendants of the founding family of New Utrecht, owned farm tracts along Fifth Avenue and others farther east. Jaques's son Peter owned the Vechte house, notable for its role in the Battle of Brooklyn; it was reconstructed in 1933 and is known as the Old Stone House, near Fifth Avenue at Third Street, close to its original location.

[8] Literally "country in city," creating an illusion of countryside in an urban environment, typically through gardens.

fashion. The rich as a class prefer to avoid the expense of two establishments and like to go about in the Summer wherever they choose. Their money is judiciously invested in forgeries of Rousseau and Diaz and Troyon[9], not in grounds and nurseries of young trees and large villas requiring a troop of servants for their maintenance. They find the former more easily disposed of, and it is no doubt true that it is extremely difficult to sell villa property along the Hudson for anything like a fair price. But this is not the case with the villa properties that are upon Fifth Avenue, in Brooklyn, for the former owners are now all dead, and the property is being divided up among the numerous heirs and is in the real estate market, and rich investors are clamoring for it, not to hold for speculative purposes but to build upon. And buildings are rising up along the line of the avenue in a way that is astonishing. In fact, there is no part of Brooklyn where there is such an intensity of life, such feverish energy of purpose as here.

One cannot help feeling some pangs of regret at the feeling of the tall-tufted trees in the old homesteads, and the carting away of the soil from the old gardens, which in many places are above the level of the sidewalk. But what is being done is inevitable, and the wonder grows when one comes to think of it that anyone should have created a villa upon a thoroughfare that could not fail of being a tremendous artery of traffic. The temptations were great beyond question, for this was the first uninterruptedly high ground on the whole stretch of Prospect slope[10]. It was well named, for never did a more magnificent sight gladden the eyes of humanity. It is the same landscape as is unrolled before the dwellers upon Columbia Heights[11], but the additional distance has lent a new enchantment to the view, has softened and mellowed, and refined has made the shadows more transparent, and

---

[9] Beginning in the 1840s, the rise of private art dealers sparked a correlating rise in forgeries. E.R.G. is mocking wealthy art investors.
[10] Park Slope.
[11] See Chapter 11.

glazed with a finer purple the mountains of New Jersey in the background, and has given to the movement of the vessels upon the bay the interest of life without the restlessness and pain of visible effort. There is animation without the sense of "toil and endeavor" as Longfellow aptly says in his one really fine poem[12]. The colossal statue of Bartholdi is exceedingly visible here, painfully so, for the front aspect is perfectly rigid and devoid of grace, the upraised arm making, with the drapery of the body, one long, stiff line. Seen from the Brooklyn end of the bridge, the statue has both dignity and charm, although the torch in the hand is not sufficiently clear and does not disengage itself with sufficient force to preserve the arm from the appearance of undue length. But from Fifth Avenue it looks like a piece of machinery and is less imposing than a Corliss engine[13]. The heirs are quite right in selling their portions of the family property, and James C. Jewett[14] and others who are putting up tall blocks of houses that will hide the ungainly thing are public benefactors. Quick! to the rescue! gentlemen of means, and build up Prospect slope, for the landscape that gladdened the eye of old Brooklyn has been marred by charlatanry and vile speculation and will delight no more.

Fifth Avenue is built up thoroughly near Flatbush Avenue for a few blocks, and then there are gaps that are being rapidly filled in, along the whole stretch of the thoroughfare until one comes to about Fourth Street. From that point right to Green-Wood Cemetery this street is thoroughly devel-

---

[12] "The Day is Done," from *The Belfry of Bruges and Other Poems* (1845), includes the lines: "Come, read to me some poem, / ... Not from the grand old masters, / Not from the bards sublime, / Whose distant footsteps echo / Through the corridors of Time. / For, like strains of martial music, / Their mighty thoughts suggest / Life's endless toil and endeavor; / And to-night I long for rest."
[13] A large stationary steam engine with flywheels, patented in 1849, used to provide power in factories.
[14] A noted developer at the time, especially in Park Slope.

oped. Upon Saturday nights there are such throngs of people doing their marketing that there is a local legend firmly believed in, that there are bigger crowds on Fifth Avenue than on Fulton Street. At present this is not altogether true, for this street is now strictly a market street like Smith Street and Myrtle Avenue combined, having the concentration of butcher shops and other purveyors of provisions of the former, and the open-air huckstering and country wagons of the latter. None of these will create a crowd, a perfect jam, such as one often experiences on Fulton Street, but this is caused by the highly reprehensible conduct of certain merchants of dry goods, who dress up their stores on Saturday night in so brilliant a style and with such bewildering display of fashionable novelties that the feminine heart cannot withstand the temptation of feasting the feminine eyes, and the feminine feet are fairly frozen to the pavement. But this is coming to Fifth Avenue, too. I see it looming in the future. With prophetic previsionings I descry whole blocks given up to this nefarious traffic somewhere in the neighborhood of President, Carroll and Union streets. The husband of the future will not be able to lie down on the sofa and plead that he is too tired to go downtown to help his dear spouse do her shopping. "It's only on the next block, darling," his wife will say, for the foes of his pocketbook will seize a central point and hold it as Corse did the fort that Sherman was so anxious about[15]. Go he will and must, and the savings of months will be on his wife's back in an incredibly short time. Does she want money for housekeeping? He will not be able to excuse himself upon the ground that he has only a check, for she knows that there is a bank on the corner of Carroll. Will the poor fellow now be able to absent himself from home of evenings on the plea of business? She can follow him up and

---

[15] General John Murray Corse is best remembered for desperately defending the Allatoona Pass during the Civil War, during which he received a famous message from General William Sherman: "Hold the fort, for I am coming!"

prove that his business can be transacted right here upon Fifth Avenue. He does not feel like going to the theater and taking his wife and her mother, doesn't he? Well, now that the Casino is turned into a theater[16], he can escort them to the door only four blocks and come for them when the performance is over, as the young men of the Roman Catholic faith do with their girls who go to church. The capacities of development of Fifth Avenue are so great that I fear to dwell upon them[17]. The heart of Brooklyn for a long time has been upon Columbia Heights, but I cannot conceal from myself a strong impression that in twenty years it will be upon Prospect Heights[18].

Some people are, perhaps, not aware that the first house in Brooklyn and, perhaps, on Long Island, most certainly in Kings County[19], was built either on or near Fifth Avenue, somewhere between Twenty-fifth and Twenty-eighth streets. This was the site of the old hamlet of Gowanus and the tract of land called Gowanus was purchased from the Indians in 1636 and the sale recorded at Fort Orange (Albany) by William Adriance Bennet and Jacques Bentyn. Their tract was

---

[16] The Fifth Avenue Casino stretched from Union to President, behind a row of storefronts on the west side, with an entrance at No. 214. It wasn't a gambling hall but rather offered, at various times, roller skating, bowling, billiards and live music. It burned down in 1893 and was replaced by athletic-club headquarters and eventually, as E.R.G. predicts, a theater—the Alhambra, which showed movies until 1934.

[17] Within a couple of years, an elevated train was constructed down Fifth Avenue, from Green-Wood Cemetery to Atlantic Avenue (and then to Fulton Street, after which it followed the Myrtle Avenue line all the way to Park Row on the other side of the Brooklyn Bridge). A few years after that, it stretched south to 36th Street, then turned down to Third Avenue and continued to 65th Street. The line remained in service until 1940 and was demolished the following year.

[18] Park Slope.

[19] Today, Brooklyn and Kings County are coterminous, but not then: Flatbush, New Utrecht and Gravesend remained independent towns until 1894, and Flatlands until 1896.

930 acres in extent and reached to the present city line at Sixtieth Street, where the township of New Utrecht begins. Mr. Stiles records this interesting fact, and further states that the name of Gowanus, which has been such a puzzle to philologists, is purely Indian and was applied to all the land fronting on Gowanus Bay and traversed by the creek of the same name. I strongly doubt this, for the reason that Bennet is not a Dutch name but is most emphatically Scotch, being of undoubted Gaelic origin and belonging to the same category as Bains and Benton and Bainbridge and Benson and Bennington and Bentham and Bentley, etc. The record was no doubt made by a genuine son of Holland who succeeded in giving the name something of a Dutch air, but the Gaelic character peeps through the disguise after all. If William Adriance Bennet was a Scotchman, what could be more natural than that he should give a name to his property as all Scotchmen do? What could be more natural than that he should call the beautiful slope of the fairest, natural meadow land the eye of man ever saw as it lay before him sprinkled with large-eyed daisies—the gowans, which is North British for the daisies. Nor is this pure hypothesis, for in the early documents cited by Mr. Stiles, this district is called "the Gowanes," and also the Gouanes, and I submit that when one has subtracted the element of personal error, arising from a man writing something in a foreign language, the gouanes is as near to the gowans a man could wish to come[20]. It is also to be remembered that Mr. Stiles was for the translation of Dutch records and other documents indebted to friends who did not know the importance of apparently insignificant details, and who only cared to give the sense of the original. If the original records were to be presented in *puris*

---

[20] Gowanus is usually said to have been named after a local Native chief, Gouwanes, but Joseph Alexiou reports in *Gowanus* that there are no contemporary records of such a man. Its origin remains unknown, perhaps unknowable, but I like E.R.G.'s theory.

naturalibus, it is very possible that some queer facts would be discovered.

For example I should like to learn something more about Jacques Bentyn, the alleged partner of William Adriance Bennet. He appears in that document and then he disappears forever. The Bennet Laird of the gowans begot sons and daughters, and the family filled an honored place in the annals of Kings County, but no one ever heard of Bentyn with the French name of Jacques. I strongly suspect that he never existed save in the brain of the worthy recorder, and that the latter mistook for a partner the locality to which Mr. Bennet belonged and that he affixed his name as Scotchmen always do[21]. Macaulay, to a Scotchman, was not a historian[22] but the brother of Macaulay of that ilk, in other words to the gentleman to whom belonged the woods and heather and ploughed rigs of Macaulay, that being the name of the locality. Mr. Bennet probably recorded himself as being Mr. Bennet of somewhere, and the Dutch recorder twisted this into the name of a suppositious partner. Forced, as this seems to be, it is strengthened by the fact that only one house was ever erected, only one family was ever known, and there is no record of transference. Mr. Bennet, who was so particular to place on record his purchase from the Indians, would have been equally particular to also place on record the fact that he had purchased from Jacques Bentyn his undivided half of the same tract. The element of personal error in the records of those days must have been very considerable, for the men stationed at Fort Orange were a compound of traders, sol-

---

[21] Bentyn was a Dutch West India Company man who arrived in New Netherland in 1633 aboard the *Santberg*. In 1636, he became *Schout-fiscael* of the colony, something like a modern comptroller. He held the job for two years, then held other posts in the local government. He returned to Europe in 1648. E.R.G.'s theory is intriguing, but wrong.

[22] Catherine Macaulay was an English historian best remembered for her multivolume *History of England from the Accession of James I to that of the Brunswick Line* (1763–83).

diers, diplomatic agents, interpreters and seamen, and the recorder must have been a man of many occupations and possibly of limited education. A proof of this is given unsuspectingly by Mr. Stiles. He says: "In June, 1636, one of the officials, Jacob Van Corlaer, purchased from the Indians a fiat of land called Castateouw on Sewanhackey or Long Island between the bay of the North River and the East River which is the earliest recorded grant to an individual in the present County of Kings." Andries Hudde and Wolfert Gerritsen purchased the flats next west to Van Corlaer, and, shortly after, the tempting level lands to the eastward were acquired by the director himself, amounting to 15,000 acres of land, a tract that was afterward part of New Amersfoort, now Flatlands. I have turned this information round and round in my brain and for the life of me cannot see that the Corlaer tract refers to any tract save Governor's Island[23]. Nor can I understand how Sewanhackey comes to mean Long Island for Algonquin Indians always called the Dutch Sewanecken[24], and therefore if Sewanhackey refers to any locality at all it must be Manhattan Island. But I rather believe that the whole record is a forgery to get over the unpleasant fact that William Bennet, a Scotchman, was the first settler on Long Island, and he probably was from the New England colony[25]. If it is not a forgery, it is a series of blunders.

E. R. G.

---

[23] Van Corlaer's name is associated with a few places in New York history, most prominently Corlear's Hook, on the Manhattan side of the Williamsburg Bridge. But he's not associated with Governor's Island, which was purchased in 1637 by Wouter van Twiller, director general of the Dutch West India Company.

[24] I have not found this claim repeated, and historians believe Sewanhackey was a Native name for Long Island, referring to its abundance of shells.

[25] He was an Englishman living in the Netherlands who immigrated directly to New Netherland in the seventeenth century.

18

Navy Street

A VIEW OF NAVY STREET.

The First Thoroughfare That Crosses Fulton.

Destiny Against It—The Neglected City Park and the Ugly School House—It Was a Swamp. The Approaching Tide of Manufacturing Life.

Sunday, March 6, 1887

Streets have their destinies as well as individuals, and the fates decreed that the fortunes of Navy Street should be less than humble and should even verge upon degradation. Navy Street runs from the angle made by York Street and the United States Navy Yard into Flatbush Avenue[1], and it is one of the streets over which candidates who are being examined for office by the Civil Service Commissioners moan and groan. For it is the first street that crosses Fulton Street[2], and this important fact in local topography the commissioners consider ought to be known as a matter of general information by anyone who seeks to feel the ecstasy of getting a warrant monthly for pay and having the same disbursed to him in the neighborhood of the City Hall. How much better after

---

[1] Today, Navy Street stops at Myrtle, swerving to meet Ashland Place, once Raymond Street, rather than run parallel to it. The rest was lost to midcentury superblock developments of public housing, apartment buildings and Long Island University during urban renewal. The southern part of the street, from Dekalb to Lafayette, was renamed "Rockwell Place" in 1889.
[2] See Chapter 7.

all are these local questions than those which Mr. Dorman B. Eaton used to put to men who wanted to serve their country as Custom House Weighers[3]. He would say to Mr. Morse Bloodtub, a protégé of the amiable Mr. Theodore Allen[4], "The planet Jupiter, Mr. Bloodtub. I have no doubt you know accurately the computed distance of that planet from the sun, and also from the earth. Be so good as to tell me, how you would calculate the distance in inches from the central point of Brooklyn Bridge to the nearest portion of Jupiter's disk at 12 o'clock today, Washington time. I am not asking the distance, you understand, Mr. Bloodtub, but only the manner in which you would compute it." Our examiners rather delight in catch questions, but there is more sense in them than in puzzling problems of a highly equational character. It is certain that had it not been for the Civil Service reform and the energy of Mugwumpian reformers, Navy Street would have been unknown to the vast majority and would have slumbered in obscurity, like the fat weed that rots on Lethe's banks[5].

It must be exceedingly disagreeable to those highly respectable people who live on Navy Street, between Fulton Street and Flatbush Avenue, to be obliged to give their address to casual acquaintance. As they mention the name, they observe with distress but without surprise an involun-

---

[3] Eaton was a lawyer and civil-service reformer who served as the first chairman of the national Civil Service Commission, established just four years earlier, following the assassination of President Garfield by a disgruntled and delusional office seeker.

[4] A notorious figure at the time, tied up in a mix of crime, saloons and politics. He's intended here as a symbol of the corruption Eaton opposed—a sort of lesser (and Republican) Boss Tweed.

[5] In Act I of *Hamlet*, the Ghost says, "I find thee apt; / And duller shouldst thou be than the fat weed / That roots itself in ease on Lethe wharf, / Wouldst thou not stir in this." Lethe in Greek mythology is one of the rivers in Hades; its waters cause humans to forget their earthly lives.

tary smile bubble up from the inner depths of the person with whom they may be conversing, and they at once enter into explanation concerning the superiority of their part of Navy Street and run over the list of families of good standing who live on the same block. Because in other parts of the street the Italian maketh his lair and the colored population have their dwelling place[6]. I do not recall to mind a single store, from Fulton Street until one arrives within hailing distance of Flushing Avenue, save a cobbler's stall, kept by an Italian of the resonant name Antonio Di Giovanna. There are no grocers, no butchers, no bakers, no fish shops, and the people of this part of the street probably do their marketing on Myrtle Avenue. This cannot be due to any fear of losses from pilfering, to which, according to the voice of slander, the children of the colored people are somewhat addicted. For one single fact shows with marked positiveness the honesty of the inhabitants of this street, and that is that almost every street door is open. Why this should be the case, when February winds are blowing so keenly and the thermometer is about twenty degrees, or twelve degrees below freezing, I do not pretend to say, but it marks the confidence that all families have in each other. It may be that the landlords will not furnish door keys to all of the multitudinous families that swarm in all of the wooden or brick houses, for as far as external observation goes, I believe that each house is rented out in rooms. Certainly, this is the case in the block between Will-

---

[6] This surely inspired the drive to rename a portion of the street Rockwell Place just two years after this column was published—to distinguish it from the parts of Navy Street perceived to be less reputable. A scathing Brooklyn *Eagle* editorial in 1889 suggests "Rockwell" was chosen "perhaps because in the minds of some thoughtless ... individuals the title is more high sounding."

oughby and Bolivar[7], on the east side[8], a row of as badly built houses as can be found in the United States. They are frame houses and were once painted, but there are no areas, and apparently no collarage. The doors are in the center and there are two doors on each side. A staircase leads to the upper story directly from the door, which is always open, so there is nothing of the decency of privacy to which poor families are as much entitled as anyone else, and that is invariably secured to them in tenement houses erected at the present date. This row has the fatal look on it of a locality doomed to get the full benefit of every epidemic and contagious disease that may visit Brooklyn, and I believe that an inspection would reveal a total neglect of every sanitary precaution that should be taken by the inhabitants of great cities. Swarthy Italians and good-humored colored men stared at my notebook, and the Italians frowned and glowered, from which circumstance I have no doubt that the Board of Health has been going [on] its rounds of late.

Nowhere can the colored population be seen to greater advantage than in this locality, for here they are the dominant element. I had the pleasure of seeing a full-blown professor, at least I imagined so, walking with much dignity with massive folio under one arm. He wore gold-mounted spectacles and his hands were encased in stylish gloves, and he gave the unencumbered arm to a colored lady whose furs were something dazzling. There is a kindliness, good humor and warmth of friendly feeling among male colored men that endears them to white men, with whom they are great favorites. But this is not the case with the dusky beauties of the race, who are apt to be exceedingly sour and ill-tempered in their intercourse with white people. I was caught in the act of taking notes of their street by the worthy pair, and the man

---

[7] One of several streets around there that no longer exist, it ran at an off-grid angle for a few blocks between Myrtle and Willoughby, ending at Fort Greene Park.
[8] Nos. 187–203.

smiled and nodded as if firmly believing that I could be actuated by a right motive, and that the result would be good. But Madame, who did not wear glasses, scowled at me with her natural orbs and muttered loudly and audibly something about the "imperence[9] of white trash." Even the children that came from District School No. 14, at the center of Concord Street[10], were not frank and smiling as darky children used to be. Ten years ago they would have been all grins, but now they walk sedately and severely past the affable stranger who patted them on the head, and looked through their glasses at him in rebuke of the liberty he had taken. Schooling seems to have a bad effect upon their eyes, for a very large percentage were obviously myopic, and a bad effect upon their temper, for they were undeniably cross-grained. It is possible that the white children torment them, or sent them to Coventry[11], or lead them unhappy lives in some way, and it is strange that this should be so, for in South Brooklyn, where there is no concentration of the colored element comparable to that on Navy Street, the little darkies appear to be on the best of terms with their white schoolfellows. But the cause may lie deeper, for when I was in Jamaica and San Domingo I remember to have noticed the marked unfriendliness of colored women to all white people.

There is hardly a good house from Fulton Street to the Navy Yard upon this street. There are some that are tolerable and some that are quaint, notably a liquor saloon, which has immense glittering signs upon it. The building itself seemed to have been erected in part with ship timbers, and

---

[9] An archaic word meaning "impertinence."
[10] On the northwest corner, it continued as a schoolhouse into at least the late 1930s. It was then used as a warehouse before becoming, for members of the armed forces during World War II, a canteen—an informational and recreational center. Today it's the site of P.S. 287, built ca. 1953 as part of the broader urban-renewal project in Downtown Brooklyn and Fort Greene.
[11] A British expression meaning to ostracize.

after some examination I came to the conclusion that the signs had once been the name plates of schooners or barges. They were highly patriotic, having large gilt eagles at the ends, and I have no doubt are much admired by the marines and others who use the house. On the opposite corner was a vacant lot fenced in with palings that were falling to pieces. An obliging stranger informed me that there was no owner for it, and that some of the neighbors had clubbed together and bought it at the last tax sale. He was an old residenter and remembered the time when the water in the marsh overflowed the ground where we were standing[12]. None of the houses, he said, in the neighborhood were much more than thirty years old, but they looked older than that, because they had been badly built, and in some cases [out] of second-hand materials. He thought that the street was not worthy of good buildings. The district school not being affected by these local impressions might have been made an oasis in the desert, but unfortunately it was built in 1858, a bad time for educational architecture; for the notion prevailed at that time that beauty was a thing to be avoided, in the interests of the taxpayer, and accordingly the edifices of that date are hopelessly ugly masses of brick. The structure on the corner of Concord Street was reared upon foundations that were not as broad as they should have been, considering the marshy character of the ground, and there has been a settlement, which has been general and even and therefore has caused no real damage. But it has cracked the brick work and split the stones in nearly every part of the building.

Opposite to the school is the City Park[13]. Here was another opportunity to ameliorate the fortunes of Navy Street, but the destinies had decreed that Navy Street should not be lifted up from the mire. This park is completely neglected,

---

[12] The land surrounding Wallabout Bay was once a tidal marsh.
[13] The oldest park in Brooklyn, acquired in 1836, it was renamed Commodore Barry Park in 1951, after Revolutionary naval hero John Barry, who helped establish what became the Brooklyn Navy Yard.

for it has been found impossible to do anything for it on account of the limited amount of the appropriation for park maintenance. The Commissioners of the Park Department have also argued that Washington Park[14] is so close as to render the City Park unnecessary. But this is hardly true, for the former is situated on the boundary line between the poor quarter and a quarter where there are almost exclusively well-to-do families. Myrtle Avenue is at the end of the one and DeKalb at the beginning of the other. Washington Park does not in any sense minister to the enjoyment and moral and material improvement of the low-lying section between the Hill[15] and the East River, whereas City Park would do so if it were made worthy of its name. There never has been any comprehensive effort to make a true park of it. It is filled-in land to begin with, and about four feet down one would probably strike water. Under these conditions there was an admirable opportunity to plant hemlock evergreen trees, which grow naturally in swamps and would not find the circumstances unfavorable to their well-being. Of course, poplars do well in moist soils, and the silver poplars of the City Park have grown exceedingly well. But they have not the charm of the hemlock, which is an imposing and majestic tree. Moreover, the poplar harbors insects, especially the orgyia leucostigma[16], whose masses of white eggs are deposited in the cracks of the bark. No attention is paid to the spread of these insect pests, and they start out from the City Park and from that center devastate the shade trees of the entire city. As a matter of public policy and democratic justice, the City Park ought to be as fairly treated as any other local park in Brooklyn. A good model for an enclosure of this size and conditions is Tompkins Square[17], which has a broad

---

[14] Officially renamed Fort Greene Park in 1897.
[15] Fort Greene–Clinton Hill.
[16] Better known as the white-marked tussock moth.
[17] Tompkins Park, in the heart of Bed–Stuy, between Marcy and Tompkins avenues, Lafayette and Greene, was acquired in 1857 and

outer border of evergreens, flowering shrubs and plants and green sward, then a gravel walk, and the remainder is given up for a playground and croquet ground. The City Park ought to be treated in the same manner, making such variations in the trees and general plantings as the peculiar conditions require.

Having crossed Flushing Avenue, one side of the street is occupied by the wall and iron railing of the Navy Yard, above which rise the long, low buildings where the lumber is stored away. They were erected before ships were built of iron and steel, and now they are practically useless, because seasoned timber is no longer wanted. On the other side are wooden structures that are neither better nor worse than the average house of the street, but through holes in a fence one gets glimpses of other buildings in the last stage of dilapidation standing in the rear. The very last house in the street[18] is one of the oldest and probably was a quiet, comfortable home before Comfort and Joshua Sands sold the big slice of the Rapelyea property to Uncle Sam for a Navy Yard[19]. It is sufficiently obvious that the level of the sidewalk is not what it was when that poor house was built. It has a basement of red sandstone roughly squared, and above this are two stories of wood, covered in cedar shingles. The timber part was once painted, and this has cracked and crumbled until its

---

designed in 1871 as a public square. It was named for Daniel D. Tompkins, governor of New York and vice president under James Monroe. The park underwent many renovations in the twentieth century, and it was renamed Herbert Von King Park in 1985.

[18] No. 242, which last appears in the newspaper record in 1929. It appears on a map from the same year.

[19] Joris Jansen Rapelje bought 335 acres from the Natives in 1637. The family owned the property until the Revolutionary War, after which it was confiscated because they had been loyal to the British. The Sands brothers, patriots both, bought 160 acres in 1784, encompassing modern Downtown Brooklyn, Vinegar Hill and DUMBO, but the Navy Yard property was purchased by John Jackson, who established a shipyard that he sold to the federal government in 1801.

decay has given it a picturesqueness akin to the mosses on an old manse. The basement door and the first-floor door are both in the center, and there are two windows on each side provided with green shutters, on which are conspicuous announcements of apartments to let. A wooden archway over the basement with a flight of wooden steps gives access to the first floor. There was once a garden in connection with this place, but the corner house on York Street[20] has destroyed it, leaving a narrow gore fenced in, as if to guard the half dozen blades of frowsy withered grass and the promise and expectancy of a weed or two in Springtime. The buildings of the United Sates opposite are all painted a bright hospital yellow, so that the location is as cheerful as a quarantine smallpox station, and the disinclination of the public generally to hire the rooms is not amazing. Poor house! It has outlived its usefulness, its beauty and its decency, and it is time that it should be converted into kindling wood. Why does it cumber the ground[21]?

Commerce has not quite forsaken Navy Street, for it contains one factory, that of an electric company[22]. But it was not necessary in that instance to build a heavy structure, and the fact that Navy Street does not afford a good foundation is plainly the cause of its neglect. The schoolhouse shows this, but it must be remembered that a good architect can always counteract marshy soils by specially constructed foundations. This was done under far more difficult circumstances by George B. Post, the architect to whom Brooklyn is indebted for the Long Island Historical Society's building. The Pro-

---

[20] 123 York Street. Both it and its neighbor were within the present site of the Farragut Houses, near what's now a basketball court.

[21] A reference to Luke 13:7, in which Jesus tells a parable about a man who notices a fig tree in his vineyard has failed to produce fruit for three consecutive years and tells his dresser, "cut it down; why cumbereth it the ground?"

[22] The Excelsior Electric Company Works, at the southeast corner of the intersection with Willoughby, now the site of the LIU Athletic Center.

duce Exchange in New York, at the foot of Broadway, is as heavy and solid as it is magnificent, and yet the ground was even worse than that of the lower part of Navy Street[23]. Factories are being built on Sands Street, just one block from Navy, and it is a reasonable hope that the strong flood tide of manufacturing interests that is doing so much for Brooklyn will at least sweep onward to Navy Street and give it a new life and a new nature[24]. No old denizen of Brooklyn or New York can think of smallpox without a shudder, for it has been more deadly than cholera and more persistent than a hungry politician soliciting an office. And there are blocks upon Navy Street that no one can look upon without dreaming of smallpox[25]. The Health Department is vigilant, as we all know, and as the recent experience of Butler Street proved conclusively[26]. But somehow I had rather trust in the effects of a progress that will replace these suspicious build-

---

[23] Post designed the New York Produce Exchange Building, opened in 1884 at Bowling Green, where commodities futures were traded. A magnificent icon of Victorian New York, it was torn down in 1957 and replaced by the thirty-two-story skyscraper 2 Broadway.

[24] By 1929, a handful of factories and other large industrial buildings had been built on Navy Street.

[25] In 1907, twenty-three-year-old Minnie Jones was taken to the hospital with smallpox from her home at 242 Navy Street.

[26] In January, Joseph Mauri, a druggist and one-time streetcar conductor who lived at 111 Butler Street, died of smallpox, as did three of his sons, including an eight-month-old. His other three children were infected but seem to have survived. The case was covered extensively in the local papers. A vaccination for smallpox had been available since the turn of the nineteenth century, but Joseph was passionately against it, telling a doctor that "if he knew he was going to die of smallpox tomorrow, he [still] would not submit to vaccination." With cajoling from a doctor, he did finally allow his children and wife to be vaccinated, though it didn't take, for unknown reasons. The health department followed regulations to contain the spread, though not without controversy; some objected to the forced removal of infected patients to the smallpox hospital in Flatbush.

ings by factories where there shall be a steady hum of wheels and a buzz of industry.

E. R. G.

19

Washington Avenue

ON WASHINGTON AVENUE.

Through the Heart of the Fashionable Hill Region.

Beginning in the Wallabout Truck Market—The Primeval Character of the Navy Yard Swamp—Traversing the Ancient Site of the Hamlet of Cripplebush—The Aristocratic Part of the Thoroughfare—Uniformity and Individuality in Houses—The East Side Park Lands.

Sunday, March 13, 1887

I think that Washington Avenue, take it all round, is the most representative thoroughfare in Brooklyn, and therefore the most thoroughly American, since it is conceded by all that Brooklyn is par excellence a truly American city. Those who are hot-headed extremists are apt to declare that it is the only American city in the East—above a certain line of latitude, that is to say—but this is doing an injustice to Boston, which is also a truly American city, and a very noble one. But at the Hub[1] they are so desirous of not being Anglomaniacs, like the silly children of Gotham, that they go in the opposite extreme and are eternally quarreling with their mother tongue and starting fads about pronunciation. Every little while some purist from Beacon Hill rises in his might and announces that the h must be pronounced in wheat, or that

---

[1] In 1858, Oliver Wendell Holmes joked in *The Atlantic* that the Boston state house was "the hub of the solar system," but proud Bostonians embraced it and soon considered the entire city to be the hub of the *universe*, or just the Hub.

there is no h in sugar, which must not be sounded as if it were spelled shugar. About these things we do not trouble ourselves in Brooklyn, but we pronounce as we hear those doing who are around us. But we have great faith in Boston as an American city, and we despise the current talk about codfish aristocracy[2]. Our own upper classes, if they have not a codfish in their armorial shields, have a truck wagon, which is not a bit loftier[3]. And yet they are as good, and as well educated, and as refined and in every way as fit to be leaders of our city world as if their escutcheons boasted griffins, wyverns, "salvage" men or even fleurs de lys and lions rampant or couchant. And it is very essential that this should be clearly understood, because Washington Avenue, which traverses the very heart of the fashionable Hill district, begins, not to make any bones about it, in the Wallabout Market[4].

This splendid thoroughfare begins at the drawbridge over Wallabout Creek[5] and runs pointing nearly due north and south into Flatbush Avenue, in the Village of Flatbush,

---

[2] A derisive term from Massachusetts for the nouveau riche that made their fortunes in codfish.
[3] He means the corresponding aristocracy in Brooklyn made its money in farming.
[4] A bustling complex of dozens of buildings, it was in the nineteenth and twentieth centuries a clearinghouse for wholesale foodstuffs patronized by grocers, restaurateurs and others. It was within the present boundaries of the Navy Yard, east of Washington Avenue. It closed during World War II, over security concerns and because the Navy needed the space, replaced by the Brooklyn Terminal Market in Canarsie. Today, Steiner Studios occupies the site.
[5] Washington Avenue extended through the present Navy Yard to intersect with Kent Avenue at about Clymer Street. In 1887, the Wallabout Canal, now called Wallabout Channel, did not stop at Washington Avenue as it does today; it extended southeast as far as Hewes Street, almost to the present Brooklyn–Queens Expressway, servicing the many factories and coal and lumber sheds along Kent. Washington was the only street that crossed the canal, over a bridge.

just by the fine grounds and trees of the Lefferts property[6]. At its commencement it represents old Brooklyn with a surprising fidelity. On the west side of the street is the marshland belonging to the Navy Yard, pretty nearly in its primeval condition. The Government, with a friendliness that speaks volumes for Secretary Whitney[7] and the Cleveland Administration, now permits dumping, and a narrow thread of carts can always be seen passing through the enclosure and going to the appointed place. In the immediate neighborhood of the fence on our avenue, however, the Jamestown weed[8], whose seeds are so fatal to poultry, spreads its long arms and displays its finely shaped leaves and handsome white flowers just as it did when Mareckiawick[9] was a factor in the everyday life of the white men living on Long Island. On the other side of the avenue is the Wallabout truck market, reaching from the creek to the elevated railroad[10]. Now, as in the oldest times, the market gardens of Long Island[11] are a constant source of prosperity, and now, as then, we feed our over-weening neighbor on the other side of the East River. Pretty nearly the whole extent of this long stretch of ground from the creek to Flushing Avenue is occupied by commission houses doing business not only in the produce of our Long Island farms but in similar merchandise from Connecticut, and in West Indian and Italian fruits, and in early vege-

---

[6] Washington and Flatbush avenues intersect at what's now Lincoln Road (then East New York Avenue), south of which was the Lefferts estate. See Chapter 2.
[7] William Collins Whitney, secretary of the Navy, 1885–89.
[8] Also known as jimsonweed.
[9] A Native American settlement. See Chapter 13.
[10] The Park Avenue line opened in 1885, though its route was modified a few years later to connect with the Brooklyn Bridge. There were a few more marketeers on Washington between Flushing and Park, including those making or selling flour; mineral water; and hay, straw and feed.
[11] Or the vegetable farms in the rural towns, such as Flatbush and New Utrecht, and farther east.

tables from Southern ports along the Atlantic seaboard. Their stores are not remarkable for height or for splendor, being, in fact, for the most part, of only one story, and bearing a marked resemblance to the buildings on the one sole commercial street of a new town in the great West[12]. But they do a tremendous business, supplying a large part of the fruits and truck[13] devoured by 800,000 souls. And by the pleasantry of fortune and the conservative spirit of Uncle Sam, opposite this market, which could not exist except through an enormous concentration of population, is the primeval marsh over which Governor Van Twiller may have floundered[14], groaning in spirit and smoking his big Dutch pipe.

This region is supposed to be the Wallabout, which has been such a problem to the investigators of early history on Long Island. Out of sheer despair the conjecture that this name refers to a colony of Wallom settlers has been tacitly accepted[15], but it is to be noted that even those who offer this do not pretend to explain the word itself. What the last syllable means is absolutely unknown. I do not think those who have attempted to solve this riddle have gone at it in the right spirit. There has been a constant assumption that all names in the western end of Long Island must be either Algonquin or Dutch, but this cannot be maintained. No philologist who values his reputation dare now affirm that Ihpetonga is Algonquin[16], for it would be as absurd to maintain that

---

[12] The market was redesigned in 1894–96 as a sort of Flemish village, with a "town" square, spires and a prominent clocktower. Many photographs exist of this more architecturally impressive design.
[13] Produce from market gardens.
[14] Wouter van Twiller was director of New Netherland, 1633–38. In his satirical *History of New York*, Washington Irving portrays him as being incapable of making decisions. He owned considerable land in the colony, including "the Red Hook." See Chapter 12.
[15] See Chapter 13.
[16] See Chapters 12 and 13 for more of this nonsense.

Hochelaga, the Indian name for Canada[17], was Algonquin also. It is beyond dispute that Hochelaga is Huron, and that Huron is Iroquois, and it is equally beyond dispute that Ihpetonga is Iroquois also. There is a soft musical murmur in Iroquois names so different from the harsh, rock gutturalnesss of Algonquin nomenclature that no one with a philological ear can mistake. Now Washington Avenue, beginning as it does in the Wallabout, traverses the sites of the old hamlets of Cripplebush and Bedford[18], and an old official document actually places them in the Wallabout. All the inhabitants of Brooklyn can give a pretty good guess at the site of the hamlet of Bedford, and, there, the implication that either it or the Village of Cripplebush that lay north and west of it was in the Wallabout must come as a tremendous surprise[19]. The fact is that the documents dragged from obscurity by the wearied industry of Mr. Stiles and published in his "History of Brooklyn" are contradictory and inconsistent with each other, so long as we maintain our present views. They are stubborn facts, however, and those who prefer to cling to old ideas can only do so by ignoring them. The plain truth is that they require to be carefully analyzed and studied, so that all the facts will present one harmonious view.

I am strongly tempted to believe that Wallabout should be Wallabot, or Wallaboth[20]. It is one of the misfortunes of the English language that it has discarded the Saxon runic thorn, giving the sound of the th as one letter. For by the

---

[17] Hochelaga was an Iroquois village in modern Montréal.
[18] Cripplebush was east of Wallabout, around the modern border of South Williamsburg and Bedford–Stuyvesant, closer to Nostrand Avenue. Bedford was south of that, around the modern border of Clinton Hill and Crown Heights, in the vicinity of Bedford Avenue.
[19] Cripplebush was started by Wallabout settlers and later incorporated into Wallabout Village; E.R.G. may be misinterpreting that to mean it was located on Wallabout Bay.
[20] Some outlandish etymological logic follows. You could skip this paragraph and the next.

present system there is no method by which an aspirated t can be expressed, and in Irish and Welsh names this is constantly required. It is obvious from the frenzied efforts of early historians to spell Wallabout that something was needed that the Roman alphabet did not supply. Many a student must have bemoaned the day when the rich runic futhore of forty characters was abandoned for the scanty abecedarium of Rome. It was like putting the clothes of a boy upon a six-foot Kentuckian. Wallabot is in all human probability the Iroquois equivalent for Mareckiawick, the Algonquin name for the Indian town that was somewhere near the meeting point of the Eighteenth, Sixteenth and Twenty-first wards[21]. In the documents that the industry of Mr. Stiles has made accessible to every student of Long Island history, Mareckiawick is found also as Reckiawick, and this in a paper of the very highest character, clearly confirming my previous statement that ma was simply a prefix to denote greatness, and that the place itself was the ruling town of Long Island, the Algonquin headquarters in this region. The lands belonging to this town are described as in the Mareckiawicking, the particle ing being an addition made either by Dutch or English for it belongs to both languages, and this fact can only be explained by the supposition that my view is correct. When the great Chief Penhawitz summoned the Dutch to a conference, the place was designated by the latter as Reckiackey (now Rockaway[22]), but it clearly obvious that Reckiaki means the men of the ruling tribe. My explanation for one is good for all the variants, and it is based upon the two axioms that Indians of this race (coasters) have no names for local-

---

[21] Wards were akin to modern city council districts. These three didn't intersect; if he meant the Twenty-seventh instead of the Twenty-first, those three intersected at Flushing and Bushwick avenues.

[22] Penhawitz was a leader of the Natives at Canarsee. In 1643, he brokered a peace agreement between the Dutch and many Native leaders of Long Island at a conference in Rockaway during Kieft's War. It didn't last.

ities unconnected with individuals, and secondly that European languages contain many roots that belong to this race, which is distributed in nearly every part of the globe, and which alters little because it always lives on the same food. Language is based upon diet, and everywhere those who feed on shellfish and seafood will have the same sounds to express the same things.

Now Walla is a word belonging to the race of serpent worshipers who claim to be the children of the great serpent[23]. Originally, they were fruit eaters and cannibals, but in their migrations they have often been compelled to change their diet. The Iroquois had enslaved a race of agricultural savages, the Hurons, who taught them the secret of maize cultivation, and they lived exclusively on maize, but the cannibal pushed out in battle, according to the account of Father Jaques, a Jesuit missionary[24]. There can be no doubt that they had received some ideas of government from white men, either from Asi Marsson, the Irish Dane[25], or from Prince Madoc, the Welshman[26], or from Tottee sources still more remote. But the word Walla is genuinely of the serpent vocabulary and will be found west of the Rocky Mountains, among all the tribes of the Shoshoni or Snake Indians. Walla-Walla is a well-known locality in Washington Territory[27], giving not only the word but the plural form by reduplication. Its meaning is rulers and inhabitants of a

---

[23] He means the Iroquois. See Chapter 12.
[24] Père Jacques Marquette (1637–75) explored the Mississippi River with Louis Jolliet and wrote an account of their proselytizing expedition that describes the customs of the Native peoples they met.
[25] Ari Marsson, according to Icelandic legend, reached Great Ireland, or White Men's Land, said to be a six-day sail west of Ireland, near Vinland, or modern Newfoundland.
[26] A Welsh prince who, according to folklore, sailed to America in the twelfth century.
[27] Millard Fillmore created the Washington Territory in 1853, and it was admitted to the union in 1889, more than two years after this column.

country. The European representatives of the Sons of the Serpent used the word precisely in the same double sense and called the Romans Walla and Wallaki from Russia to Wales. This will explain why those who call themselves Roumanians up-on the banks of the Danube were called Wallaki by the Tar-tars and the Poles. It must not be forgotten that the warriors among the Poles, Tartars, Cossaki and Turks shaved their heads, leaving a scalp lock, just as the Iroquois did. The great nobles did not, because they were long haired Saxons and to have shaved the head would have been a descent to the ranks of the "salvage" men who were their supports, not only heraldically, but absolutely. Walla therefore means rulers. Now bot or both means an unfortified town of wooden houses or huts; in Scotch, bothles; in English, booths. This root is general and is found in Indian as bad, e.g., Allahbad, Ferozebad, Ahmedabad; in Hungary as Buda; in Scandinavia as Leifsbudir; in England as Badminton and Bodmin; in Roumania as Botoshani; in Scotland as Bothwell and Bute; and as these localities embrace nearly all the linguistic elements of population, it is impossible to say to what race it belongs. The two words Walla bot mean ruler town, the precise meaning of Mareckiawick.

As soon as Washington Avenue has passed Flushing Avenue it is no longer on the low land of the Wallabout in its present restricted sense but is upon the rise of a hill[28]. No doubt this hill was the old Cripplebush, which sheltered on its bosom a little hamlet of the same name. Cripple is certainly identic with the Scotch criffel and means a broken, contorted, twisted summit of a hill—one of those picturesque and poetic terms with which dialects of the Gaelic abound[29]. The hill is smooth enough now. Very soon the traveler comes

---

[28] South of Flushing, Washington goes uphill—the hill that gives Clinton Hill its name.
[29] More likely it was adapted from the Dutch word "kreupelbosch," meaning undergrowth.

to lines of handsome houses, but when he is nearing the crest he is in the heart of the villa region. Running from west to east, and therefore traversing Washington Avenue, are Willoughby, DeKalb, Greene and Gates avenues and Fulton Street, where ends the present series of fine residences on this thoroughfare, and running parallel with it are Adelphi Street, Carlton, Clermont, Vanderbilt, Clinton and Waverly avenues to the westward, and to eastward a great number of new streets and avenues, including Franklin, Bedford, Marcy and Tompkins avenues, which are the most important. The villa region seems to radiate from Washington Avenue, and as one gets further away from it one finds one's self surrounded by long rows of buildings comfortable, no doubt, far more than respectable, giving many evidences of wealth and refinement, but painfully monotonous and distressingly uniform. Every house is exactly like the houses to the right and then left—their window curtains, the paint on their doors and their very door plates are the same. I wonder how it is possible for a man who has been dining out and who has partaken even in moderation of salmon and new potatoes, a diet notoriously clouding the intellect, to find his way to his own domicile. The resident of 2,002 I should fancy would be eternally attempting to enter 2,004 under such circumstances, and if the door happened to be ajar might walk in and proceed to take off his boots in the passage under the belief that he had surmounted all difficulties and had arrived home safely, to the fearful anguish of the two maiden sisters, the lawful proprietors of the house, who would take him for a burglar and be in ecstasies of fright. But in the villa region every house is either wholly apart or semi-detached, a very pleasant style of building that permits people of comparatively modest means to the enjoy the luxury of a garden at a small cost. There are numberless villas whose yards, as they are called down South, must be perfectly exquisite in Summertime, and there are not a few whose windows are glorified by lovely blossoms even now. There seems a prejudice against the old-fashioned conservatory built out over the portico, or in an angle of projecting walls on the side, and if one may accept Washington Avenue as a true indicator of the present style, people prefer to have their flowers in the recessed windows of their drawing rooms. One of the villas of this avenue is of wood, but quite large and obviously very comfortable[30]. It has not only a glimpse of floral loveliness in a window, but it has a splendid lawn and a noble rhododendron covered with buds, which are only waiting until Winter is ashamed of lingering in the lap of Spring to burst forth in utter gorgeousness. And there is an iron facsimile of the Warwick vase[31], which will, I presume, be filled with the blue creeping lobelia and variegated colenses. No one can help noticing this villa, because it is next to the noble Graham Institute for Respectable Aged Indigent Females[32]. This is a very large building and has the air of a college or scientific institution rather than of a home for the ship-wrecked in life's voyage. In fact, it is not homelike. Should it be my hard fate to wear out the gray evening of life in some home for destitute journalists, I do hope that the windows will be small and the ceilings low and the passages and corridors narrow, because there would be a sense of homeliness about it. But in the proud halls of a place like the Graham Institute I should

---

[30] No. 336, it was owned by John Underwood, the typewriter manufacturer, and occupied a large, almost square lot 250 feet long. He died in 1937; in the 1950s, his widow and daughter donated the family property to the city, which tore down the house and built Underwood Park.

[31] A marble vase discovered at Hadrian's villa in Tivoli and moved to Scotland, where it was restored and became something of an attraction in the nineteenth century. Cast-iron replicas became popular garden ornaments.

[32] Today, No. 320. It was opened in 1851 by philanthropist John Graham to provide older women with some of the comforts to which they may have become accustomed. In 1899, the name was changed to "The Graham Home for Old Ladies." It was converted into condos ca. 2001. See Chapter 15 for more about Graham.

have the feeling of being eternally on inspection and part of a charity show, under obligation to smile when visitors came around and to make pleasant answers to the dull jests of would-be witty gentlemen who had lunched copiously. I am sorry that a place so unhomelike should be a home, and that it should be situated on an avenue where there are so many true homes, as pleasant and as refined as any in America.

It is delightful to me to lounge about this avenue in this villa part and to notice the little flourishes of individuality here and there. The dull, decorous uniformity of some streets makes me unhappy, and when I come across a house where the proprietor has done something showing that he takes pleasure in his belongings and is not afraid of criticism I am thankful to that man. Now on the corner of Greene Avenue is a villa of a gentleman who has a fondness for statuary[33]. The villa is of brick, handsome, substantial, well-proportioned and commodious. In the center is a porch. Under the shadow of each of the two pillars is a red iron lion with white eyes. On the lawn to the left is a marble representation of Paul and Virginia[34] when they were babies nestling in a huge shell of white marble, after a bath, of course, and while their nurses were preparing their toilets. In front is an iron statue of a boy holding up a boot, contrived as a fountain. When the waterworks are in operation a pipe concealed in the boy's arm fills the boot with water, which overflows and falls upon his toes. This is not quite so poetic as an Undine, but it is as good as the fountain that used to be in front of the New York Court House[35], where an iron Grecian nymph standing on one toe poured water from a bedroom jug down the throat

---

[33] Likely No. 395, which is still standing, though without the statues. It was likely built by Freeborn Smith, a leading citizen and piano manufacturer; his family moved out ca. 1885.

[34] Or Paul et Virginie, the title characters of Bernardin de Saint-Pierre's very successful 1788 novel, regarded as a classic in the nineteenth century.

[35] Today it's the Tweed Courthouse, built 1861–81 behind City Hall.

of a swan. On the right side of the lawn is an iron basket filled with lycopodium. This is supported by a stag's head, and the basket fits in with much exactness between the horns. In the rear garden there is a change of level, so that all that is visible is the upper part of an iron negro boy gayly painted. Nearly opposite to this artistic villa is a public school built in 1881[36]. It is an excellent specimen of what can be done by a good architect with such perfunctory structures, for it is well-proportioned and actually impressive, and what is very strange is that, though built a generation before the Queen Anne craze, it is far more in the spirit of Queen Anne architecture than any building of the present date. There are two semi-detached villas between Gates and Fulton[37], one of which seems to me to be a model of a comfortable home, for it has been touched everywhere with the marks of a home-loving spirit and an artistic nature combined and is just the sort of nest that should by rights belong to a journalist and an art critic[38].

It is of brick that has been painted a cold Turkey red, but this is relieved by a modified mansard of slates with semi-dormer attics, and by a heavy wooden veranda painted a dark, warm green. The carving of the latter is in the most exquisite taste and shows that the designer thoroughly understood that all form must depend upon the quality of the material. The flooring of the veranda forms a roof for the area of the basement, which is shut in by very handsome and original lattice work. One can see that this is either an old house restored or that the designer deliberately went back to the old order of things, believing it to be more comfortable than any other. The door is of oak, perfectly original in com-

---

[36] PS 11 then stood next to what's now Greene Playground (which opened in 1961 on the old site of the Summerfield Methodist church). The present, much larger school building was built in the early 1960s.
[37] No. 481–3. The former still stands, though much altered (e.g., it has lost its front porch). The condo complex next door was built in 2007.
[38] He means himself.

position, and the upper part is an arrangement of the beautiful glass created by Louis C. Tiffany. The central panel is open and is filled with light, graceful, metallic scrollwork. The plate of the doorknob is in repoussé brass work, etched in with acids, and the bell plate is in the same style. The villa is much larger than its front would indicate, and its side extends inordinately, but with projections and broken surfaces. At the very end is a large room with windows facing to the south and east[39], so as to catch the Summer breezes from the sea, and above it is an open large balcony of heavy carved wood, like the veranda, for after dinner smokes in the heated season. The gardens of both run down to a stable that must front on Clinton[40], and are both evidently cared for by people who love flowers and shrubs. I haven't the least idea who lives in this beautiful home[41] but should not be surprised if it were some commission merchant doing business in potatoes and onions in the Wallabout at the other end of Washington Avenue. For men of that class are really our best citizens, always progressive, always ready to receive new ideas, always home loving. If politics are to be redeemed it will be by these men and not by the great banking and railroad magnates, whose interests are too large and too special to allow them to be disinterested patriots.

I shall not say many words about the gorgeous brick and terra cotta flats with brownstone basements in this part of

---

[39] This suggests he's talking about No. 483, which had one more room than its neighbor, at the rear.

[40] There was a wooden private boarding stable behind these semidetached homes, on St. James Place.

[41] The house was purchased ca. 1886 by George W. Shiebler, who spent $10,000 that year to add the backroom. In 1889, he opened a factory on Underhill Avenue that produced renowned silverware. In 1897 he spent $130,000 to erect the Shiebler mansion at the intersection of Plaza and Union streets, across from Grand Army Plaza—a celebrated Park Slope landmark until the 1920s, when it was replaced with the flatiron apartment building 47 Plaza Street West.

Washington Avenue. There are commendable architectural features no doubt, and much beauty of decoration. But it seems to me that they are in the wrong place, even admitting them to be the right things, which is not certain. I am disgusted at a proprietor who is determined to build upon every inch of his ground and as high as the law allows coming into a region of villas where the idea of every other proprietor seems to be to create a garden spot open to all God's sunshine and ozone. There is a selfishness about it, a contempt of the unwritten rights of others, which shocks the moral consciousness of the just of soul. Neither shall I say much of the Washington Avenue that stretches beyond Atlantic Avenue to Flatbush. Very much of it belongs to the East Side Park Lands and rests in status quo, a barrier to progress, a source of delight to the shantyman. If it be true that an error once made by bodies wielding the law of eminent domain is irretrievable, then the law conflicts with common sense and the common law of England[42]. But the opinion of lawyers is by no means all sufficient in the matter, and they are exceedingly apt to be wrong, for they are too versed in the letter to comprehend the spirit. Law is in the abstract the most perfect justice, and to condemn the city to permanent loss for the alleged oversight of some Park Commissioners would be the most perfect injustice to the taxpayers. Nor will I say much of the churches upon Washington Avenue, which were built of brick at a time when the inherent quality of brickwork and its power lending itself to noble decoration were undreamed of[43].

E. R. G.

---

[42] Some of the East Side Lands was developed as the Brooklyn Botanic Garden, bordered on the east by Washington Avenue. See Chapter 14.
[43] The aforementioned Summerfield Church, torn down in 1931, looked very much like the still-standing Washington Avenue Baptist Church (now Brown Memorial Baptist, since 1958), on the corner of Gates. Neither seems to warrant E.R.G.'s dismissal.

20

Lafayette Avenue

ON LAFAYETTE AVENUE.

A Well Paved and Attractive Thoroughfare.

Contrast With Smallpox Concrete—The Baptist Church—People Who Live "on the Hill." Houses and Gardens.

Sunday, March 20, 1887

At this precise moment, when General Newton, over on the other side of the East River, proposes a thorough repaving of the more important thoroughfares of New York[1], the inhabitants of Brooklyn point with pride to the pavement of Lafayette Avenue and view with alarm the pavement of a part of Schermerhorn Street contiguous to Flatbush Avenue and connected with Lafayette Avenue by the nearest ties of civic geography. For though to the uninstructed eye it may not appear so, yet the fact remains that Lafayette Avenue is a continuation of Schermerhorn Street; but very fortunately for the former the concrete pavement at the end of the latter was not continuous. Had it been, the pavement would have been as full of holes as the face of a negro after the smallpox; but fortunately the star of Lafayette Avenue was in the ascendant, and it was paved with Belgian blocks and is in consequence one of the best paved streets in the metropolis

---

[1] John Newton, a Union general and one-time chief of engineers, was in 1887 New York City's commissioner of public works. He was famous for leading the immense controlled explosions of several dangerous rocks in Hell Gate in 1885.

of Long Island[2]. And as, moreover, Lafayette Avenue is upon the slope of the big hill of Brooklyn, it enjoys splendid facilities for surface drainage and for that inexpensive kind of street sweeping that is done by the winds. And that is the only system in vogue at present in Brooklyn, the readers of the EAGLE, more especially those live on Court Street, will comprehend the full force of the statement that in spite of the thorough neglect Lafayette Avenue is still clean and decent[3]. The winds and the rains and the slope and the pavement have all contributed. Therefore, a man without getting any hints from the Health Department could, just upon the visible facts, take an affidavit that Lafayette Avenue is remarkably healthy. The children upon the sidewalk show it, the grown-up people walking up and down demonstrate it, and the general exuberance and demonstrative character of the quarter testify to it.

There can be no question that the people on Lafayette Avenue are very conscious that they live on the Hill. That fact peeps out in the nomenclature of the lawn tennis clubs[4] and the associations for the support and maintenance of the noble game of croquet. It appears in the formation of the Oxford[5] and the "W. C. T. U. of the Hill[6]," and in the build-

---

[2] Belgian blocks are often mistakenly called cobblestones. The former are rectangular, like bricks, the latter round.

[3] Henry Berau had been contracted by the city to clean the streets—including picking up trash and emptying ash barrels—but his men did not do a good job of it; the streets were filthy. One alderman in March called the state of Fulton "a disgrace." The *Eagle* reported on "the street cleaning problem" and "the garbage nuisance" often in 1887.

[4] There was, for example, the Brooklyn Hill Lawn Tennis Club.

[5] The Oxford Club built a clubhouse in 1880 on the southwest corner of South Oxford Street and Lafayette, No. 103–9. An exclusive private social organization, it had an impressive library and art collection. The site is now occupied by the Griffin, a hotel built in 1931 and converted to co-ops in 1987.

[6] The Women's Christian Temperance Union on the Hill was founded in 1879, an offshoot of a national organization that would help drive the

ing of grand churches where the people of the Hill can worship without being crowded by people from less-favored districts. But though there are many churches on this avenue the only one that really merits attention and comment is near Washington Avenue[7]. Cruel and unjust as this sentence may seem to those who belong to the brownstone church at the corner of South Oxford Street[8], or the Puritan Congregation Church[9] near Tompkins Park[10], it is nevertheless true. There are churches that are purely mechanical efforts, being simply places enclosed by walls for the purposes of religious observance, having no originality of conception, nor beauty of ornamentation, having been made without any regard to the quality of the material employed, purely perfunctory and with no more consciousness in them than a matchbox. It may seem absurd to speak of the consciousness of a building, but this is certain, that, whenever a man puts his soil into the thing that he is making, something of the ethereal essence lingers about it as long as it endures. Now, in the church near Washington Avenue on this thoroughfare, this quality is patent. The architect who designed it[11] burned to express the intense admiration he felt for the transitional architecture of the Twelfth Century, and he did this not by servile copying some French or English structure of that period but by designing something in that clef, as the musicians say in their

---

ratification of prohibition in 1919. Its headquarters were at 17 Greene Avenue. It's last referenced in the newspaper record in 1910.

[7] Emmanuel Baptist Church, still on the corner of St. James Place, opened a few weeks after this column was published.

[8] The still-standing Lafayette Presbyterian Church was built 1860–62.

[9] On the southwest corner of the intersection with Marcy Avenue, the church was built ca. 1869. A hundred years later, it was destroyed by fire. Today, the old church site and that of a few neighboring buildings forms the Hattie Carthan Community Garden, established in 1991.

[10] Now Herbert Von King Park. See Chapter 18.

[11] Francis H. Kimball is remembered especially for some early skyscrapers in Manhattan. His other most notable building in Brooklyn was the Montauk Club, in Park Slope, which opened in 1891.

technical jargon. No one can regard this building without admiration, for the towers and the central mass of the façade are of exquisite beauty, and the architect has used the articulated column of that time with wonderful force and discretion. Yet this is a point about it to which I must demur, and I trust that in so doing I shall not displease the Baptists, to whom it belongs. When one remembers how fifty years ago this denomination prided itself upon the ugliness of its ecclesiastical buildings, one cannot but hold up the hands of astonishment at surveying such a church as this. But the fact probably was that the Baptists of that day were poor, and whenever one of them became rich he incontinently abandoned the fold and pastured with Episcopalian sheep. Now, on the contrary, the rich Baptists cling to their creed, and what desertions there still are take place among the poorer brethren. Perhaps the Baptists are going to be the fashionable denomination of the next century. But this is a digression.

In the transitional churches of the Twelfth and Thirteenth centuries the façade where the main entrances were situated divided itself naturally into three masses, because of the nave and lateral aisles. It is obvious that no one can be satisfied with internal arrangements of that character now, because the columns of the clerestory not only tend to darken the place but prevent people from seeing each other, which they naturally wish to do. The efforts of those who wish to revise the ecclesiastical feelings of the Twelfth Century must be futile, for the people of today cannot without hypocrisy pretend to feel as the others felt. If he who is gone[12], and whose lips were far more eloquent than those of St. Bernard of Clairvaux[13], had preached a crusade against the Mor-

---

[12] A reference to Henry Ward Beecher, who died less than two weeks before this column was published. See Chapter 5.

[13] An abbot from Burgundy who gave a famous sermon in Vézelay in 1146 CE that convinced many Christians to join the Second Crusade.

mons[14], he would have shocked his hearers, and he would not have been obeyed. But when St. Bernard preached his crusade, kings left their thrones, counts their castles, boors their cottages, merchants their stalls, and all rushed with one mad impulse against the followers of Mahound[15]. Yet St. Bernard was not a greater man than Beecher, and the difference between them lay in the difference of their times. The Baptist church on Lafayette Avenue has externally the three divisions, the central mass and the tall, flanking towers, but within there is a great open space and the galleries are supported by iron trusses resting upon four columns in the corners of the church. There are no grand processions of stolid monks and cross bearers and boys waving censers, passing up the nave with chants and chanted prayers. All that is as much gone as the crusades, and those who revive it commit an anachronism. But architecture has not yet devised an exterior that shall be in harmony with the interior, and therefore we have flanking towers, with their exquisite fluted columns. But I believe that we might have the fluted pillars without the towers, and that the latter are as much an anachronism as the processional of the High Church party[16].

Then again in the central mass I am not satisfied that the gable end should have been treated in the Queen Anne style, so popular nowadays, with finials and croquets superadded from the decorated Gothic. It is to be noted that in the architecture of the transitional period there was a grand horizontal line of arcade gallery work, instead of a pointed gable, and this was connected with smaller galleries on the towers, so that there was one magnificent sweeping line at the top across the whole breadth of the edifice, and the towers

---

[14] Members of the Church of Jesus Christ of Latter-Day Saints were at that time still practicing polygamy in the Utah territory.

[15] An archaic name for Muhammad.

[16] A movement in the Episcopal church that favored older Roman Catholic traditions, as opposed to the Low Church, which preferred newer Protestant ones. See Chapter 6.

seemed to rise from that line and not from the ground. Here, as it seems to me, the architect might have followed in the old path to great advantage, but, instead of doing this, he has given a disconnected piece of simulated asculine in the center of his façade and has then carried it upward to end in his Queen Anne gable. This is worse than weak, for it is pretentious without force. No one can maintain that an architect must follow rigidly the style of any period, and I think he did admirably in presenting a large and most noble window full of tracery and of many bays instead of the great rose window and the geminated small windows on each side, which are usual in transitional Gothic. And though the fluted columns terminating in sculptured corbels on each side of his grand window are purely decorative, and belong to the interior of Gothic churches, where they served to hold up the timber roof, yet they are effective, and would be still more so if there had been no peaked gable. And I think he was right in making the entrances very simple, because we are not capable nowadays of creating the richly sculptured recessed arches of early Gothic porches. There is little decoration to these except that the spandrels are adorned with very spirited water dragons, in which the sportive mind may find a gentle allusion to the tenets of the congregation. But in spite of all these points in which I have presumed to differ from the accomplished architect, I have found no edifice of an ecclesiastical character in Brooklyn that has pleased me so much. It is in a fine cream-colored sandstone that will mellow to an exquisite tone in the course of a few years.

With the exception of its pavement and its churches, Lafayette Avenue presents no features of striking general interest[17]. It is a street of dwelling houses generally handsome and comfortable, and of stone or brick, up to a certain point,

---

[17] Construction on the striking Brooklyn Academy of Music theater at 30 Lafayette Avenue would not begin for another almost twenty years, after its home in Brooklyn Heights burned down.

and there wooden houses begin to show themselves, increasing in number so tremendously that long before one reaches Broadway, into which Lafayette Avenue debouches, every house is of wood[18]. The good folks who inhabit this section obviously do not belong to the Hill. It is not, therefore, surprising that the excellent pavement was not extended throughout the length of the avenue, for the cost would have been great, and the circumstances would not have warranted it. It would be unjust to the department that controls these things to say that the rich are better treated in the way of pavements than the poor, for the idea of paving has evidently been based upon considerations of traffic and communication with other centers. Clinton Avenue, the pearl of the city, the queen avenue of the Hill region, or, as the sporting men say, the boss avenue, is paved with a cobblestone pavement of the vilest description. Cumberland Street, where it intersects with Lafayette, has a concrete pavement of the smallpox kind. Vanderbilt Avenue is vilely cobbled, so is Washington Avenue, but Clermont Avenue is paved with very superior cobble work, the stones being small and even, a proof that cobble pavement, the cheapest of all, need not necessarily be bad. One might have expected that the good granite block pavement on Lafayette Avenue would have extended at least to Tompkins Avenue and the lovely little park located there[19], but such, unfortunately, has not been the case, and the cobblestones in that region are most uneven and rocky, so that substances that corrupt and make bad gases when lodged between them are not washed away by the rains. The Froebel kintergarden schools are on Lafayette Avenue in this neighborhood[20], and the wooden buildings are on as small a scale

---

[18] He exaggerates—there were homes made of stone or brick as far as Broadway, but east of Classon Avenue they became scarcer, with many more wooden neighbors.

[19] See Chapter 18.

[20] Friedrich Fröbel was a German educational reformer in the nineteenth century, best remembered for the concept of kindergarten

as possible and are, moreover, atrociously homely. The Queen's County foxhound kennels are handsomer structures[21]. But perhaps the Froebel system inculcates a detestation of the beautiful as a necessary part of the education, fitting human beings for the practical side of life[22]. Well, well! Froebel was a German, so that there is nothing very strange in such an idea. But I hope the influence of American love of the beautiful will permeate the Froebellian expounders and induce them to make their schools as attractive as their means will allow, so that a fondness for whatever is lovely may sink deep into the childish hearts of their scholars.

Lafayette Avenue cannot boast of many attractive buildings, and the finest are flats, of which after one leaves the summit of the hill there are so many that they form a distinct feature. The most remarkable structure is a combination of four villas, a sort of tetrarchy, between Clermont and Van-

---

(which E.R.G. misspells). The Froebel Academy was directly across from the park, at No. 686–89. It was founded ca. 1876, and the schoolhouse on Lafayette was built ca. 1883, then expanded ten years later. By 1898, it offered ten years of instruction, beginning at kindergarten, to prepare students for high school. It moved to 176 Brooklyn Avenue in 1919 and closed in 1953.

[21] In 1877, a group of sportsmen founded the Queens County Hunt, a foxhunt across the farms and fields of Long Island. (What's now Nassau County was part of Queens County until 1898, when the western part joined New York City.) It was later redubbed the Meadow Brook Hunt; the kennels were in East Meadowbrook. An illustration of "The Meadow Brook Kennels," from 1897, shows a low, unglamorous wooden frame building. His point is that the princeliest dogs had better accommodations than the kindergarteners.

[22] Even after the building was expanded and improved, the Brooklyn *Citizen* reported, "The building is not as fine, architecturally, as the trustees and teachers would desire, yet it is ample enough for present needs," suggesting the quality of the building's appearance was a practical matter, not an ideological one.

derbilt avenues[23]. There are two in front and one on each side, standing like the brave Highlanders, shoulder to shoulder. In front of those that face upon Lafayette Avenue is a sort of park-like garden in which are many tall trees and a number of evergreens that do not seem to have prospered. This garden sweeps round to the entrances of the tetrarchs facing on the other avenues, but these cunning people evidently have got the better of their co-mates, for they have a garden enclosed by a high fence, and the rear part of their houses is within this enclosure. The smell of spruces and pines and firs is very grateful no doubt, but there is no way by which such trees can be prevented from giving a forlorn appearance to the villa garden in which they have been planted. Grass will not grow underneath them, and as they shoot up into the air, they cease to be attractive in themselves. Villa gardens have their limitations like everything else, and the vaulting ambition that wishes to make parks of them doth o'erleap itself[24]. Good green turf, rhododendrons: kalmias, hydrangeas and dwarf viburnums make an admirable surrounding for a villa, but the tall trees and evergreens of this tetrarchy only shed gloom over the houses, which are in the Italian style, of brick and stucco, and not particularly ornate. I have no doubt that the enclosed garden is a thing of exquisite beauty throughout the Spring, Summer and fall, not because I have seen any indications to that effect but because it is hidden by the high fence, and, being hidden, I conjecture all sorts of beautiful things in it, which perhaps are not there. Perhaps there are no banksia roses trained against

---

[23] These buildings occupied the north side of Lafayette, Nos. 191–209 (alternatively numbered 305–23 Clermont and 296–316 Vanderbilt). Half this lot became the Brooklyn Masonic Temple in 1906, the other half Our Lady Queen of All Saints church in 1910–13.

[24] He paraphrases the end of Macbeth's soliloquy at the top of Act I, scene v: "I have no spur / To prick the sides of my intent, but only / Vaulting ambition, which o'erleaps itself / And falls on the other."

one corner of the house, no masses of Tartar honeysuckle, no laburnum sweeping to the ground, its long branches crowned with golden blossoms, no wisteria-covered arbor, no line of hollyhocks against the fence, no plat of blue nemsplutas and orange eschscholzias rising out of the shaven turf, no standard roses, no bushes of fuschias, no masses of verbena and lantana, no bavaidia nor deutzia trees, no geraniums and pelargoniums, no clumps of irises in the wet places. But then again there may be all these things, when the Spring comes, because you see the fence hides them, so that they may be there, almost invisible. But what no one can deny is the magnolia tree in front of the boarding house facing the Oxford Club[25]. That is plainly visible, and what is more, it is in bud, and will soon be in flower. The Spring, perhaps, comes earlier to the Hill part of Lafayette Avenue than to other places.

Perhaps the trees of this tetrarchy would not be so melancholy if it were not for the ruin on the other side of the way. Of all ruins none are so thoroughly saddening as those of uncompleted buildings. This was to have been a great church, almost a cathedral, apparently, from its dimensions[26]. The

---

[25] Of the rowhouses on the south side of Lafayette, between South Oxford and South Portland (which are still standing), only No. 86 advertised furnished rooms to let in the Brooklyn *Eagle* at this time.
[26] The Catholic Church owned the entire block between Lafayette and Greene, Clermont and Vanderbilt avenues. It planned to build on most of it the Cathedral of the Immaculate Conception, which would have been the second-largest Catholic structure in the country. The foundation was laid, and St. John's chapel was built close to Greene Avenue, but the funds to finish it couldn't be raised. Today, much of the land is occupied by Bishop Loughlin Memorial High School and its schoolyard. Previously on Jay Street, it moved to Clermont in 1933, the same year it was renamed for the Very Reverend John Loughlin, Brooklyn's first Catholic bishop. The Episcopal residence was built before the cathedral project ran out of money, at 367 Clermont Avenue, in 1883–7. It still stands, now used by Bishop Loughlin as a separate boarding school for struggling students.

first courses were laid and were carried to a height of about twelve or fourteen feet and then the work was stopped. The end upon Greene Avenue, which included ecclesiastical buildings and the apse of the church, with its seven mystical windows, illustrative of the seven sacred folds of the divine hood[27], over the altar, had been completed before the end came, and this gives the whole a look as if it had been destroyed by fire and all had toppled down save the apse and the clerical houses on each side of it. But it was not so, nor did a flame ever touch it, but it stopped growing and remained what it is now—a ruin. Seeds of grass, scattered by the winds, have been blown upon the topmost course, and finding the mortar a satisfactory substitute for soil have prospered amazingly, so that there is quite a flourishing topping of turf. There are also young shoots of shade trees that have sprung up and will live a year or two and then must die for want of nourishment. Meanwhile they live cheerily and feel a mighty exultation in the coming of Spring, and each one whispers to the grasses and the sparrows that hop about, "The Spring has come and I'm glad of it, for I was tired of that long, dreamless sleep." Little do they forebode how soon they are to sleep forever. But the grasses live on and flourish and wave about in the wind, for they are humble-minded and content with little, not like the towering maples on Lafayette Avenue, whose seeds, blown hither and tither, alighted on the ruined walks and sprang into life. After all, it is better for them to have lived and known the ineffable sweetness of the blue sky and the sailing clouds and the whispering winds and the golden sunbeams, even for two or three short years only, than to be ground into dust under the feet of the horses and trampled by the heels of the pedestrians. Nature produces her seed by uncountable billions and all are equally

---

[27] The Book of Revelation mentions the seven spirits of god, which Christians understand to be the ways the holy spirit manifests itself in people—wisdom, counsel, etc.

fit for life, but only those survive that are blessed by fitting surroundings.

E. R. G.

21

East Baltic Street

ON EAST BALTIC STREET[1].

A Pessimistic View of the Physiognomy of a Thoroughfare.

Criminal Suggestions of Gowanus Canal—A Possible Confederation of Thieves—The Model Cottages of Cleveland Place and Whitewashers' Row—An Interesting Relic of Days Gone By—The Badness of the Highway on Sundays—Gamblers of the Sidewalk.

Sunday, March 27, 1887

Streets have their physiognomies as well as men, and if ever the Police Department has a rogue's gallery of streets we may be certain that East Baltic Street, from Hoyt to Nevins[2], will be represented. There is not the least doubt in my mind that this is due to the proximity of the Gowanus Canal. The police of this city are morally certain that in the neighborhood

---

[1] Today there is just one Baltic Street, without cardinal distinction. It was divided into east and west, at Court Street, in 1852, along with neighboring Warren Street. The two names were commonly used into the 1870s, but even by the time this column was published, "East Baltic" was rarely still employed. In fact, E. R. G. was the last person to use it in the newspaper record. It arose, like Rockwell Place in Chapter 18, from the desire of the people of one section of the street to distinguish themselves from those of the other.

[2] Today, the block between Hoyt and Bond is occupied on both sides by the Gowanus Houses, ground for which was broken in 1948. Between Bond and Nevins, there are mostly nondescript, low-lying industrial buildings.

of this detestable plague spot are scores of houses where stolen goods are concealed. But it does not seem to have entered into the heads of those who control the department that the choice of such a locality is due to the facility that the schooners and canal barges give for the transference of plunder from one point to another. The proceeds of robberies from other sections are brought by innocent lumber schooners and sloops laden with bricks and barges filled with tobacco bales to this unfortunate city, to be disposed of in New York or here; and the insolent and motiveless burglaries that have terrorized our citizens and made one weeping widow are the consequences of the congregating at this one point of thieves, robbers and burglars from many regions. I remember reading long ago an account of the interior magnificence of the lumber barges coming from the border line of Canada, near Niagara Falls, to the Gowanus Canal, and how the daughters of one barge captain were on board and had a piano in the cabin and had dances in the hold after the lumber had been disembarked. But I have seen nothing of the sort although I have narrowly scrutinized the canal and its vessels for the past twelve months and have come to the conclusion that a large percentage of the men who frequent the place and work about it on barges and in yards are allied with the criminal classes. They may not commit crime themselves, but they wink at it. They harbor criminals and give passages to men who are at odds with justice, and they carry the fruit of robberies for a consideration to and fro, being under the rose a sort of Robbers Express Company. I cannot doubt that there is a complete confederation of criminals, whose headquarters are here in Brooklyn, in the immediate neighborhood of the Gowanus Canal. It may become the duty of the citizens to take picks and shovels and fill it up, which would be a cheaper method of ending the evil than of doubling the present rate of taxation for a police force capable of grappling with the concentrated crime of many cities harbored so comfortably here. The death of Lyman S.

Weeks[3] and the absurd and ridiculous robberies of the past month in Brooklyn can only be explained by the braggadocio of criminals who find themselves in great numbers in a city almost denuded of police. There is so little for them to get here that they would not be here under ordinary circumstances. A city of poor homes is no place for a burglar. But they are here because this is their headquarters, and they break in and steal towels and tidies out of sheer wanton insolence and to keep their hands in. If the Gowanus Canal were filled up, the receiver's occupation in this part of Brooklyn would be gone for good.

The first block, from Court Street to Smith, contains many respectable homes, obviously the homes of respectable people. Here, also, is located an admirable Catholic educational establishment, St. Francis' College for boys[4], which, like almost all the structures belonging to this faith, is remarkable for nothing save its neat sobriety of aspect and its suitability for its work. In the next block, from Smith Street to Hoyt, we descend the hill literally as well as figuratively, yet the houses here are the abode of poor people, and of vicious ones. Still, the system of building that now becomes visible is

---

[3] Lyman Smith Weeks was a hat-company executive who lived at 1071 Dekalb Avenue. On March 15, 1887, less than two weeks before this column was published, he was roused from bed by his wife, who'd heard a noise, and surprised a burglar in the basement of their home. Weeks was shot once, and he died while trying to say goodbye to his wife. John Greenwall was convicted of the murder, perhaps wrongly, and hanged at the Raymond Street Jail on December 6, 1889—the last person to be executed that way in New York State, which the following year began using the electric chair.

[4] St. Francis Academy was founded in 1859, the first Catholic school in Brooklyn, at 300–10 Baltic Street. In 1884, it had acquired six rowhouses behind the school, on Butler Street, and the following year it evolved into a college. The school continued to grow, and in 1963 it relocated to Remsen Street, in Brooklyn Heights, where it remains. Parts of the old Baltic Street property are now occupied by various public and charter school buildings, built in the twentieth century.

injudicious from sanitary reasons, and it may be doubted whether a health department alive to the interests of the city would in past years have permitted the state of things now existing to have grown up. In former years, the houses and cottages in this street had in front of them a long strip of garden, and when land became valuable for business purposes the owners disposed of a certain portion of these gardens and buildings were erected on them, so that Baltic Street is a sort of double street, and for a considerable extent has on each side of the way two rows of houses, one behind the other. It must be acknowledged that there is often quite a considerable courtyard between them, and that this state of things is preferable to the erection of towering flats upon the whole of the ground, as has been done in some parts of the city to the manifest detriment of the neighboring houses, where sunlight in Winter and cooling breezes in Summer are intercepted by the monstrous mass of brickwork, climbing into the blue vault of heaven. But the double rows of Baltic Street are famous for the accumulation of filth and garbage, for the city is not served in this particular as it should be, and the police know well that the occupants of these rear homes are not alone in fault. It seems reasonable to allow owners of real estate to make the most of their property, but some limit must be drawn as to the powers of ownership in the interest of the community.

Now there is a way by which the two things can be conciliated, and this is shown on a block farther down Baltic Street, in the neighborhood of Third Avenue. Here, instead of pursuing the time-honored practice of building a row of houses parallel with Baltic Street, the owners have built at right angles with it, running a short cross street called Cleveland Place, from Baltic to Butler[5]. They named this place in

---

[5] Cleveland Place ran parallel to Third Avenue just behind the storefronts on its west side. It appears on a map from 1929 but was probably soon after demolished; I found no records of it from the 1930s, and it does not appear in the city's tax-photo archive from

honor of the President because he was a reformer, and they considered these cottages a reform. And so they are. They are very neatly built of red brick and have a sufficient yard behind for laundry purposes, with a fence high enough to prevent the incursions of the juvenile bandits who lurk around. Cleveland Place, not to put too fine a point on it, is only just outside the jaws of the lion, being between Nevins Street and Third Avenue, so that the neighborhood is a drawback, as the projectors have discovered. These cottages have two floors and a basement, and the rooms are small and cozy, and well adapted for respectable mechanics, being very much on the order of those built in Philadelphia for this class of occupants, but neater and more artistic. There are twenty-four of them, twelve on each side of the little street, which has a fine, refreshing strip of green turf in the center. They were to be rented for $25 a month, but the first occupants were of the tough variety, and they were got rid of, and to tempt a better class the rents were lowered to $18, with precisely the contrary effect, for the newcomers were still tougher than their predecessors. Finally, the projectors kicked out all the white rowdies, raised their rents to the normal figure, $25 a month, and announced that the row would be reserved for colored people of the utmost respectability. This plan succeeded, and the occupants are such refined people, such thorough ladies and gentlemen, that though the women are nut-brown maidens and the men have more or less coffee in their complexions, one feels instinctively that they are more akin to us than the ruffians of the Gowanus Canal and its neighborhood. When they walk on the street the young rowdies shout out "nigger alley," "nigger alley," but this is all, for there is a stern janitor, and hence their windows are not

---

1940. The New York Public Library has a photograph of a corner house from 1924, showing a low concrete gate at the entrance to the street, with a narrow opening for pedestrians. E.R.G.'s description of the street seems to be the most detailed record of it. Its former site is roughly now occupied by a nondescript industrial building, No. 540.

broken, and they are not otherwise molested. And what is more, the cry of "nigger alley" is raised not because they are colored people, but because they are so well dressed and so refined that they are tacit reproaches to East Baltic Street[6]. For there is on the block between Third and Fourth avenues a whole row of old houses[7] occupied entirely by colored people, but not of the same high class as Cleveland Place, the women being washerwomen and the men so addicted to calcimining and whitewashing that they might start a Limekiln Club, like the darkies of Detroit[8]. They are honest, hearty, hard-working folk, but they do not gall the white people around them by obvious superiority, as do the inhabitants of Cleveland Place, some of whom are journalists and clergymen, and others are connected with well-known caterers. Baltic Street, therefore, hates the one crowd, but loves the other, and the observer will notice young whites and the young darkeys of this block gambling together, pitching pennies in the most amicable style and cursing each other with the good-humored fervor of true fraternal feeling.

Sunday is the great gambling day. Then, on both sides of the way for some four blocks, the sidewalks are occupied with groups of boys and young men pitching pennies. These are first thrown against a wall, and he whose cent comes in its rebound nearest to a line drawn on the sidewalk gathers up all the cents, places them on a piece of wood, to which he gives a dexterous heave that sends the coppers in the air, and then claims as his own all those that come "heads." The men

---

[6] Cleveland Place remained an African American enclave until its unrecorded disappearance. (In 1925, for example, No. 19 was home to The Cleveland Place Colored Republican Club.) This perhaps explains why the media were indifferent to its erasure.

[7] On the north side of the street, where today there's a public-housing complex and luxury condo buildings.

[8] Starting in 1878, Charles Bertrand Lewis began publishing tales of Brother Gardner's Lime Kiln Club in *The Detroit Free Press*. They were fictional and racist stories of a Black fraternal organization.

stand around and spit and smoke, and the women generally sit at the windows of the front rooms and discuss the passersby. One good dame, with a handsome, determined face, has an arm larger than that of any fat woman in any museum in these United States, and, with a generosity and public spirit that does her infinite credit, shows it liberally. But the inhabitants of Baltic Street have seen it so often that their curiosity is satiated, and it is only the casual observer who gratifies the lady's vanity and rewards her for the display by unequivocal admiration. Strings of half-grown girls, flashingly dressed, with their hair frizzed and falling in great masses to their waists and with astonishing revelations of muscular legs, go pushing through the groups of gamblers and repay the execrations of the one who has just heaved the wicher and is hunting up the results of blasphemies as outrageous and by looks and words of utter disparity. These things are not caused by poverty, for, in many parts of Brooklyn, there are girls as poor as can be imagined who are as pure as they are good looking, and that is saying not a little. It is the cousinship with crime, the alliance with criminals, that breeds vice and that makes this neighborhood morally pestilential. And the unlighted courts and numerous alleys offer as many opportunities for the vicious as they do points of propagation for epidemics and contagious diseases. These things exist because of the Gowanus Canal, which is uncontrolled, unwatched and utterly neglected by the authorities. It is time, now that a foul murder has been committed out of pure braggadocio by a criminal, that this state of things shall continue no longer[9].

All the little gardens have not been obliterated by the front buildings necessitated by the present concentration of population. There are still spots where there is turf and

---

[9] Though Weeks lived a considerable distance from the canal, on the border of Bed–Stuy and Bushwick, E.R.G. places responsibility for all crime in Brooklyn on the Gowanus Canal.

where lilac bushes spread perfume through the nights of June and where flowers are cultivated in leisure hours by the industrious and honest people who still linger here. In one of these long, narrow gardens there is a strange relic of some eccentric being who probably has long since passed into dust. It is a wooden bust and pedestal painted white, of that beautiful Greek bust in the British Museum that is called Clytie for want of another name. This most exquisite creation was long a puzzle to art writers, for the features are not classical, and one writer even advanced the idea that the features were Britannic, and that probably the model had been a beautiful British slave[10]. But the terra cotta statuettes of Tanagra[11] have shown the world conclusively that the so-called Hellenic type was purely ideal, and the Athenian, Corinthian, Spartan and Theban beauties were infinitely less classical, some of them even had retroussé noses. Think of it, ghosts of Michael Angelo and Raphael! The Hellenic girls had snub noses. So, in all probability Clytie was a portrait bust of some sweet wife and mother in old Athens. But whose freak was it to have a copy (and a good one, too) carved in wood for the decoration of his garden? It may have been old Mr. Blake, who owned the house at the southeast corner of Baltic and Court streets, and indeed that whole row was called Blake's Row[12]. The young bandits of the street have smashed every

---

[10] This marble bust, still in the British Museum, continues to bemuse scholars; one theory is that a Roman portrait of Antonia Minor, Marc Antony's daughter and Claudius's mother, was reworked in the eighteenth century to elevate its eroticism.

[11] Naturalistic figurines from before the common era, discovered in that Greek city in the later nineteenth century.

[12] Anson Blake, a speculator and developer in what's now Cobble Hill, bought in 1839 what became the east side of Court Street, between Butler and Baltic, before Court ran south of Atlantic. "A country road ran past the site of the new block," the *Eagle* later explained. After fire-related delays, the homes were ready by 1842 and sold quickly to fine families. The eight homes were known as "Blake's Row," and numbered as such (1 Blake's Row, 2 Blake's Row, and so on). Blake's house was

individual pane in one of the side windows and have pulled out half of the old slats in the Venetian blind, so that they can see into a deserted room, where there is nothing. They have also commenced to smash the panes of the bay window above but have done little damage so far, as it is rather out of their reach unless they make open and obvious onslaughts. In the rear of this forsaken house there was once a fine garden, and it may be that Clytie belonged to it in the days gone by.

As a rule, the houses in the rear row where Baltic Street is desirable are better in construction and appearance than those in front. Many of the latter have the air of being derelict wrecks—houses belonging to other regions which were sold for a song and dumped down here. They are not as rectangular as they should be, and not a few have one corner higher than the other. As a rule, the houses are of wood, and all different; but the row of frame houses which is honored by the presence of the fat lady is an exception[13]. It is singularly like the bad row on Navy Street and boasts the same peculiarity of house doors that are never closed. If burglars enter there it is because the inmates are glad to see them, and the only human beings they can possibly care to keep out are the police, the overtaxed, overworked police of the district. And as such, doors would not keep them out if they really wanted to enter, why, there is after all no real reason why doors should not be open, unless for decency's sake. But I fear, I greatly fear, that counts for little in this part of Baltic Street. Let the observer contrast the blocks from Hoyt to Nevins with the whitewashers' row on the block be-

---

No. 1, later 243–5 Court Street. Contemporary mentions of "Blake's Row" last appear in the newspapers in 1864. The former site (and then some) is now occupied by what was I.S. 293, constructed in 1968, now home to the Boerum Hill School for International Studies and other schools, which were the subjects of the podcast *Nice White Parents*.
[13] Probably those extending east from the northeast corner with Hoyt, Nos. 385–97, now part of the Gowanus Houses complex.

tween Third and Fourth avenues; let him notice the decency of the latter, the closed doors, the windows filled with geraniums and other pot plants, the pleasant blinds, the clean steps, the respectable yards in front of the houses (which were badly built originally and are not easily kept in order), and he will comprehend that there is nothing so lowering as the indifference born of despair that vice and criminality create in the human heart. That makes the vaunted white man lower than the despised African. The consciousness of honesty and of the will and power to labor give to the latter a moral hopefulness that have made his surroundings pleasant and homelike and tend to develop that feeling for decoration and color that belongs to the black race.

E. R. G.

22

West Baltic Street

ON WEST BALTIC STREET.

South Brooklyn May Lose Its Well to Do Population.

Tenement Towers Migration to Prospect Heights On One Side—Development of Docks and Warehouses on the Other—Dirty Streets. Prosperity of the River Front—The Custom House of the Port.

Sunday, April 3, 1887

So completely do the inhabitants of Baltic Street on the west side of Court feel the necessity of segregating themselves from the people living on the same street on the east side of Court that they have adopted the plan common in other cities, but unusual in Brooklyn, of calling their thoroughfare West Baltic. They are so addressed in letters, and West Baltic is proudly painted on the corner houses[1]. The first block of West Baltic is only remarkable for the extreme smallness of the houses on the south side[2], and one wonders if the proprietors of building lots that must be valuable should allow such structures to remain, as they cannot make heavy returns in the way of rental. But everyone knows his own business

---

[1] "West Baltic" last appears in the newspapers in 1902, though it was rarely used outside of legal contexts after 1896.

[2] There were roughly half a dozen narrow, two-story buildings, Nos. 244–52, most of which were replaced by 250 Baltic Street, the cornerstone for which was laid in 1936. The one-time "Red-Hook Gowanus District Health and Training Center" now houses various healthcare and social-services organizations.

best, and it is far easier to notice things than to give explanations of them. Reflecting men are not certain about the future of South Brooklyn. Ten or fifteen years ago it seemed roseate enough, and the influence exerted by such streets as Clinton, Henry and the Places was naturally so great that no one hesitated at putting up two or three good dwelling houses as a matter of investment. But since that date the big blocks of real estate on Prospect Heights[3] have come into the market, and the progress made on Fifth Avenue and parallel thoroughfares has been wonderful and unexampled. There is no doubt about the value of South Brooklyn building lots, for population is steadily on the increase in that quarter. But cautious men are not certain as to the kind of buildings that should be put up there, for the development of South Brooklyn is not what it used to be. Formerly professional men, merchants, well-to-do clerks, bookkeepers, bank cashiers, etc., made their homes here, but they are migrating to the Heights. And then, upon the other hand, there seems no limit to the growth of docks and storehouses along the water line of South Brooklyn, and this is introducing an element of population for whom homes must be provided. Now, there is more money for the investor in houses for the poor than in houses for the well-to-do who are not rich. If South Brooklyn is to be in the main peopled by the poor, then it is better to wait a while and build for them than to put up brownstone fronts and have them tenanted by the landladies of workingmen's boarding houses. Civilization is inexorable. Sands Street was once the fashionable quarter of Brooklyn; only yesterday it was occupied by the very poor, and once again a gleam of prosperity, a sort of Wintry sunshine, has fallen on it, for its proximity to the bridge has made it desirable for a better class of tenants.

    There are nice houses on Baltic Street—West Baltic, I should have written—but there is nothing about them wor-

---

[3] Park Slope.

thy of a chronicle. But when the observer nears Hicks Street he cannot but be aware that the buildings about him are of a very unusual character. He has, in fact, arrived at the wonderful Brooklyn "Towers,"[4] about which so much has been written that the fame thereof has been wafted across the Atlantic and English members of Parliament have been desirous of acquainting themselves with all the facts in the case. The Towers are in reality tenement houses of a special character and of prodigious size, providing homes for 1,100 people, and their true title is the "Improved Dwellings Company." They are so popular that a vacant set of rooms is an unusual thing, and this is due to two main factors, the good quality and comfortable character of the accommodation and the manner in which the agent comprehends his duties. Tenement houses have the fault of promiscuity, but this has been very artfully avoided by the architect of the Towers, who has so arranged his passageways as to give to every set

---

[4] These buildings were the brainchild of social reformer and businessman Alfred Tredway White, whose motto was "philanthropy plus five percent"—he intended to make small profits off his public-spirited projects. (He was also an early benefactor of the Brooklyn Botanic Garden, where a memorial to him by renowned sculptor Daniel Chester French stands at the center of a small outdoor amphitheater.) White also designed the Riverside Apartments, on Columbia Place in Brooklyn Heights, and Jacob Riis spends the last few pages of *How the Other Half Lives* praising White's buildings as models for tenement design. The first phase of the Baltic Street project, the Homes Buildings, were built in 1876–77, and they still stand on the southeast corner of Baltic and Hicks, stretching in both directions, forming an L. The even more impressive Tower Buildings were built across the street, on the east side of Hicks, spilling onto Baltic and Warren, in 1878–79. (White also built the "workingmen's cottages" that still line Warren Place, or Mews.) By the 1970s, many of the apartments were vacant or boarded up; local real estate broker Frank Farella bought the buildings in 1975 and spent a decade restoring them, and today the Cobble Hill Towers stand gloriously at the edge of the Brooklyn–Queens Expressway—even if they're now condos.

a commendable degree of privacy. There is, however, the common stair, which in Scottish cities has been found to be the bane of young people too poor to marry but not too poor to love, but this has been made like the corkscrew stairway of a Gothic tower, and is so dark, so winding and so generally uncomfortable that no one is likely to linger there, and people pass, repass without recognition. The arrangements for water supply and disposition of bathrooms are also most commendable. But the chief merit of the Towers is that the company deliberately sacrificed valuable space so that there should be the freest possible passage of air and no dark rooms. All over America at the present moment, flats are being built both for the well-to-do who are not rich and the very poor in which the number of rooms that are dark and have no ventilation is almost equal to those that have light and air. On the next block from the Towers, on West Baltic Street, there is another tenement house, built subsequently to the Towers, and much superior to it externally, in which there are sets of rooms running from the front to the rear, of which two rooms out of the four are dark. Nothing can be more monstrous than this, nor can I quite understand how an inspector of buildings can permit it, for I suppose he has some discretionary powers and is not limited to seeing that the mortar contains a proper amount of lime and sand and that the walls are of a legitimate thickness.

But the poor have too much trouble on their hands to bother about these things. Their work takes too much out of them every day to allow them to fight about their sleeping accommodations. They know when they are well treated, and they are in the Towers. The agent is one of those typical Americans who are prototypes of what man will be in the millennium, gentle as a woman, yet dauntless as a lion, careless about himself, careful about others, constantly working and dreaming for perfection in what he undertakes. He saw that the city's neglect of the streets had an inevitable reaction upon the dwellers in the Towers. The dead cats in the gutters, balls of horse dung between the cobblestones, the juicy squash flung out by the grocer's boy and ground into a thick unctuous mud by passing wheels, the ashes in the barrels upon the sidewalk dumped out partially by an eager Italian who discovered in the middle strata something worth having; these things made the population under him careless and untidy, and he told the company that the Towers would have to sweep and water its own street sections and remove its own ashes. The company thought he was right and gave him the necessary authority. Throughout this wretched Winter the vicinity of the Towers has been constantly swept and garnered. When people in the aristocratic region of the Heights on Montague and Pierrepont streets have looked with dismay upon the accumulated snow and filth and wondered what was going to happen to Brooklyn, there was not a vestige of snow on Hicks Street, between Baltic and Warren, and the cobblestones were as clean as if a mountain torrent swept over them daily. At present, garbage dwells upon the mind of the agent. There are garbage boxes allowed in the Towers, but very few, and his request to the tenants is to burn their parings and peelings and bones if they will be so good. But last Summer a lady from the South whose husband works on the docks stumped him with the query as to how the rind of watermelons was to be got rid of. "You can't burn it," said she. "I think you can, if you try very hard," said he, mildly and persuasively. "Mercy! Mr. Agent," she reiterated, "my husband and I are very fond of watermelon and eat a good deal of it. If you have only one during the Summer, you may gradually burn the rind, but how can you when you eat three a week?" The result was that a limited number of garbage boxes was issued, but the question has not been settled and still weighs upon the agent's mind. The city is supposed to do all these things, but it is notorious that it does not, and there is a strong probability that the garbage will be removed by the company as the ashes now are.

What can be more intolerable than the present condition of Brooklyn? Upon Court Street, south of Atlantic Avenue, the filth has accumulated in such quantities on each side of the car rails[5] that it looks not like a paved street but like a veritable dirt road. I cannot understand why men having fast trotters do not take them down Court Street, but they must be quick about it or there will be such a thickness of stratified beastliness that the wheels will sink to the hub. Upon Union Street, which has a fine concrete pavement laid with remarkable care and of superior quality and very easy to keep clean, there is a thick selvage of dust, which is nothing less than desiccated dung. There is a dead cat there which has been driven over until nothing remains save a mummy of skin and bones, everything else having become dust, blown about by the March winds into the lungs of young children and tender girls and delicate invalids. There are boxes and barrels of ashes all over South Brooklyn, and the wagonmen dump the contents so carelessly or with such careful maliciousness that ladies' fur sacques are covered as if a volcano were in eruption and a fine shower of ashes were falling. Garbage is boldly thrown into the streets everywhere. There is no decency, there is no comfort, there is no regard for sanitary laws. The municipality of Brooklyn does not govern in any one of the essential things that concern the housekeeper—the man of the house. The officials do not protect his property or his life from burglars; they apparently cannot discover the existence of confluent smallpox until there have been several deaths from it; they do not clean the streets; they do not remove garbage and dead animals, and the ashes are taken in an improper, slovenly and untimely fashion. If these things continue, let us give up municipal government, for it is expensive and it does not pay. Let us return to the village system of trustees and make the people of each block responsible for the cleanliness and sanitary condition of their homes and

---

[5] Public transportation on Court Street at the time was by horse car.

streets. That plan has been resorted to in self-defense by the Improved Dwellings Company, and it may be that we must all come to it. With them it has been a success, but it is hard to keep a dog and do one's barking—to pay taxes to the city to do these things and then have to pay others to do them.

Let us thank heaven that if Brooklyn is in throes of anguish through a positive syncope of municipal energy, the city itself is prosperous. One has but to walk to the end of West Baltic Street to discover that[6]. Here is a long and comparatively broad dock at which a tramp steamer is unloading hogsheads of coarse brown sugar. She wanders about the Bahamas, and the countless isles of the American Archipelago, picking up sugar in casks and bags, and then straightaway hastens to Brooklyn, which is the center of the sugar-refinery business upon the Atlantic shore. Over in California there are big sugar refineries, not due entirely to enterprise, as are those of this city, but to the persuasive powers of a gentleman named Claus Spreckels[7], who has managed to convince the United States that sugar ought to be allowed to come into this country from the Sandwich Islands[8] free of duty. If it did not, he argued that the Sandwich Islands would be very angry with this country, and something terrible might happen. Queen Kapiolani[9] might invite the French to come and rule the Sandwichs, or might make a present of Tatuiti to Queen

---

[6] The block from Columbia Street to the waterfront, now blocked off from public access, contained a lumberyard as well as the Baltic Stores, several free (and one bonded) storehouses on the south side of the block that also stretched up neighboring Harrison (now Kane) Street.

[7] A German American businessman who founded the Spreckels Sugar Company, which is still in business and once dominated the West Coast sugar market.

[8] A name for the Hawai'ian Islands given by explorer James Cook for John Montagu, the 4th Earl of Sandwich, a distant cousin of the husband of the eponym of Montague Street.

[9] Kapi'olani was the queen of Hawai'i, 1874–91.

Victoria for her jubilee birthday[10], or might even sell the lease, goodwill and fixtures of the entire group to those intriguing Prussians and Prince Bismarck. In consequence of these representations, Claus Spreckels does all the sugar refining of the Pacific Slope, and Brooklyn does pretty nearly all the remainder. So, the tramp steamers that catch cargoes of sugar know that they have a sure market in Brooklyn and come to our docks as soon as they have stored enough big barrels under hatches. Two or three are seen to be partially stove in, and one can see what brute sugar is like. It resembles sand: reddish moist sand that has a little thickening loam in it. One hogshead has to be weighed by the Custom House men, and the great barrel is opened and the contents dumped upon the planks of the dock, but away from the water, and under the shadowing wall of the great storehouse. Then it is shoveled back and again, and a couple of bustling coopers get to work and fasten the top. Lumps of brown sugar dot the whole place, and the sparrows try it, but don't like it, very much preferring the good, wholesome bird food in the vicinity of the giant elevators[11]. There are long rows of barrels of syrup in one part of the plaza in front of the six-story bonded warehouses[12], and near there is a flock of sour-mash whiskey barrels from New Haven. The latter are being sent rapidly to the sixth story of the huge building, which must be of great strength if its highest floor can endure so heavy a weight as whiskey barrels. Everywhere men are in a high state of bustling activity, except those who are waiting for a job and who place their backs against the wall of the

---

[10] The fiftieth anniversary of Queen Victoria's coronation was celebrated a few months after this column was published. It was attended by dozens of British and foreign royals, including Kapi'olani.
[11] The nearest grain elevators, ninety-four and a hundred-twenty feet tall, were on the waterfront north of Degraw Street, between it and Sedgwick Street, which was demapped in 1991.
[12] Likely the Robinson (or Congress Street) Stores, on the north side of Baltic Street, at the waterfront.

storehouse and chew meditatively, keeping a sharp lookout, however, for a possible call from one of the bosses. There are the men who live with their families in the Towers, and these growing docks and multiplying storehouses give occupation to the entire neighborhood.

The foreign commerce of Brooklyn is colossal. Our docks are differently constructed from those of New York, being much more elaborate and accompanied everywhere with warehouses, but they are not so much in view as those of New York, which are in plain sight of all who walk along the riverside streets. In consequence of our warehouse system this is not the case in Brooklyn, and to know what its commerce is you must leave the streets and venture around the warehouses. Then its colossal character begins to break upon the mind. It seems strange that with so vast a foreign commerce Brooklyn should not be itself a port of entry but should be considered a part of New York and under the officials of the New York Custom House. Even if New York had the larger foreign commerce of the two cities, a well-considered system of statesmanship would have placed the Custom House in Brooklyn[13]. For nothing is so obnoxious to the Democratic policy as concentration of interests and powers, and in New York there is a concentration of money that ought not to be placed in juxtaposition with the concentration of political power in the hands of the Collector of Customs. As the case stands, with the larger motley of the foreign commerce of the port actually in the possession of Brooklyn, a sense of what is just should have awakened Democratic politicians to the propriety of transferring the collection of customs to our city. The more the matter is regarded, the more obvious it becomes that where the money power is so strong the political power should not be. It should be the aim of the Democratic party to build Brooklyn as an equipoise to the overweening pretensions of New York and the

---

[13] He revisits here a pet issue, covered in Chapter 12.

dangerous power given her by the concentration of banking interests. Not only should the Custom House be in Brooklyn, but the Sub Treasury[14] also and every other department of the United States Government.

E. R. G.

---

[14] The Subtreasury building on Wall Street, now known as Federal Hall, was a part of the Independent Treasury system that managed the country's money supply. It was replaced by the Federal Reserve system in 1913.

23

Adams Street

A PRODUCTIVE CENTER.

The Transformed Conditions of Adams Street.

Historical Facts—John Graham's Enterprise. The Old Building Where His Company Made Acids—John Robertson's Activities—The Fate of the Thoroughfare Farther Up the Hill. The Architectural Points of the City Hall District Police Court.

Sunday, April 10, 1887

There must have been a time when Adams Street was very famous and in fact in the mouth of every Brooklynite, and this was when Brooklyn was still a village but was beginning to shake off the long depression caused by the Revolutionary War and to appreciate and utilize its great natural advantages. Much of the remarkable spirit of enterprise then displayed would, in my opinion, have still lain dormant had it not been for Hezekiah Beers Pierrepont, whose influence must have been very great[1]. He was a gentleman, a man of education, a merchant in the grand old sense of the word, a traveler and one who had encountered dangers and undergone hardships and had thereby received that true education that experience gives. The enthusiasm that he felt for Brooklyn, he who had seen so many cities, at first evoked sneers and then astonishment, but finally it awakened conviction. The men of Brooklyn comprehended that they did possess

---

[1] See Chapters 6 and 9.

advantages, and they went to work to develop them. One of the first and greatest undertakings was the Brooklyn White Lead Company, established in 1825 chiefly by John Graham and his brother Augustus. The works were located in a building upon Adams and Water streets that had been used as a distillery. At that time there was no movement against distilleries[2], of which there were not a few in Brooklyn. There was no pretense that the man who ran a distillery was dragging his fellow creatures to perdition and was to be made a mark for pulpit peltings and the intemperate howlings of frenzied teetotalers. The distilleries disappeared because the economic reasons for their existence ceased to be. As population increased within the area that we now call Brooklyn, there was a demand for the corn which was raised on Long Island, and it was no longer necessary to utilize a surplus by converting it into gin or brandy. There is so much feeling upon this subject that the mere suggestion that the Graham Brothers were interested in that old distillery would be regarded as wantonly staining the memory of John Graham, the noblest citizen, take him for all in all, that Brooklyn ever possessed[3].

So many additions and changes have been made since 1825 to the block of buildings of the Brooklyn Lead Company that it is hard to say what parts are relics of the old distillery. Probably the building at the corner of Adams and Water is one of them[4]. It was used by the company for their

---

[2] Temperance had become a mass movement by the late nineteenth century.

[3] See Chapters 15 and 19.

[4] A row of two three-story buildings and one single-story building on Water Street, off the southwest corner of Adams, identified on an 1887 map as the "Kalsomine Finish Fact'y." These buildings and the entire Brooklyn White Lead Works, occupying the whole block from Front to Water streets, Adams to Washington, were replaced in 1909 by one of paper-goods manufacturer Robert Gair's many DUMBO factories, 55 Washington Street—the same year the Manhattan Bridge opened,

cooperage shop, and no doubt it answered the same purpose in prior times. In the revolution of industries brought about by steam and machinery it has been found cheaper to buy barrels from manufacturers of barrels, and therefore the White Lead Company have abandoned their cooperage and leased the building to a Mr. Moore[5], one of the dearest friends of the colored race[6], and one of the direst foes of aesthetic long-haired exponents of the True and the Beautiful upon the lines laid down by John Ruskin[7]. Mr. Moore, in fact, manufactures that superior article of whitewash that is used in calcimining, and his name is known and blessed by the colored practitioners of the art on Baltic Street, on the block between Third and Fourth avenues[8]. Mr. Moore's establishment is on the southern corner, and on the northern corner on the opposite side of Adams Street is another old building which belonged to the White Lead Company, although not upon the same block[9]. It was used by them for the rendering of sulphuric acid from iron pyrites, a work that the philosophic mind regards with the most beaming approval. Now the Lead Company no longer finds it necessary to make its own acids, for that work is also done for them. There are no grander monuments of human ingenuity and power than the acid works in what may be called North

---

forcing formerly straight Adams Street to curve westwardly into Water Street.

[5] Benjamin Moore began his paint company with his brother in Brooklyn in 1883. Their headquarters at 51 Atlantic Avenue burned down in 1885—Benjamin was briefly missing, and his family worried he'd died—and the brothers relocated to Adams.

[6] Moore was not a noted advocate for Black people; rather, E.R.G. means laborers appreciated his quality calcimine.

[7] He's making a joke that the Romantic theories of influential English art critic John Ruskin (1819–1900) were at odds with Moore's simple whitewash.

[8] See Chapter 21.

[9] Across the street was the company's storage yard, which included a long, three-story structure on the corner.

Brooklyn, away out by Newtown Creek, where the worthless of substances is turned into a material of the utmost value to scores of great manufacturing industries. The Kalbfleish Acid Works[10] furnish the life blood, as one may say, for innumerable pursuits that give employment to hundreds of thousands in this and other cities. And yet in the dawning of industrial development in Brooklyn, the White Lead Company had to manufacture their own acids. In the path of industry one step clears the way for another. The creation of one center of industry gives birth to germs that in their turn develop into centers, and they again shoot out germs that develop and become centers themselves. And so humanity progresses, and so a city grows and grows.

This old building on the northeast corner of Adams Street does not look as if it had been built for the manufacturing industry to which it was destined. It has all the look of an old warehouse and has many features in common with that old warehouse on Furman Street, which is now used as a stable by the Brooklyn Car Company[11]. It must be remembered that at the date to which I am referring, when Hezekiah Beers Pierrepont, Joshua Sands, John Graham and Gentleman Hicks swayed the destinies of infant Brooklyn, Water Street was the river street, and some considerable warehousing must have been done there. It was not particularly well built, or perhaps it is nearer the truth to say that it was put to usages for which it was not intended, and part is

---

[10] The Bushwick Chemical Works were founded in 1829 by Martin Kalbfleish; Henry Stiles puts its campus between Metropolitan and Grand avenues, occupying several acres, the largest acid works in the country. Kalbfleish was also instrumental in the unification of Brooklyn with the town of Bushwick, later serving as an alderman, congress-member and several-term mayor of Brooklyn.

[11] The Brooklyn City Railway Company owned 8 (Old) Fulton Street, on the southeast corner of Furman, which still stands. Behind this was a two-and-a-half story stable, No. 3–7 Doughty Street, which was probably not the carriage house there today.

now in a high state of dilapidation. It may have been the acid making that should be held responsible, or it may have been the subsequent industrial pursuits of which it was the theater, or it may have been the time, but at any rate there is a stack of chimneys at the eastern end of the structure that has deviated from the perpendicular and is nodding to its fall. It forms a part of the works of the Atlantic Steam Engine Company[12], which was started in 1845 by William Arthur[13] and John Robertson. And here the reader will observe that Adams Street becomes connected with another of the great historic names of Brooklyn, for among the dazzling scroll of American inventors there is not one name more honored, more widely known than John Robertson[14]. He and Arthur graduated, if one may use the term, from the Burdon Iron Works, on Front Street[15], which are even older than the

---

[12] He previously placed the building on the northeast corner, but the Atlantic Steam Engine Company was on the southeast corner. Across the street was William Taylor & Sons Columbian Iron Works.

[13] William Young Arthur was born in Glasgow in 1836 and immigrated to the United States at about the age of seven. He died at his home, 66 Fifth Avenue, in 1924 and is buried in Green-Wood. It's likely, if the firm was founded in 1845, that Arthur came on later. It first appears in the newspaper record in 1854—with William Arthur. Perhaps E.R.G. or the typesetter transposed the numbers.

[14] Born in Scotland in 1809, Robertson spent a decade in India with the East India Company before moving to Canada in 1842 to farm. He moved to Brooklyn two years later and established himself as a notable mechanical engineer, best known for founding the Tubal Cain Iron Works in 1863. Five years later, he partnered with his son-in-law, James Hardie, to form John Robertson & Company. "The concern designed and built practically all the hydraulic lead-pipe extension presses and lead-encased underground cable presses now in use in the United States, Canada and South America and shipped many machines to Europe," the *Eagle* reported in 1919, in Hardie's obituary. Robertson had died in 1896, at his home, 203 Sterling Place, and is buried in Green-Wood.

[15] On the corner of Pearl—though it's unclear which corner—it was by this time being used by another concern, probably the Brooklyn

White Lead Works[16], and bought the old building from the lead company, adding it to an extensive annex four times its size on Water Street. And in it, John Robertson remained for more than twenty years, and then he started the Tubal Cain Works, on Water Street[17], for the development of hydraulic machinery, to which his genius has been devoted for many years. I am sorry to say that the Atlantic Steam Engine Works are now either defunct or in a bad case of suspended animation[18]. The fact is they have been closed for the past six months, which accounts for the neglect to repair the erring chimneys. If a man has a liking for chimneys, and as it is the age of specialties, perhaps there may be a traveler within our gates who wanders from one manufacturing city to another, gloating upon the tall chimneys of each, such a one is cordially invited to examine the chimney of the White Lead Company, which is as nearly opposite as possible to the stack of chimneys of the Atlantic Steam Engine Company that seems inclined to fall[19]. That great white column that goes soaring into the blue air must have for manufacturers the fascination that lofty towers and climbing spires have for the artistic and the aesthetic. Industry has its romantic and picturesque side if a man but will look for it.

I need not dwell upon the rolling mills and the brass works and the decorated tin-can company that adorn the

---

Brass & Copper Company Works, which occupied the other half of the block shared by the Atlantic Steam Engine Works: Adams to Pearl, and Water to Front, most of which is now occupied by Manhattan Bridge anchorage.

[16] The Burdon Iron Works were established in 1836, but the buildings were renovated in the 1870s.

[17] On the northeast corner of Washington Street, roughly the site today of 31 Washington, a landmarked former ironworks built in 1896 and converted to condos in 2001.

[18] The *Eagle* reported, in 1898, "The firm went to smash in 1887."

[19] The two chimneys were almost directly on either side of Adams Street, just south of Water.

lower part of this street. The last establishment is upon the rise of the hill[20], whose apex is traversed by Sands Street. Obviously at the very time that the Graham Brothers were starting their great enterprise at the foot of Adams, handsome dwelling houses were being built on the brow of the hill in the vicinity of Sands, and this part of Adams was fashionable, yes, fashionable[21]. Good old John Graham seems, however, to have had a predilection for Washington Street when he founded the institute, and there was in those early times a marked rallying to that beautiful thoroughfare. The consequence was that Adams Street socially had to play second fiddle to Washington Street and lost caste earlier than it. The great industrial enterprises at the foot of the street employed thousands of hands, and they naturally sought homes as near to the scene of their labor as possible. In the mute struggle for position that followed, Adams Street was conquered by the working men as high up as Prospect Street, not at once, but bit by bit, block by block, house by house, and they might have won the whole street but for two important actors. The bridge has brought over from New York a multitude of gentlemanly young fellows, clerks in offices and big mercantile establishments, who above all things want rooms contiguous to the bridge. This has created a renaissance for Sands Street and its neighbors in which Adams Street has shared. But the greater factor is that the important buildings that are being erected on Washington Street must have an immense effect upon it and Adams Street, its second fiddle. There will be in the immediate future a great extension of banking facilities in Brooklyn, and there is a high probability that the neighborhood of the United States building will be the center

---

[20] The Ilsey & Co. Tinware Factory was on the southeast corner of York Street.
[21] Today, this part of Adams is dominated by the Brooklyn–Queens Expressway to the west and the former Jehovah's Witnesses' printing press, built in 1950 at 117 Adams Street, to the east, which replaced various brick buildings, probably a mix of industrial and tenement.

of financial operations[22]. We learn from one source and another that this structure is to be extended to Adams Street, so that it will cover half the block between Adams, Washington, Johnson and Tillary. The financial influence of these structures is already felt by the boarding-house keepers, who have raised their prices, either because their landlords have raised their rent or because they have threatened so to do. They are in high good humor, because their rooms are constantly inquired for, not by New Yorkers principally but by people doing business in Brooklyn. The signs are that there will be a tremendous development of local business and a concentration of it in the immediate vicinity of the new structures.

Barring these new buildings, Adams Street does not shine architecturally. It does, however, boast of one edifice that has legitimate pretensions to be considered one of the notable structures of the city. I do not know in what manner all the rooms of its many stories are utilized, but on the ground floor is the City Hall District Police Court[23]. It is remarkable for two things: the boldness and originality of its decorative details and the exceedingly poor quality of its terra cotta. It looks very much as if someone had employed an architect of genuine talent, and then had endeavored to have the work done in the cheapest possible fashion. One of the most impressive features is the cornice beneath the mansard roof. It is recessed and pendent, and has a look of the old Alhambra palaces, but much of the effect is marred by the bad quality of the terra cotta of which it is composed, which is totally deficient in the fine sharpness of edge that is one of the main

---

[22] Planning for Brooklyn's original federal building began in 1885. It opened in 1892 with a post office and courts, and it still borders Cadman Plaza East (then Washington), Johnson and Brooklyn Bridge Boulevard (Adams). See Chapter 15.

[23] No. 318–22, on the west side of Adams, between Myrtle and Johnson. It was replaced in 1958, along with its neighbors, by the Kings County Supreme Court building.

charms of this material. This defect is equally noticeable in the course between the second and third stories, which is decorated with a fine flowing band of entre lacs with hints of scroll work. This course contains in the center the date 1885 beautifully arranged in scrollwork, and here the terra cotta is of excellent quality, which only enhances the regret that it is not so elsewhere. The emblematic disks, for example, on either side of the date are so poorly executed as to be illegible. The southern part of the building is arranged as a round tower, a good system in American cities where structures have greater height and no breadth, and the manner in which the windows have been worked out shows high architectural capacity. Those on the ground floor are framed in terra cotta, which simulates the roughness of tree branches, a rustic effect infinitely preferable to the rocky style of the rococo period of the Renaissance, both in its appearance and in the moral sense of fitness for the work and the position. Whether the architect did not go beyond the mark in introducing terra cotta ashlars with simulated vermiculations may be fairly asked, but the result is bold and pleasing. This, however, is partly due to the fact that the effort at imitation of vermiculated effects in masonry is a failure, and the terra cotta looks like a roughened brick. Here is a hint that might be worked out advantageously. Houses of great beauty might be built of large terra cotta bricks roughened. They would never require painting or pointing; they would be an exquisite color; they would admit of greater harmony with terra cotta decorations, and they would be practically everlasting. A slight convexity to the bricks would be a marked advantage.

There is an imposing and pretentious portico to this building that is essentially Roman in spirit and treatment, but I do not like it, because the main effect of the Roman triumphal arch from which this portico was elaborated depends as much upon the side columns as upon the central arching. Here the columns are double and of terra cotta, and decorated with bands in the center. Everything tends to make them look weak, even to the broad capital that tops both shafts on each side. Terra cotta columns have a crumbling air that is contrary to the essential spirit of a pillar. A stone column has an air of immense strength, as if able to support enormous weights, whereas a terra cotta column does not seem to support itself. The arch is good, and the tore or cable decoration of the inner edging is fine in conception, though marred by the bad quality of the terra cotta. The abacus protrudes in a very singular fashion, unauthorized either by Greek orders of architecture or Roman imitations of them. It is shallow, like that of the Ionic order, and, in spite of its eccentricity, one recognizes that it would have a telling effect with other capitals. In the window of the ground floor upon the other section of the building, the bays of division are terra cotta columns, and here the abacus disappears entirely, and in its place is a perpendicular stone like the central voussoir of an arch. The effect is good, and something might be evolved from it, though the principle involved seems to apply more to metal working than to stone or terra cotta.

E. R. G.

24

Henry Street

VIEWS OF HENRY STREET.

Remarkable Variations of a Singular Thoroughfare.

A Long Sweep from Fulton to Gowanus Bay. Beginning Poorly it Rises Gradually Into Grandeur—The Rheumatic Steeple of the Castellated Church—A Miniature Renaissance Palace—The Becar Mansion.

Sunday, April 17, 1887

There never was so singular a street as Henry, which, though it may be classified as a sort of second fiddle to Clinton, has yet a life of its own that offers the peculiarity of changing as the neighborhoods change. It is a long street, beginning at Fulton Street, below the bridge, and ending its career in a vastly elongated slip upon the muddy waters of the Gowanus Bay. It once had another name, given to it by the Middagh family, who really created it, but when it grew to the point where it came in contact with the quarter that Hezekiah Beers Pierrepont was laying out he made it entirely his own, and it was renamed after his son Henry, the present Henry E. Pierrepont[1]. Until Henry Street arrives at right angles with Pineapple, it affords no indication that it is, higher up, a street of particularly fine residences, for the houses and stores are of quite a humble character. But from that point

---

[1] See Chapter 6. Henry Evelyn Pierrepont was a prominent citizen of Brooklyn, designing the street grid, helping to establish Green-Wood Cemetery and much more. He died a year after this column was published.

the houses begin to improve in quality, and the street itself wears another air[2]. Possibly this is due to the character at that part of Hicks Street, its neighbor to the westward. The structures beyond Clark were once the solid homes of solid men, and it is evident that at the time when these were built, solidity was the great desideratum and not beauty nor any fashionable style of aestheticism in architecture. Almost all are of brick, with a frontage of twenty-five feet and with doors and door frames of commendable strength. One cannot say that in this part of Henry Street there is anything that specially calls for notice, and yet one has the sense intuitively that if one of these houses, plain and unadorned as it is, were set alongside of a modern Queen Anne structure, the former would be the more impressive and would create the effect of being the home of a very well-to-do man who could afford to live in a generous style. Whereas there are not a few exceedingly artistic mansions, built within the last few years, that create the impression that the people who live in them care more for external appearances than for solid comfort. You would not expect to be entertained with terrapin and Madeira[3] on Saturday nights in any one of them, and you would feel instinctively that you would have to brush up on your knowledge of music and ascertain satisfactorily, before you pressed the electric knob, whether it was Schumann or Schubert who wrote the music considered by the aesthetic [to be] superior to Beethoven. For my own part, I confess, I can never recollect which of the two is the real simon-pure of the musical world, though I have a pointer. I know one of

---

[2] If E.R.G. is Edward Rowland Greene, his father's house, which he would later inherit and occupy, was on Henry Street between Pineapple and Clark.

[3] Turtle soup, prepared with terrapin meat, cream, butter and Medeira (or sherry), was such a popular delicacy from the mid nineteenth century to the early twentieth that it almost wiped out the diamondback terrapin. When Prohibition illegalized the wine, its popularity plummeted.

them wrote "Teaumerei," and that the other is the right one[4]. And this is an important matter, because in such houses if you get this little business right you are treated as one of the elect, but if you name the wrong man you are a Philistine, loving the cheap, popular, melodious music of the outer barbarians.

Solidity, though an excellent quality, can be carried too far, and I think this was the case in the First Presbyterian Church[5], which has a central tower and two square aisles built of heavy blocks of brownstone and decorated with carbellated cornices. I can conceive circumstances under which such a structure would not be out of place. Were it surrounded by a churchyard where modest graves nestled among the long green grasses and heavy yew trees reared their pyramids of dark green foliage on every side of it, the square tower would be in keeping, and would be a reminder of those unhappy days when the village church was the rallying point of defense against enemies of all the Commons of England— the men who tilled their land "in common," and owned no feudal land, and had, therefore, no castle with its men at arms to protect them. But here on Henry Street, in the deep tranquility and assured repose of American life, this ponderousness is an exaggeration of solidity and is out of place and unmeaning and ungraceful. It is a reminder that church architecture in crowded cities must be constructed in harmony not only with the surroundings but with the essential requirements of modern churchgoers. This same fault is far more conspicuous in another church upon Henry Street, situated where it intersects with Remsen[6]. Here there are

---

[4] Schumann composed "Träumerei," one of his *Kinderszenen*, in 1838.
[5] No. 118–26, just south of the corner of Clark Street. It's still there, with the same name.
[6] Then called the Church of the Pilgrims, it was Brooklyn's first Congregationalist church, built in 1846. In 1934, its congregation merged with nearby Plymouth Church, and the building was sold to a

flanking towers from which you expect to see a flight of arrows, and a central façade which has the air of having been built to resist the shot of culverins. If the Mormons should ever become conquering fanatics like the followers of Mahomet, then this church will be able to stem the tide of invasion; but until that event is brought about, its martial and fortified style seems out of place. This church has a peculiar spire, which is one of the first things noticed by strangers in our city. It looks as if it were afflicted with inflammatory rheumatism, which has caused a swelling at the joints calculated to fill the architect with the deepest anguish.

But while we have skipped from Clark to Remsen, in pursuit of architectural offenders, we have passed into another region. Henry Street here has risen to grandeur, and there is not a better quarter in this city, but this is due to the cross streets rather than to any intrinsic life on the street itself. However that may be, the houses are evidently occupied by the foremost and wealthiest citizens, and at the corner of Joralemon and Henry we meet with a structure that is even palatial in character[7]. It belongs, architecturally, to the earliest period of the renaissance, when castles had become unavailing strengths in consequence of the introduction of artillery, and there was, therefore, no need to sacrifice comfort, light, air and convenience in the arrangement of rooms to the one thought of defense. Palatial mansions, in fact, date from that day, and the curious observer who studies this house on Henry Street cannot fail to see that it is, in fact, a sensible modification of a castle. The keep has become a façade, and battlements are replaced by a peaked gable with some charming terra cotta diaper work; but, in the rounded turret with a peaked roof, there is an obvious survival of the bartizan flanking towers. The portico has just as plainly been

---

Maronite Catholic congregation that renamed it Our Lady of Lebanon, which it remains today.

[7] He refers, probably, to 245 Henry Street, replaced with some of its neighbors by an apartment building of the same address in 1957.

annexed from a church and as the pointed arch lingered in the ecclesiastical structures of the Fifteenth Century, after the introduction of squared windows in the dwelling houses that were springing up; the portico is Gothic and very beautiful, too, with side piers most dexterously managed. Of course, this delightful house is only a miniature of the great renaissance palaces of France, but it was planned with uncommon tact and skill and with little touches of exquisite decorative work that are most pleasing. It occupies a great frontage, and its courtyard is connected with a stable, located in a mews or street of stables in the center of a block of dwelling houses[8]. This is an excellent arrangement, one very common in England, but which does not seem to be very popular here. There is an idea that everything of that sort ought to be hidden away like dirty linen or ashes or garbage. For my part, I think a mews more interesting than the streets of which it is the humble dependent and am never tired of watching the operations of carriage washing and horse grooming going on there. Nothing is more ludicrous than the injured air of a carriage horse whose tail is being operated upon by a groom with a currycomb and a pail of water. This is heightened by the gravity with which wandering dogs survey the business, especially some big mastiff who is on friendly terms with the sufferer. His sympathy is obvious and resembles most laughably that of one boy whose teeth are all right with another boy seated in the dentist's chair and about to have his grinders operated upon.

The block from Joralemon to State is very long and contains a series of well built, handsome mansions, such as any

---

[8] The house backed onto Hunt's Alley, probably named for John Hunt, a nineteenth-century local landowner. In 1929, it bore an unofficial street sign proclaiming it "Hunt's Lane," though on maps it remained an alley. That year, a resident petitioned the Board of Aldermen to change it to a lane, after the post office couldn't figure out where to deliver a package from her aunt addressed to Hunt's Lane, rather than admit she lived in an alley.

man might be glad to dwell in, no matter how rich he might be[9]. We may be sure that there are none of those villainous devices called modern conveniences, such as stationary washing basins with hot and cold water, and furnace heating and other allurements of the serpent. I notice three large, roomy houses with proto-Doric doorways and know instinctively that they were the handiwork of the famous builder Colonel Underhill[10], so that these houses were built at least fifty years ago and all this time we have been retrograding in domestic architecture, not progressing! *Ay de mì Alhama!* [11] We alter what our fathers did and call it improvement. From State Street going southward there is a slow, steady deterioration in Henry Street which comes to a climax in the blocks connecting with Atlantic Avenue. The houses are poor and of the tenement order, and there are stores with not very much exposed in the windows, nor much more concealed in the interiors. One of the blocks between Amity and Pacific, the western one, is occupied by the Long Island College Hospital, an institution of which Brooklyn is justly proud[12]. It was built at a time when classicism was rampant, and it is a compromise between common sense and Attic architecture. The building is well planned, well-proportioned and infested with a certain air of dignity by its great size and well-bal-

---

[9] These brick and brownstone homes are mostly still standing.
[10] See Chapter 12.
[11] The refrain in a traditional, anonymous poem about the siege and conquest of the strategic town of Alhama in Granada in 1482, part of the Catholics' campaign to take Spain from the Moors. Lord Byron translated the poem in 1810, rendering this phrase as "Woe is me, Alhama."
[12] Founded in 1857, LICH was the country's first teaching hospital. The Henry Street building opened in 1858 and several more buildings were added over the years until it occupied the whole block. In the 1980s, the hospital traded some lots on Henry Street to the city, which became the playground there today. The hospital closed in 2014, and the building is now a combination of emergency room, healthcare facility and condominiums.

anced manes. In the center is a grand tetra-style portico of the Ionic order, whose columns would have been majestic had they been of stone. But in that case, they would have overpowered the rest of the building, as they do even now. I should be glad to see them removed and to have the central façade of the same plain, unpretentious, useful style as the rest of the building. Then the fine trees in front of the hospital would become in harmony with it, which at present they are not, for trees and classical temples do not belong to the same category, as Captain Trent would have remarked. A fountain and a statue and a plot of green grass are all that can be permitted, and it was an error to plant maples in front of our City Hall, whose classical front is most impressive and is accentuated by a most noble flight of stairs. As these young trees will not grow and were obviously dying last Fall, it is to be hoped that the Commissioners will recognize the expediency of removing them.

The houses begin to improve as we move southward down Henry. When we arrive at the block between Warren and Congress, there is one of the old-style mansions belonging to the days when a man wanted a whole square for himself[13]. He built his house in the center thereof, surrounding it with a splendid garden full of contemporaneous trees. This special house is of brick with a high stoop and shallow portico of gray granite, and with well-worked granite trimmings to the windows, and a heavy cornice surmounted by Italian balustrading around the flat roof. The stonework is partic-

---

[13] 380 Henry Street stood on a lot that occupied almost half the block between Henry and Hicks, Congress and Warren. The other half was occupied by St. Peter's—church, academy, hospital. But the hospital soon outgrew its building, and the year after this column was published, the new St. Peter's Hospital was completed, replacing No. 380, its spacious garden and a few brownstones on the corner of Henry and Congress. The hospital closed in 1962, and the building became a nursing home; it was landmarked soon after and has been partially restored.

ularly fine, especially the consoles of the stoop. If a man were to pay diamonds for day wages, he could not today get such stone cutting, because the apprentice system has broken down, and even superior workmen when they can be found cannot do good work, because their hearts are not in their craft. Their souls are in their great battle with capital, which absorbs all their energies, so that their handicraft is purely perfunctory, and mechanical. I shall not go into the Becar history of this old house[14], because its present tenants are a million times more interesting. They are Sisters of Mercy connected with those admirable institutions of which St. Peter's on Hicks Street is the nucleus. From it radiate, like so many rays of vivifying love, a school, an infirmary for sick and incurables, and a kindergarten. There is a sort of cloister walk of light-construction in the garden, plainly visible from Henry Street, for the house is surrounded on all sides by its grass and trees and flowering shrubs. Here the sisters walk in their black robes and hoods, breviary in hand, but with eyes open to all the beauties of nature around them. They are such gentle and loving ladies that attacks upon them are as outrageous as the trampling into ruin of exquisite flowers, and yet in Thackeray's "Irish Sketch Book" there is such an attack, and many devout Christians have a horror of these sisterhoods[15]. These gentle virgin mothers are actually the

---

[14] Noel Joseph Becar (1798–1856) was an early resident of Brooklyn, a lace importer who rose to prominence in the burgeoning city.

[15] Protestants and Victorians disfavored Catholicism, monasticism in particular. Thackeray spends a chapter visiting the Ursuline Convent in Cork. The sisters demonstrate nothing but humility and satisfaction, but he's dismayed by the cloistered austerity. "I came out of the place quite sick, and looking before me,—there, thank God!...—liberty, sunshine, all sorts of glad life and motion, round about; and I couldn't but thank heaven for it, and the Being whose service is freedom, and who has given us affections that we may use them—not smother and kill them; and a noble world to live in, that we may admire it and Him who made it—not shrink from it, as though we dared not live there..."

purest representatives of Heavenly love upon Earth and live for nothing save the noblest ends and the kindest purposes. On Easter Sunday I watched one of them walking in the cloistered garden, holding her breviary, but all the time observing the actions of two little girls from the Orphanage who wait upon the sisters. The sisters had hidden in the garden Easter eggs for them, and they were hunting for them with the wildest energy, and shrieks of delight unchecked by that dear lady whose sympathy with their happiness was obvious. While they ran and raced over the grass and peeped into every hole and corner, there came pealing strains from the organ and choral bursts, for high mass was being performed in St. Peter's. There was no primness, no straight-lacedness, no awed cry of "hush" although the service was going on, and she herself was an avowed daughter of the church. She seemed to believe that infinite love is delighted with human happiness and demands and desires no suppression of innocent enjoyments.

When Henry Street arrives at Harrison[16] the style of the houses improves very materially, and there are some residences with frontages of thirty feet, and proto-Doric doorways that are either imitations of the Underhill style or specimens of his handiwork. On the other side of the way are some flats built modestly and in good taste, and not with that violent architectural assertion of themselves that is but too frequent and looks as if they were proud of themselves and felt a glory in invading home life and suppressing the homely virtues that grew out of it. An interesting little bit is a two-story house of red brick on the corner of Degraw[17]. Obviously it was once a villa, a *rus in urbe,* and the proprietor, finding that the day had gone by for that sort of thing, submitted to his fate like a sensible man and made the best of it—not the

---

[16] Now Kane Street.
[17] 491 Henry Street was built ca. 1844–50 for George Jarvis, a grocery wholesaler. In the twentieth century, it was disfigured by a white-painted brick façade, but ca. 2007 it was restored.

worst, like the Goelet of Broadway, who persisted in keeping his cows and poultry and garden when a million people were roaring around him, and the front of his house was a very maelstrom of activity[18]. Our friend of Henry Street almost suppressed his basement, leaving only a foot of lattice work visible, pulled down his veranda and left the wooden floor of it as a sort of broad step to the house. A low stone-step in the center brought him to the level of the street. The lower windows are of the French style, opening upon what was the veranda, and there is a row of four upon the upper floor, and above them in a neat, somewhat heavy cornice. In the rear of the house one sees another story, and it is possible that originally the front of the house was toward Strong Place, and that the garden reached to that point. Possibly the picturesque Gothic church on the corner of Strong Place is built upon land that once belonged to that house[19]. The vestrymen have had the good taste to preserve the garden on the west side of the church, and it is wonderful to see how the gothic style harmonizes with grass, trees and flowers of a certain kind. But the poor old house has very little garden left for itself, and what space there is is chiefly occupied by a trellised arbor. Nor is this by any means the only example of the old *rus in urbe* order of things that once prevailed in this part of Henry Street, for not to speak of others less perfect, the Luqueer mansion opposite Third Place, is still as it used to

---

[18] Until he died in 1879, the eccentric wealthy bachelor Peter Goelet owned a mansion at 890 Broadway, on the corner of 19th Street, north of Union Square, surrounded by a yard. There, he kept exotic birds (peacocks, pheasants, storks, cranes) as well as egg-laying hens, horses and a cow—the last to graze on Broadway—persisting in a rural lifestyle even as the city grew up around him. It formed a preposterous juxtaposition that seemed mostly to delight passersby.

[19] The Strong Place Baptist Church was built in 1851 and converted into condos in 2013.

be, and stands surrounded by the old hereditary trees[20].
Dead leaves must fall, but oh! how they hate to drop.

E. R. G.

---

[20] 618 Henry Street once housed the eponyms of Luquer Street (though they spelled it with two Es), local landowners and millers. Today, the lot (and some of the neighboring lots) is occupied by PS 146, formerly PS 142.

25

Union Street

ALONG UNION STREET.

Unfavorable Effect of the Gowanus Canal.

The Italian Population—Residence of the First Citizen of Brooklyn—Comfortable Quarters of the Father of Prospect Park.

Sunday, April 24, 1887

It has sometimes occurred to me that there are two destinies for some people and for some streets and that there is a constant struggle going on between the two, to see which shall rule. Union Street was, I think, originally intended for noble ends, and in the outset its destiny was to have been the one thoroughly grand, fine thoroughfare going from west to east in South Brooklyn. But another destiny interfered, a hateful, malignant destiny, in the form of the Gowanus Canal, and the consequence is that Union Street's grandeur is a thing of shreds and patches, belonging to the early days of the war and to the propitious fates that then smiled upon it. What could be as regards mere planning a better scheme than such a street running from the Hamilton Ferry due eastward and debouching into the plaza in front of Prospect Park? The Eastside Parkway that was possibly intended by the Park Commissioners to go to New Lots (only it doesn't get there)[1]

---

[1] Eastern Parkway originally stretched from Grand Army Plaza to Ralph Avenue. The first parkway in the country, designed by Olmsted and Vaux, it was intended to continue east on what's now called Pitkin Avenue, into and beyond New Lots; it's labeled as such on maps from

is, in fact, a continuation of Union Street, and the estimable planners of the latter, no doubt, saw in their minds' eye a vista of comfortable, even splendid, homes and a line of fast trotters speeding to and from the park. Union Street was obviously the natural line to the park for the whole driving population of South Brooklyn, for Clinton and Henry streets, for the Places, even for the villa world of Gowanus. But the wisdom of the Scottish bard has taught us that "the best laid schemes of mice and men gang aft aglae[2]." The unfortunates who planned this thoroughfare reckoned without their Gowanus Canal.

And within recent years another development has been made in Union Street at its western extremity, which could not have been foreseen and which cannot now be viewed with unmixed pleasure. It has been chosen by Italian immigrants for their headquarters, their corso and their chiaja[3]. Here are their stores, here their Santa Croce, here their levatrices or midwives, here their padrones. Are you a businessman requiring unskilled labor and have you a blind, unreasoning hatred against the Irish? Make your way straight to the edge of Union Street and see a padrone and hire gangs of Italians. So long as you satisfy their padrone you will satisfy them, but if you do not, these matters may go ill with you, for these men carry knives as certainly as wasps have their

---

the year this column was published, and the addresses on Pitkin are continuations of those on Eastern Parkway. But a few years later, Brooklyn got the idea to reroute the planned "Eastern Parkway Extension" northeast, to connect Prospect Park to the newly acquired Highland Park. The project was never finished, however, and Eastern Parkway now peters out at Bushwick Avenue.

[2] A famous line from "To a Mouse" by the Scottish poet laureate Robert Burns. Its Scots dialect ending is usually translated as "often go awry."

[3] In Italian, corso means, among other things, path, while ghiaia, corrupted as chiaja, means gravel. Chiaia is also a well-known neighborhood in southern Italy's largest city, Naples. I think he's trying to say colorfully that it's their main street and district.

stings and use them as readily and as unscrupulously. Never before has the American power of assimilation been put to so tremendous a test as now, and there are wise men who doubt if it will be able to accomplish its work of turning these men from the Heel of the Italian Boot into American citizens. If it is done at all it will be through the Irish, with whom the Italians manifest a desire to be on friendly terms. These men from the Basilicata and Calabria and Apulia[4] evidently look up to the Irish as a superior race, or rather as superior beings of their own race. It does seem next to marvelous that these tough citizens, who have accepted just as much and as little of the teachings of the church as suited them, and whose ignorance is proverbial, should know that they are of the Keltic family and should recognize the Irish as the head of that family, as they undoubtedly are. Why! Greek and Carthaginian and Roman, Astrogoth, Lombard, Vandal and Norman have marched over them and trampled upon their upturned faces. But nothing has blotted out of their minds the fact of their race, not even the blurring of thousands of years. Here are men who have preserved in secret the traditions of their ancestry, and who laugh to scorn the Indo Germanic theory and the successive waves of emigration from Aryana, for they know that the Kelts marched from west to the eastward, just as Lluyd, the great Keltic archæologist[5], two centuries ago said they did. But they will not speak of their traditions to me who has not their shibboleth, yet they betray it in their actions. And to them the Irish, hated, even detested, by the Anglo Saxons, tolerated and liked contemptuously by the Anglo Americans, are still the grand old people, the uncrowned kings of the western world. This is their one redeeming feature, their fealty to their old leaders, and without

---

[4] The southernmost regions of Italy. These are not just Italian immigrants—they're Southern Italians, which carries for E.R.G. stereotyped connotations of low class and criminality.

[5] Edward Lhuyd (1660–1709) was a Welsh naturalist and linguist.

it they would be a most dangerous element in the population of Brooklyn.

Brooklyn is essentially a city where the children are prettier, cleaner and better dressed than anywhere else in the United States. But the visitor who lands at Hamilton Ferry house[6] and walks up Union Street will find an exceptional state of things there. The children are wonderful. They are clothed in ill-fitting, dirty, voluminous garments and have filthy stockings divorced from garters and uncut, uncombed shock heads of hair that resemble exactly the thatch of an Irish shealing[7]. Their faces are dirty with the accumulations of days, not with the honest muck gained by a recent fray in the gutter. They do not shout and scream and race and run like other children, but they sit upon doorsteps phlegmatically and consider the ways of things. Occasionally one of them gets candies, which he immediately shares with one comrade of either sex and drives all the other babies away. The two put their arms around each other and munch contentedly while the others longing and admiringly gaze on them from a distance. One does not see these children studying the contents of the pastry cooks' stores in the basements, pointing out good things and telling each other what they would have if they had five cents. They have much of the stolidity of [American] Indian children, and not a few of their mothers have strong resemblance with Indian squaws. One would think that they would be attracted by the heaps of big chestnuts and by the figs strung into long lengths, and by the nameless wonders of their grocery stores. Not they. Occasionally, when some pretty Irish girl living in the quarter comes tripping along daintily, in well-made garments of good material, with silky hair neatly braided and coiled in

---

[6] The Union Ferry Company's Hamilton Ferry waiting rooms were at the intersection near the waterfront of Sackett, Union and Hamilton Avenue. The ferry was reached by a short walk down a pier, a wharf and another pier. See Chapter 1.

[7] A shepherd's hut.

what some people call a Greek knot, but which is as purely Irish as the word Biddy, these stolid children look up and cry, "Ecco[8]"; but, as a rule, they vegetate and show less life than the grasses growing on an old wall and waving in the wind.

The Italian part of Union Street only extends up two blocks (from Hamilton Avenue to Van Brunt Street and from the latter to Columbia Street)[9]. What may be called the good part begins after one leaves behind Hicks Street and increases in quality as one goes [east]ward. It can hardly be said that there is anything especially interesting in any of these houses, with the exception of that occupied by one of the best-known citizens of Brooklyn and one of the fathers of Prospect Park[10]. His house and grounds cover nearly half the block. The house has only a frontage of twenty-five feet, but it is very long, and its real front is upon the garden, which occupies the whole of the front on Clinton Street, between Sackett and Union. The garden fence does not come flush with the sidewalk, and between the two there is a strip of pleasant green grass and some trees and evergreens, guarded from enterprising boys by a handsome iron railing. A sleek Durham cow is occasionally allowed to wander in this pleasaunce and to make a pretense of grazing, but she generally lies down and chews the cud, gazing upon the public on the other side of the railing with calm eyes full of meditation. Over the garden fence one can see the tops of fruits trees, which are generally a mass of exquisite blossoms by the end of May, but whether they will be this year depends upon the weather. One can also see the large hothouses and greenhouses, so that the old Park Commissioner obviously has a park of his own in miniature. In the next block there is a

---

[8] An Italian word without equal in English, best translated as "voilà."

[9] There were many tenements on these two blocks, but there were also several coal yards, a lumber yard and a large wallpaper factory. Some of the homes survive, I suspect, on the south side, between Van Brunt and Columbia.

[10] James S.T. Stranahan lived at 269 Union Street. See Chapter 1.

house that is isolated something in the same way, but the gardens are by no means extensive and furnish simply a sort of foreground for the stabling. An Italian nobleman lived here a few years ago in the strictest seclusion[11]. No one knew why he came, what he did, or where he went, and the enterprising reporters who came to extract from him his mystery were baffled by a courtesy that would have disarmed tigers. The neighborhood still preserves memories of him, and he will, no doubt, someday become legendary and the hero of a Brooklyn myth.

So strong was the impulse given to Union Street in early happier days that the houses of quality survive the shock of crossing Court Street, and the next two blocks are charming. On the block from Court to Smith, on the north side, are two houses which are built in a peculiar way, and one that seems to be a very good way[12]. The lot must have been about eighty feet frontage, and the houses are built at the two ends, leaving in the center a broad carriage way, leading to a handsome and commodious double stable in the rear. There is nothing especially attractive about the architecture of the

---

[11] E.R.G. means the same block, between Henry and Clinton, No. 223. It was an "elegant brownstone mansion," according to an 1876 ad in the *Eagle*, with a "brick stable and carriage house, conservatory, plant house, choice fruit trees, gardens beautifully laid out … with all modern improvements and in first class order." The grounds were almost 162x100. In 1868, it was occupied by a Peter Smith; in 1876, by Joseph C. Dimon, butter and cheese merchant of Fulton Street; and a little later, the Thynes family. None of these names are Italian. Around 1894, the grounds were replaced by "a row of new flats," according to the Brooklyn *Citizen*. "They are five stories high, and are double flats, with apartments on either side of the hallway. They are the only flats in the immediate neighborhood, and are rather pretentious buildings, viewed from the street, being of brick, with ornate stone trimmings." The home today at 223 Union, as well as its neighbors, seems to have been built in the early 1980s.

[12] Nos. 329–31 and 333–5. The apartment building today at 329 Union Street, which occupies the former site, was built in 1914.

houses, but they have a maximum of light and air and sun by this system and have no abominable dark rooms. Still, it is to be considered that to gain these advantages two houses have been built upon what are now deemed four lots and, therefore, to men who prefer sound pecuniary returns to considerations of health and comfort, this system must seem deplorably wasteful. Upon the next block, there is a group of three houses built upon another system, equally based upon a desire to obtain all the ventilation, sun and Summer breezes possible. These houses, instead of being built with the butt end, as it were, facing the street, are turned in the natural way, and their greatest length is upon Union Street[13]. The door is in the center and there are two windows upon each side of it and five windows in a row above. This was the dear old English way that once prevailed, and of which a fine specimen is still extant upon Washington Street[14], facing the bridge extension. The modern way is due to Dutch economy and has led to most monstrous building abuses that call for legislative reform as speedily as possible. These houses on Union Street are handsome structures of brownstone as regards their fronts, but without any architectural pretensions. They are not specially æsthetic, but they must be excessively pleasant to live in, and one of them has the additional advan-

---

[13] No. 366–68 and No. 370–72 were two boxy, three-story, semidetached homes with main entrances that opened onto airy side yards, rather than onto Union Street. The smaller No. 374 also had a side door, opening onto the same yard as No. 370–72. The latter was last used as a boarding house for women by the YWCA, who abandoned it ca. 1910 for the Grosjean mansion on Schermerhorn and Nevins, which was larger and nearer its offices. No. 374 seems to have been briefly a rooming house, but developers who preferred sound pecuniary returns soon built apartment buildings on the site of the two larger houses. The smaller seems still to exist—just now with a proper front door, as an apartment building abuts it to the lot line.
[14] Probably No. 99, between Prospect and Sands. That whole block is now just expressway infrastructure.

tage of a great garden space, which is, in truth, more of a child's playground than a garden.

The grade is downhill from Court Street, and we descend very fast as we approach Gowanus Canal, which is furnished upon Union Street with a stone bridge. All South Brooklyn mourns and weeps and will not be comforted because of this canal, which is becoming more and more pestiferous every year. It is clear that the authority that the Congress of United States claims over navigable streams and harbors was never meant to apply to such a creek or inlet as that of Gowanus. That it does so now is due to the fact that such places have been found convenient excuses for that corruption that is exhibited yearly in the River and Harbor bill[15]. The principle at the base of that monstrosity is undoubtedly sound, but it has become a source of such manifest and disgusting jobbery that everyone who is a true patriot winces at the mere mention of the yearly crime, and there is a steady desire to stifle it, which occasionally succeeds, as it did this year. But the innocent suffer with the guilty when that is done. The Hell Gate improvement is an admirable and necessary work, and the delay in its completion that has resulted is a blow against the development of Brooklyn[16], which will profit from it when finished many times more than New York, until their Harlem ship canal is constructed[17], and that is an engineering dream, easily done as far as the engineer is concerned, but difficult to get underway on account of jarring and irreconcilable interests in the land. It seems to me that

---

[15] See Chapter 12.

[16] Treacherous rocks were exploded in 1885, but it seems to have taken at least a few years to clear the rubble. See Chapter 20.

[17] The long-planned canal finally opened in 1895. Spuyten Duyvil Creek, which separated Manhattan from the Bronx, was a narrow, winding waterway that large ships couldn't navigate. The new canal provided a wide, deep and straight(er) path, connecting the Hudson and Harlem rivers, thus enabling boats to travel to and from the East River and Long Island Sound without having to go around the Battery.

there ought to be a discrimination in Congress and that navigable streams less than 1,000 feet in width and with a less average depth than fifteen feet ought not to come within their bailiwick but should be under the direction of the municipal or other local authorities. The attention of all the Congressmen of this State ought to be directed toward the obtaining of such a discrimination by law, for it is contrary to common sense and humanity and to the best interests of Brooklyn to allow the Gowanus inlet, for canal it is not, to remain as it [is] now. The great Democratic party must unite upon this question and purge itself of the stain which the River and Harbor bill has made upon it.

The grade rises materially east of the Gowanus Canal, but the moral influence of that black belt of infamy has clearly ruined Union Street. There are no dwelling houses upon it until one arrives at Fifth Avenue[18], and these are not of the character one would expect from the style of Union Street before it falls a victim to the Gowanus Canal. They are small, cheerful, well-built houses, not better in any way, as far as casual external observation shows, than those of Cleveland Place[19].... As one breasts the steep hill there is some improvement, but still not as much as there should be when one considers the vicinity to the park and the magnificent character of the location[20]. The whole sweep of Prospect

---

[18] On either side of the Canal, Union was lined with lumber and coal yards; a lime, brick and lath yard; and a box factory. From Nevins to Third, there was a sash and door factory, as well as a carriage house, a paint shop, a storage building and other miscellanies. From Third to Fourth, there were no buildings. Housing began just past Fourth Avenue, with rowhouses starting at No. 638, which is still there today.

[19] He uses offensive language here I have omitted. See Chapter 21.

[20] He omits two mansions, perhaps because he didn't travel as far as Eighth Avenue or they had not quite been completed yet. What today is called 70 Eighth Avenue, built the year this column was published, still stands, a splendid Queen Anne/Romanesque Revival home on the northwest corner, converted in the 1990s into condos. Across Union Street, there was what on maps appears to be an even larger and more

Heights[21] is unexampled as regards healthiness and fine air and good foundation soil. What filling was done in early times in the vicinity of the canal I can only know from hearsay, but people generally are of the opinion that it was mostly of the wires of crinoline hoopskirts, tomato cans and dead cats[22]. My own eyes have shown me that the filling in of today is of the very best character, consisting entirely in some places of loam, gravel and stones. In others, in former years, it was more miscellaneous, but a spasm of common sense has fallen upon the sinning owners of real estate, and they have comprehended at least what fools they would be to nullify by cheap filling in their really wonderful advantages. To those readers of the EAGLE who are not residents of Brooklyn it may be necessary to explain that the heights of the Gowanus tract were originally rolling meadowland, and the authorities wisely graded up, not down. Had they chosen the latter system, as Italians would have done, Prospect Heights would have been a series of picturesque terraces with Prospect Park for a crowning glory. This would have been very fine, no doubt, but there could be no driving fast teams under such circumstances, and the meat men and grocers, instead of driving about and getting orders, would have been compelled to lead donkeys laden with paniers up the interminable flights of stairs. But it would have made an exquisite landscape from the bay, and Brooklyn would have been as picturesque as Genoa.

E. R. G.

---

impressive house, built in the 1880s by John Rogers Maxwell, a banker, cement-company president and railroad man who died in 1910. His home, No. 78, was replaced by an apartment building of the same address ca. 1923, the year its first certificate of occupancy was issued. (His widow died in 1927, on Park Avenue in Manhattan.)
[21] Park Slope.
[22] Hoopskirts' heyday was the mid nineteenth century, about thirty years before this column was written, give or take a decade.

26

Atlantic Avenue

BROOKLYN'S HIGHWAYS.

The Road to the Lost Site of Tinneacum.

Mysterious Legend of a Buried City—The Ambition to Revive Its Ancient Glories—The Failures of Atlantic Avenue and What it Needs to Redeem It.

Sunday, December 19, 1886[1]

What a vain and illusory science is history. The man who attempts to comprehend the past by reading its pages is very much like a child looking through a telescope whose lenses have been disarranged and put together incorrectly by an ignorant cleaner. There is no perspective to history when we go back a thousand years or so. If our fancy insists upon receding still further, we lose all sense of the meaning of the words before us and give to those times the local coloring either of your own date or of some other epoch with which we are more familiar. So Mark Twain, in his amusing paper upon a Yankee at the Court of King Arthur, pictured the Thirteenth Century instead of the Fifth, and gave us the tournaments and jousting of the reigns of Richard the Lion Hearted and his immediate successors, instead of the Roman tactics, discipline, armor, weapons and decorations of King Arthur. The latter was really a figure in history, like Reicimer, Odoacer and Theodoric the Astrogoth, all of whom concealed their barbaric royalty at some time or other under Ro-

---

[1] This column appears here out of chronological order as an addendum.

man titles. King Arthur by a Romanized Briton was undoubtedly considered either as the Dux Britanniarum or an officer of consular dignity. And though probably in every one of the Arthurian myths there is a local color belonging to the epoch of each myth, there can be no doubt that in every one there is a substratum of truth that we fail to recognize, because of the false perspective and the adventitious accessories.

If those who are learned and scholarly make such blunders, can it be a source of wonder that the early inhabitants of Brooklyn were led astray concerning the ancient city of Tinneacum? No one knows how the legend grew, but this is certain, that there was, and perhaps still is, a belief that somewhere toward the Eastern end of the island there had once been a famous city[2]. No one knew whether it was a Phœnician city or Carthaginian, or an outpost of that early Irish civilization whose effulgence made men esteem Ireland as venerable in the very dawn of Hellenic literature. Some even thought that it belonged to the very ancient Quinamis, who antedated in America the Maya Tzendals and Nahoas, some of whose Cyclopean structures still exist in Mexico and Guatemala. There were ardent inquirers, whose brains were not sufficiently ballasted by analytic power, who trace a marked resemblance between this part of Long Island and the city that Poseidon built for the beautiful consul who made him the father of the Atlantides. These admitted that there had been changes, and that storm and cataclysm and glacial drift had overwhelmed the work of the trident-sceptered king, but they claimed that the North River and the East River were remains of the belts which he had made around his chosen realm. However that might be, all agreed that there was somewhere in the neighborhood the site of a lost city, and it was a matter of secondary consideration whether the buried glories were truncated pyramids and white teocalli towers

---

[2] I couldn't find any other mention of Tinneacum or a lost civilization of Long Island.

flaming in the blue air or dark cyclopean structures of the round towers of Hibernian art or the stores and magazines and citadels and pharos of Phœnician and Atlantian commerce. The great and burning consideration was to find the site of the lost city, and the minds of men grew perplexed as they thought of it. It was clear that Indian nomenclature referred to such a city, but, either from the reluctance of the aborigines to disclose their knowledge or from their want of such details as could be of service in throwing light upon the matter, no progress was made by those who made inquiries of the Algonquins and Iroquois. This much, however, was ascertained: That Ihpetonga was a name given by the latter race and by the local Indians of Long Island who had been conquered and reduced to the condition of squaws. From an aged Onondaga the fact was learned that the correct spelling was Ipathonga, meaning the region of the sons of the divine serpents.

The reader must understand clearly that no one hoped to discover any traces of the lost city. Everyone comprehended that it had been overwhelmed by a fleet of icebergs and that at the same time there had been volcanic eruptions of a submarine character which had left traces in the shape of numerous boulders of volcanic trap or basaltic rock. The question that agitated men's minds was as to the probable site. History mystifies people so much that few are aware how small were the populations of the Greek cities that have filled the world with their fame. The same fact is true with regard to the Italian municipalities. The extent of Pisa or Florence was inconsiderable and yet those cities have obtained imperishable renown and both possess buildings to which artistic minds revert perpetually. It was felt that Tinneacum might not have been immense in its extent and that its population might have been inconsiderable, according to modern ideas. This fundamental truth considerably enlarged the area of investigation, since if Tinneacum had been as great as Nineveh or Babylon, its site would have covered the eastern end of the island from Oyster Bay to Brighton Beach. But so small were ancient cities of no inconsiderable renown that there was no improbability in choosing Gowanus or Wallabout or Flatbush as the veritable site of Tinneacum. Homer describes Hector as fleeing from the wrath of Achilles, and circling in his flight seven times the walls of Troy. Therefore, Troy, although famous beyond all other cities, could hardly have been more extensive than our district of the Wallabout; and, again, though the growth of the legend of Tinneacum has never been explained, yet no one has ever doubted that it came from the aborigines, and their idea of a city must have been of the vaguest. I have wandered in Arabia and remember my astonishment at the size of some of the cities that the Arabs regard with the most intense pride as the culmination of grandeur and the concentration of commerce and civilization.

No man pondered more deeply upon these things than John R. Pitkin[3]. In his hours of leisure he thought of Tinneacum until his feelings grew to be like the boy who dropped his Christmas gold eagle down the well and said that he didn't feel as if he had lost it, because he knew where it was, though he could not get it. Tinneacum was not lost but buried under stretches of lava and strata of gravel and boulders. It pleased him to think as he walked that far below him were marble colonnades and lofty ramparts and giant stairways and palaces of kings never to be known by mortal man. He read books upon the art of divination and upon the use of the witch-hazel fork in discovering the whereabouts of secret springs and of veins of precious metals, and sighed as he thought that these mystical follies were but the distempered dreams of visionary men. There was no way by which a man upon the surface of the earth could tell what was beneath him, except where there were outcroppings of metal-bearing

---

[3] An Atlanta native, John Roberts Pitkin (1794–1874) is remembered for first developing East New York and Woodhaven.

quartz, which told their own story to the initiated. Where cities had been buried under volcanic ashes, as at Pompeii, there were outcroppings in the shape of roofs, temples and public buildings, which had received no attention for two thousand years, simply because they were in a country where the ruined evidences of the mighty past exist in such profusion that men take no notice of them. Herculaneum had indeed been completely covered by the volcanic mud that Vesuvius sent up from its entrails, to fall like rain upon the doomed town. But Pompeii was a clue to Herculaneum. For Tinneacum, however, there exists no indication, and the dread forces of nature that overwhelmed it were, as Mr. Pitkin felt, immeasurably more terrible than the fiercest fires of Etna or Vesuvius.

But once when he was musing upon this terrible secret, this skeleton city closeted as it were underneath our feet, with all its population, its merchants, its matrons, its fair young girls, its buds of children entombed alive, and buried under unknown heaps of sand and gravel, a great thought arose in his soul. He had wandered out in the direction of the Jamaica and Brooklyn Railroad[4] and had insensibly left the path and was pacing slowly through fields of cabbages and early beets. He stopped abruptly and gazed around him. "What man has done," he cried aloud, "man can do." It was a sudden inspiration. In his mind's eye he saw rising around him great lines of houses, huge warehouses, giant factories whence resounded the whirr of machinery, the buzz of looms and the incessant banging and clatter of manufacturing industry. His thought was that the causes, the natural advantages that had developed Tinneacum still existed and would develop in time another city. There to the eastward lay Europe and above all England.

---

[4] Built in the 1830s, it was the first rail line to connect Brooklyn with the rest of Long Island, originally running from the new ferry at the foot of Atlantic Avenue to Union Course, a horse-racing track in Woodhaven. It was later extended.

The natives of nations might anchor outside of Long Island, or if threatened by ugly weather might run the Narrows into the more tranquil waters of the Bay and the Sound. Here he stood upon the extreme verge of one continent facing the other. What more natural, what more inevitable than that the Tinneacum of the future, the great city of the American hemisphere, should arise upon the point that vessels from Europe first make. His prophetic vision saw all the glory of the coming future. In a transport of enthusiasm, he determined to lay the site where he stood. He shook his fist excitedly at the other city upon Manhattan Island, which was intensely hated then by all the people of Brooklyn on account of the ferry exactions[5], and said: "Tyrant and monopolist, thou shalt have a rival. This shall be East New York[6]." He called a meeting of his fellow citizens; he poured out the great conception of his soul before them and his conviction gave eloquence to his language. Finally, he concluded a glowing peroration by an appeal for assistance in creating the new city and establishing lines of communication with Brooklyn. "Advance!" cried John R. Pitkin; "Progress!" cried John R. Pitkin; "Onward to Tinneacum!" and the City of Brooklyn rose as one man and forwarded.

The first thing done was to buy up all the farms in the locality indicated by Mr. Pitkin and convert them into building lots. The next movement was to create a great boulevard

---

[5] Excess profits from Fulton Ferry went to New York, which was "unjust and odious," according to an 1839 resolution, "and tantamount to the exaction of a tribute from the inhabitants of Brooklyn and Long Island."
[6] In 1835, Pitkin bought roughly two square miles of farmland and laid out housing lots on a map; he even built a footwear factory. During the financial crisis in 1837, he sold it before his dream could come true, but he remained involved in its real estate for the rest of his life. The area for decades became a stronghold of German immigrants. No other history mentions that Pitkin was inspired by reviving the spirit of an ancient lost city; rather, he saw the potential of undeveloped land near a railroad, twenty-two minutes from the New York-bound ferry.

between Brooklyn and East New York, and Atlantic Avenue was chosen, because it was felt that the new city would grow in time to the very shores of the ocean, and thus this street would stretch from the Sound to the Atlantic. The original plan was that Atlantic Avenue should be 140 feet broad and should have three driveways separated by promenades for pedestrians precisely like the Ocean Parkway that goes to the beach. Application was made to the Legislature, and an act was passed granting the necessary powers, the legislators being greatly taken by a colored lithograph of Atlantic Avenue as it would be in the time to come[7]. The genius who designed this was as innocent of true perspective as the Chinese artists, and under his expanding powers the 140 feet swelled out to something near 500, while his imagination created upon each side of the street cloud-kissing spires and turreted buildings, so that Atlantic Avenue appeared to be something infinitely finer than the Champs-Élysées of Paris. This was very fine on paper, but the parties concerned found the expenses intolerable and more than the property owners cared to incur, so they went back to the accommodating Legislature with their plan materially modified, doing away with the triple driveways and the promenade and the trees and reducing the width to 120 feet. Powers were given for this, and Atlantic Avenue became a fixed fact, and so did East New York.

But the results hardly answered the expectations of Mr. Pitkin and his friends, who were astonished that the whole world did not eagerly rush forward and settle down in New Lots[8], as the new city was colloquially termed. The appearance of Atlantic Avenue today tells the whole story more

---

[7] The New York Public Library has digitized a copy of this indeed impressive artist's rendering.
[8] Originally the eastern part of Flatbush, it was called the New Lotts by seventeenth-century farmers because it was comprised of new lots of land. It became an independent town in 1852 and was annexed by Brooklyn the year this column was published.

eloquently than words can do. It is far from flourishing, as a whole, but is bright in sports wherever it has been crossed by other and more rational thoroughfares, which naturally have been more prosperous than itself[9]. The time may come when it will have a reasonable amount of trade, but at the present moment it is a failure because it catches no distinct wave of population. Its two best localities are where it is crossed by Clinton Street and where it crosses Flatbush Avenue. At the former point there are some very fine structures, both dwelling places and commercial buildings. At the latter, Atlantic Avenue is influenced by the really grand character of the neighborhood, which is the meeting ground of some noble thoroughfares. There will come a time in the history of Brooklyn when the powers that be of the Long Island Railroad will buy that odious-looking armory and some other buildings and upon the site erect a terminal depot worthy of the location[10]. This will certainly have some effect upon Atlantic Avenue, but it alone will not be sufficient to redeem it from its insignificance. If the termination of the South Ferry[11] on the New York side were Fourteenth Street instead of Whitehall, where nobody wants to go[12], it would have the advantages of a real destination. At present, owing to the

---

[9] I suspect this column is full of so much padding and fantasy because E.R.G. felt compelled to include Atlantic Avenue in his survey of streets, especially with Brooklyn's annexation of New Lots that year, but he also didn't like it and had little to say about it.

[10] A passenger station was built on Atlantic, at the intersection of Flatbush, in 1877, but it was no grand depot. The 13th Regiment Armory was around the corner, at Hanson and Flatbush. The regiment moved to Bed–Stuy in 1892, and a proper Atlantic terminal opened in 1907, occupying, in part, the old Armory site. See Chapter 2.

[11] Since 1836, the South Ferry had connected the foot of Atlantic Avenue to Lower Manhattan.

[12] Hamilton Ferry, from Hamilton Avenue, also went to Whitehall Street.

elevated railway[13], more people use the South Ferry than in the old times, but it is after all only a sort of relief to the Fulton Street bridge and ferries. These two factors together would create an undoubted change in this avenue of great expectations. Of course, Atlantic Avenue beyond Flatbush Avenue is virtually dead, being merged in the life of the Long Island Railroad branch that goes to East New York. The railroad runs in the center of the avenue[14] and there are houses on each side, but they are by no means like the buildings in the old colored lithograph. Nor is it likely that people of means will settle there in the near future, nor probably that fine villas will dot the road to the Tinneacum, which has recently been absorbed by Brooklyn and will in about a score of years have altogether lost what little identity it ever possessed. Neither glowing fancies nor fine roads will create a city, for in that case East New York would have been a wonderful metropolis, crushing out the life of Brooklyn itself. East New York may or may not be in the enjoyment of all the advantages of the ancient Tinneacum, but one thing is proved by the fate of Atlantic Avenue, and that is that no thoroughfare however broad can compensate for the want of the first requisite of a city population.

E. R. G.

---

[13] Construction of the Fulton Street elevated line was underway in Downtown Brooklyn, presumably making travel to Fulton Ferry more difficult and unpleasant.
[14] The line would not run underground to Bed-Stuy until the early twentieth century.

27

Third Avenue, Ridge Boulevard and Shore Road

PEDESTRIAN PLEASURES.

The Foot Journey to Fort Hamilton and Back.

A Post Vacation Ramble—The Winding Road that Hugs the Shore—Disappointing Effect of the Bartholdi Statue at a Distance.

Sunday, September 19, 1886 [1]

The heats of Summer have at length passed away, and with the cooler air of the Fall the hardy and the robust begin to enjoy the pleasures of pedestrianism. He is truly fortunate upon whom a kindly nature has bestowed the gift of a stout pair of legs, for he sees the aspects of landscape scenery as no one else can. There are certain railroads that advertise themselves as specially desirable because they traverse a line of country that is singularly picturesque. But to those who have known the delights of ascending the zigzag paths of mountains or of traversing the lonely and shadowed roads that lead through great forests on foot, the hasty and unsatisfactory glimpses of the beautiful, seen from the windows of a parlor car, only irritate and vex and render feverish with longing to be on foot and wandering among them. It is undeniable that the young men of the present generation are much more athletic than their fathers, are less wedded to money making and material pleasures, fonder of yachting and of baseball, and, above all, are much better pedestrians. And now is the time

---

[1] This column predates Chapter 1 by about a week.

when the wise ones who have hoarded up their vacation until they could walk with pleasure throughout the day take their packs upon their shoulders and wander through the Catskills or the White Mountains or the Berkshire Hills or the Blue Mountains. With light heart and nimble steps they breast the Alpland and climb the crag and break through the undergrowth of the ravines. The air is cool and pure, the breeze a pleasure and movement a delight.

To those who squandered their holidays at Long Branch and Coney Island and Newport, who lounged upon the plaza and loitered upon the beach, there is no possibility of lengthened pedestrian tours now. But those who have the good fortune to live in Brooklyn have at least the privilege of short pedestrian trips of the most enjoyable character. The New Yorker is "cribbed, cabined and confined[2]" in a long narrow island shaped like an olive oil bottle, from which he must emerge before he can wander along the sound or skirt the waters of the noble Hudson. For him, therefore, pedestrianism must commence with the elevated railroad. But the Brooklynite, happy being, can start off on a short walking excursion from the door of his domicile. He has before him many trips which may be made on foot, and among the pleasantest is a walk to Fort Hamilton[3]. He need not strike Third Avenue until he is in the neighborhood of Green-Wood Cemetery, from which point it is an agreeable path open toward the bay at many spots and lined with fine trees

---

[2] A common misquotation of *Macbeth*, when the title king learns that Banquo's son has escaped his assassins: "Then comes my fit again. I had else been perfect, / Whole as marble, founded as the rock, / As broad and general as the casing air. / But now I am cabined, cribbed, confined, bound in / To saucy doubts and fears."

[3] A military installation at the foot of Fort Hamilton Parkway, still active, it opened in 1831. At the time, the village around the fort was also called Fort Hamilton, and it was like a miniature Coney Island, offering alcohol, amusements, bathing, fishing and accommodations.

and quaint old villas in the midst of old gardens[4]. Some of these have the air of being ante revolutionary and present the excellent woodwork and graceful decoration usually associated with good colonial residences in the days when George the Third was king. Both Manhattan Island and Long Island received many colonists of sturdy yeoman families of England, mingled with whom were the younger sons of the gentry. Both of these classes had a high opinion of their social standing and thought it incumbent to have good houses. So that many of these relics along Third Avenue and in Flatbush are ornamented with carved woodwork done by hand in excellent style. It is of unpretentious character, but the workmanship is often so superior as to induce the belief that it was imported from the mother country.

At a certain point in the road there is a cluster of German picnic gardens[5], for the honest Teuton has particular satis-

---

[4] Third Avenue was densely developed until about 28th Street, after which it became sparser, with occasional rows of stone and wooden houses and the occasional old house, particularly one on the east side of the street, between 33rd and 34th, near a couple of large barns across 33rd Street—the Garret G. Bergen house, torn down around the turn of the twentieth century.

[5] Schuetzen Park occupied almost two blocks, from 49th to 51st streets, between Third and Fourth avenues. It was opened ca. 1874 by William Koch and later bought by John Dobbin. "It was a spacious park area, with orchards, swings and a big dancing pavilion," the Brooklyn *Daily Times* later remembered. "It was rented by church societies and social organizations." Dobbin cut it up into housing lots in 1896, "when the growth of the borough did away with the possibilities of picnicking at the old park, the last to go to in South Brooklyn," according to Dobbin's obit. He "made a fortune" on the real estate. About ten blocks away, between 60th and 61st, Third and Fourth, Koch then opened Bay View Park. "Although Bay View Park was an ideal place for picnics," remembered the *Eagle*, "it lacked the charm and magnetism of Schuetzen Park." Koch died in 1893 and Bay View closed ca. 1899, when a reporter saw a For Sale sign and wrote that it resembled "a deserted country seat." There were other old picnic parks—Pope's, on

faction in swallowing great draughts of "schink bier" in the open air, and this is greatly increased when he has before him a fine view. No philosopher of the Nineteenth Century has worked out satisfactorily the problem presented by picnic gardens, tracing the subtle connection between the prospect of the distant water with its shining gleams like molten silver, and its gliding sails and multitudinous steamers, and the consumption of bologna sausage and Swiss cheese. But it is a demonstrated fact that when the day is fine and everything in the distant landscape stands out clearly and distinctly, the sandwiches and the schinken disappear with great promptitude and cheerfulness. But should the weather be misty, should an envious veil of haze hide the crests of Staten Island and the distant horizon of the New Jersey hills, then the appetite of the picnickers is as bounded as the view, and the attendants of the place gaze with sadness upon the undiminishing heap of these delicious dainties, which are comprehended under the generic name of wurst. A few hundred yards beyond the last of these[6] is the depot of one of the many railways that communicate with Brooklyn's sea beaches and Brooklyn's race courses[7]. Here, if he is wise, the walker will desert Third Avenue and walk along Second Avenue[8], which is a broad and fine thoroughfare, lined on one side with magnificent grounds and gardens belonging to villas not always visible from the road. These have all something worthy of an observant eye. In one instance it is a group of Paul-

---

36th Street and Fifth, and Manhattan, on 59th and Third, but they were gone by the time this column was written.

[6] While still in Kings County, he has left the city of Brooklyn, whose border with the town of New Utrecht here was at 60th Street.

[7] The Sea Beach Railroad, the future N train, met a ferry at the foot of 65th Street, then continued east to Third Avenue, then out toward Coney Island and Manhattan Beach. Brighton Beach, Sheepshead Bay and Gravesend had racetracks at this time. See Chapter 2.

[8] South of 65th Street, Second Avenue was renamed Ridge Boulevard in 1909.

ownias of great size and much symmetry, in another it is a hedge of Osage orange trees of the most luxuriant growth, and one cannot help wondering how a plant that belongs emphatically to warm countries should have prospered so greatly here. Then in a third place there is a sassafras tree of unusual size. Seldom is it higher than forty feet, but this one seems to be sixty at the very least. In another garden there are groups of grand old oaks of the large-leaved variety, in another pear trees whose branches bend down with the load of fruit, in another there are splendid evergreens, and scores of robins and brown thrushes.

The pedestrian should turn once again to the [west] when he gets to the end of Second Avenue[9] and he will have on both sides of him market gardens where men and women are picking tomatoes and filling great wagons with the deep red globes[10]. This path will bring him to a narrow road that follows the windings of the shore along the bay[11] and goes up and down and in and out in a perfectly natural and pleasing manner, much more delightful, however, to the pedestrian than to the driver of a buggy. This is a charming locality and offers continually fresh objects of interest on either side. The foot-path skirts the bank, which sometimes rises to the dignity of a cliff, and indeed is infinitely more cliff-like than the walk along the beach at Long Branch. For this is not only

---

[9] Second Avenue did and does continue to about 94th Street, where it turns toward the shore, but E. R. G. probably turned around 86th Street, after which there was little development on Second Avenue.
[10] In 1962, Grace A. Glen recalled her childhood in rural nineteenth-century Bay Ridge. "There was a kind of gentleman's agreement between the farmers and the children. Anything on the ground you could have, but no picking apples or pears from the trees—that was stealing. Tomatoes were all right however. Did you ever pick a big, red, just-ripe tomato off its vine, dust it off with your handkerchief or the hem of your petticoat and then eat it in delicious mouthfuls? If you haven't, you don't know what a tomato really tastes like."
[11] Shore Road.

very much higher at various points but at others has rocky boulders and serried clumps of cedars, many of them belonging to the remote past, when this part of the land was left in its natural condition. Mixed up with the cedars are other trees that were planted subsequently, and among these are here and there a Lombardy poplar, but generally there are splendid beeches of the European variety, and there are acacias and elms, and even a hop tree of the hornbeam family, which must have been brought from Virginia. The wild grape vines and Virginia creepers have grown in the most luxuriant way, massing themselves around the decaying trunks of dead trees and flinging their sprays like natural bridges across to other supports. The leaves of the creepers are now beginning to reflect the glowing hues of time's inverted torch, and the blossoms of the Fall, the golden rods, and the blue corn flowers mingle exquisitely with the reddened foliage. These banks and cliffs are for the most part the property of owners of the handsome villas on the other side of the road[12], and trespassing is deprecated by a multiplicity of signs, which are not always respected. For, just as the Teuton loves his beer and his lunch in spots whence he can contemplate the glories of the bay, so the tramp who has been charitably supplied with bread and meat has apparently huge satisfaction in disposing of the same, and of the half dozen ripe tomatoes that have casually wandered into his pockets, in the most comfortable and most convenient spots along the sides of the cliff in utter defiance of printed suggestions to dogs and man tramps. Come when you will along the Fort Hamilton road[13], and you will always see a tramp or two either reclining under the shade of a wide spreading beech tree surveying the glad waters of the Narrows, or else with his back against a tall cedar, taking huge

---

[12] In 1896, the city purchased all the land on the west side of Shore Road, in preparation for the park (and, later, highway) that's there today, mostly built on landfill throughout the early twentieth century.
[13] Shore Road brought you to Fort Hamilton.

bites out of a colossal sandwich. It is a surprising fact that with so much water around the tramp has never yet been discovered in the act of bathing by any inhabitant of the Fort Hamilton villas.

The pedestrian will do well to return by the village and the Third Avenue road, as he will see many noble specimens of fine trees. In the village there is a queer cottage that is in the Italian Summer house style and looks for all the world as if it was all parlors[14]. But it is larger than it seems and has a basement. It stands in a small garden that combines a glorious old sycamore of great size, a fine silver poplar with a clear trunk and a wide spreading canopy of upper branches, and some exceedingly old apple trees, whose fruit is not specially inviting to the eye. By walking down Ninety-second Street the wanderer finds himself once more on Third Avenue, and if he resists the appealing gesture of the conductors on the dummy line cars[15] who seem surprised that anyone should walk who is master of a nickel, he will not repent it. For he will travel for the most part under the shade of noble maple trees and will see some splendid masses of salvias in the grounds of the Inebriate Asylum[16], and at one point,

---

[14] Probably John Dickinson's house, on the northeast corner of Shore Road and 92nd Street. He owned a company that produced diamonds for drills used in mining and tunneling. When he died in 1897, he had "lived in Fort Hamilton about forty years and always in the same house, which is considered the finest residence on the Shore Road because of its style of architecture and the beautiful grounds surrounding it," according to his obituary in the *Eagle*.

[15] A dummy train—a passenger car pulled by a steam engine disguised to resemble another passenger car—ran down Third Avenue from Green-Wood to the fort. In 1891, the route was upgraded to electric trolley.

[16] The Kings County Inebriates' Asylum was built ca. 1869, two years after a cholera epidemic killed inmates in Brooklyn jails, including some whose only crime had been intoxication. It occupied roughly what's now 89th to 91st Streets, Third Avenue to Colonial Road (First Avenue). In the late 1890s, after corruption scandals involving the Asylum's

where the level of Third Avenue is very high, he will have an exceptionally fine sight of the splendid prospect to the south. Small as is the distance between this road and the one that winds along the shore, it is yet sufficient to give enchantment to the view. There is an added softness to the verdure of Staten Island, and there is a more tender purple to the far-off mountains of New Jersey, and the water of the bay is more silvery, more bright. One can see plainly from this point what the effect of the Bartholdi statue is to be[17], and it must be owned that it is disappointing. Even should it be all that its friends have hoped for it, and should it not be all that its critics have declared it will be, it is unfortunate in its site, being absolutely dwarfed by its surroundings. At present, though nearly completed, it makes no more effect in the landscape than the spire of St. John's Church on Staten Island, which rises gracefully from the water's edge not far from Fort Wadsworth, but of course does not seem very large, having behind it the highest point of the ridge of hills forming the backbone of Staten Island[18]. It is dubious if it is even as effective as the spire of St. John's, for there are points of view whence you can get the effect against the blue sky, and then its mass has some importance. But the statue will not unite

---

leadership, the state closed it. The Sisters of the Visitation had had an attractive home and school on the corner of Clinton Avenue and Willoughby Street, which they sold to developers in 1902 for the erection of new mansions. The Sisters used the considerable proceeds to relocate to a large portion of the Asylum grounds in Bay Ridge, then more rural and spacious than fashionable Clinton Hill. (The garden has a pond, separated from the city by thirty-foot stone walls.) Their new school and monastery opened in September 1903, repurposing the Asylum buildings; a new chapel was added ten years later. The Sisters announced in 2024 they would put the compound up for sale.

[17] The Statue of Liberty was dedicated about six weeks after this column was published. You can no longer see it from Third Avenue.

[18] The spire of St. John's Episcopal Church, on Bay Street since 1871, is still visible from Shore Road. The church is just a few blocks from Fort Wadsworth, Fort Hamilton's partner in protecting the Narrows.

with its pedestal as the spire with the church, but persists in forming two masses, one dark, one light. This detracts greatly from the appearance as a whole and makes it less large in appearance than a big sailing vessel. It is no doubt colossal in its dimension, but its surroundings dwarf it.

E. R. G.

28

Prospect Park West and Fort Hamilton Parkway

PEDESTRIAN PLEASURES.

Through Ninth Avenue, the Park and Fort Hamilton Avenue.

Views of the Colossus from Prospect Heights. The Rear of Green-Wood Cemetery—The Silly Titmice and Disingenuous Sparrows.

Sunday, October 31, 1886

No one can properly appreciate Brooklyn who is not fond of walking, for while it has many other advantages, its greatest charm is the picturesqueness of its surroundings. It seems strange that so few painters have taken their landscape motives from Long Island. Many illustrators for monthly magazines have indeed found their inspiration and their subjects in this favored land, but with the exception of Charles H. Miller, no landscape painter has seriously worked this mine[1]. The bicyclers are numerous and enterprising and go everywhere throughout the three counties[2], but the cycler cannot see as much as the pedestrian, because he goes too fast. It is the man who uses his legs for serious locomotion, and who never boggles at twenty miles or so, who takes in to the fullest extent the glories of scenery. He soon learns to look at nature with the eye of a painter and discovers bits of scenery in the

---

[1] Charles Henry Miller (1842–1922) was a successful landscape painter known for pastoral depictions of Queens and farther east.
[2] Kings, Queens and Suffolk. The western half of Queens County joined New York City in 1898, and the eastern half split off as Nassau County.

same way. Often traversing the same road, he is compelled to learn how varied is the aspect of any locality according to the conditions of light, the disposition of clouds and the time of year.

The road that in the Summertime is a miserable stretch of heated whiteness, sending up sizzling columns of air into the upper strata of the heavens and giving the general effect of an Arabian desert, plus trees and weeds on either side, becomes in the delicious robust air of the Fall a long white line of temptation, beckoning the pedestrian and coaxing him to walk upon it. Poets rave about the Spring, and there is one instance on record of a rhyming wretch who praised the beauties of snow[3], but these men derived their ideas either from other lands or from other times. In Europe there is no doubt a glorified halo of romance about the Spring, which is a long distinct season, gliding by insensible gradations into a flush and leafy Summer, which is a mature Spring as it were, resembling it as the still beautiful mother of half-grown girls resembles herself when a maiden of 15. But here in America spring is a delusion. We have intolerable summer heats in the beginning of April; we have snowstorms in the middle of May. All depends upon the winds, and they are more full of tricks and surprises than Shakespeare's Puck[4].

But in the lusty Fall, in the bracing air of Brooklyn the healthy man feels invigorated and buoyed up. There is an invisible tonic that he breathes in from his nostrils, which stimulates him and renews his youth and makes him feel that his muscles have the elasticity and firmness of steel. As he walks abroad his eyes glance upon objects of beauty in every direction, and he instinctively repeats to himself the lines in Scott's "Marmion": "Where is the coward that would not

---

[3] Possibly a reference to Ralph Waldo Emerson's poem "The Snow-Storm" from his 1856 book *Poems*.
[4] The fairy prankster from *A Midsummer Night's Dream*.

dare to fight for such a land?[5]" South Brooklyn communicates most directly with the picturesque region that stretches away until it meets the sea. An admirable jaunt is up Union Street, across the turn bridge, which ought to be a permanent bridge, and along Ninth Avenue[6] until one reaches Ninth Street. There is a diversity of opinion as to the correctness of policy pursued by the Park Commissioners in making a wall of trees, so as to shut out the view of the meadows from the avenue. Many people claim that it is because of this fence of evergreens and maples that there has been no building here[7]. They say that the families who would build fine villas along this thoroughfare are deterred by the gloomy and forbidding aspect of the trees along the park line. But it seems to the writer that there are two reasons much more cogent than this sentimental one. The first is that this avenue is rather narrow, and the second is that it is traversed by the Vanderbilt Avenue horse cars[8]. It strikes the observer also that there is a probability that the land on the western side of the avenue is held by one or two rich estates, and the owners thereof are not particularly anxious to thrust their lots upon the market. They have carefully fenced in their property with wire, as if with some forlorn hope of resisting the encroachment of boys who plunder the chestnut trees about this time. But with the tenderness for the rising generation, which is

---

[5] A popular quote from Walter Scott's 1808 epic poem, about a lord who frames a romantic rival for treason in sixteenth century Scotland.
[6] Ninth Avenue, from Union to 15th streets, was renamed Prospect Park West in 1895 at the request of local property owners, who complained that their mail was often misdelivered to Ninth Avenue, in Manhattan, and Ninth Street, in Brooklyn. They believed this problem would get worse after the inevitable consolidation with New York City, which happened three years later. Why this wasn't also a problem for any other numbered avenue in the area is unclear.
[7] Across from the park on Ninth Avenue at this time there were just a handful of structures, mostly low wooden buildings.
[8] The line extended from about the Navy Yard to Green-Wood Cemetery, after which it turned toward Windsor Terrace.

very noticeable in Brooklyn, the wire fencing is not barbed. Cows feed inside in a leisurely udder-filling fashion and seem to regard the stick-throwing boys with favor. Robins strut about, too, but they are aware that the boys are their enemies and are armed with a deadly weapon called a catapult, and they keep out of their reach. One cannot help wishing that this land may never be built upon, but will always remain as is[9], unless it should become a second Flatbush Avenue and should retain its beautiful trees.

At Fifteenth Street it becomes expedient to turn into the Park, for the fine part of Ninth Avenue terminates there, and beyond is a region comparatively dreary[10]. Before burying one's self in woodland and shrubberies the pedestrian turns his eyes to the westward. He is on the crest of a great undulating slope of what was once green meadows and was known as Prospect Heights[11]. And it was well named, for the site commands a full view of the bay and the shipping and present cynosure of all eyes, the Statue of Liberty. The waters gleam like molten metal; the distant line of Orange Mountains in the background shows like purple seen through a silver veil; the white wings of vessels of all sizes glide slowly across the extended field of vision. Amid such a scene what place does the colossal statue hold? The answer must be, a very small one. At this distance one cannot make out without the assistance of a field glass that the dark mass on the light pedestal represents a human figure, and the arm seems so slender and so long that it does not convey in the least the idea of an arm holding a torch. The head with its coronet of

---

[9] Within a decade, a few mansions and rowhouses had been built. A decade after that, many more had gone up, as well as apartment houses, filling in most of the available lots.

[10] Ninth Avenue was more developed south of Prospect Avenue, in Windsor Terrace, but it was largely commercial: low wooden buildings for feed storage and stone cutting, as well as wagon sheds and hothouses.

[11] Park Slope.

rays sinks into the body by the inevitable foreshortening of distance, and the whole figure seems dwarfed. It is to be feared that the secret of the colossal expired with Michael Angelo and has not been revived by Bartholdi. The figure looks far better from the Brooklyn end of the bridge, for there the head has some grandeur, though the neck is not visible even there, and the arm is spoiled by the torch. But from Prospect Heights the colossal image cannot be considered as other than meaningless, and there must arise in the mind of the observer a keen regret that some other locality than Bedlow's Island was not chosen. The highest point of Prospect Park would have been a most admirable site, for there the whole mass, pedestal and all, would have been against the upper sky, without another object to mar it. Had it been placed upon Hoboken Heights much of it in a distant view would have sunk into the mass of Orange Mountains. But upon the platform of the breezy outlook in Prospect Park there would have been nothing to interfere with it. It would have been the one sole form reflected against the ineffably blue skies of America, and observers everywhere would have looked up to it. Whereas from the present position of the statue nineteen-twentieths of those who see it look down upon it. The Battery Park and Governor's Island are exceptions. This unfortunate choice is due to the greediness of New York that will have everything, and it makes an old proverb true that "greediness bursts the boy."

Through the park the pedestrian gayly marches, choosing the track upon the outskirt. Foot path here there is none, for it is one of the things that is to be when the Commissioners have a little more money[12]. But there is no reason why there should be anything more than there is at present, and it may be questioned whether in the wilder parts of the de-

---

[12] Like today, in 1886 at the 15th Street entrance to the park there was a narrow pedestrian path running east, between Prospect Park Southwest (then 15th Street) and the wider West Drive. But it was not paved.

lightful park concrete is not an error and an unnecessary waste of funds that might be employed more usefully. The narrow track is good enough for the pedestrian, who mounts and descends the winding way most joyfully looking upon the unfortunates driving their buggies with an air of heartfelt pity. How stiff the muscles of their legs must feel! When he arrives at the Parade Ground, which is in splendid condition, he leaves the park and chooses one of two courses, the Ocean Parkway, which leads him to Coney Island and the Concourse[13], where he will find the same lavish and unreasonable display of concrete visible from the park itself, or Fort Hamilton Avenue[14]. As he pauses to choose, he cannot but exult in the splendor of the approaches to the park. What magnificent drives on every side! What splendid tree planting! How foreseeing has been the action of the Park Commissioners! Southward the city must grow in defiance of real estate speculation. It is its manifest destiny. And all things have been prepared for it when it begins to come this way. Who can doubt that the time will come when this region will be a succession of lovely villas, uniting with those of Bay Ridge and Fort Hamilton[15]? There is not much splendor of Autumn foliage just about here, for most of the trees are English and American elms, and they were visited with that pest,

---

[13] Near the end of Ocean Parkway was the enormous Brighton Beach Race Course, opened in 1879. It was torn down ca. 1920 and replaced with several hundred homes. See Chapter 2.

[14] Olmsted envisioned Fort Hamilton Parkway as an equal to Eastern and Ocean parkways, leafy *grands boulevards* radiating into the city and county from Prospect Park. But his ambition was never realized. Fort Hamilton Avenue opened ca. 1872 (though the section south of what's now 86th Street is decades older) and was rechristened "Parkway" twenty years later, but it was in name only, not spirit.

[15] This didn't happen. By 1905, there had been very little development on Fort Hamilton Parkway, save a few rowhouses around 39th Street, and a handful of villas around 42nd Street, until you reached Bay Ridge. By 1929, however, most lots had been developed with the low mixed-use brick buildings that still dominate today.

the din beetle, and lost their foliage. But the elm is seldom glorified by the Fall. The oak is, and there are masses of oak foliage in the park that are more magnificent than any maples. This fact decides the wanderer. He eschews the Ocean Parkway, which is elm planted, and chooses Fort Hamilton Avenue, which is not planted at all by the Park Commissioners but retains vestiges of original planting.

After crossing the Coney Island Railroad track[16] the pedestrian walks along the rear of Green-Wood Cemetery and sees it at its best, for the whole slope of the hill lies before him. Architecturally this end is not so pretentious as the other, but from a picturesque point of view it is infinitely pleasing. It is a bright and cheerful city of the dead, but it is a pity that people's monumental fancies run with such uniformity of action toward granite, which is cold in tone and does not harmonize well either with flowers or grass, unless it is unpolished. In a state of nature, the granite boulder, around which the tall grasses grew and upon which the ferns cluster, and from which the delicate hare bells hang, accords with everything around it. Some readers of the EAGLE may have had the good fortune to see a Keltic cromlech in a wheat field surrounded with golden grain and scarlet poppies and blue corn flowers, and they must have remarked how much the older monster seemed at home. Put a highly polished granite gray shaft in the same spot, and it would be a chilly incongruity. Syenite is much more suitable for a cemetery than either white marble or granite, but the real thing is red porphyry[17]. Nature welcomes her dead very tenderly, and the grass grows green, and the flowers blossom early in cemetery grounds. There may be a necropolis more beautiful and bet-

---

[16] The Culver line was a surface steam train that ran from 20th Street and Ninth Avenue (Prospect Park West) to Coney Island via McDonald Avenue (then Gravesend Avenue), starting in 1875. It was replaced by what's now the F train in 1919–33.

[17] As a strike against the Edward Rowland Greene theory, his gravestone appears to be made of granite.

ter tended than Green-Wood, but it does not seem possible. Everything goes well with it, and it has not that dreadfully crowded look so painfully conspicuous in Père Lachaise and some other famous cemeteries, nor will it ever have, for the lots are of sufficient size to prevent it. In the vicinity of Green-Wood along this avenue are many florists' grounds, who have contracts for keeping graves in good condition and surrounding them with growing flowers[18]. In the Summertime when Fort Hamilton Avenue was as hot as the great Desert of Sahara, their grounds were magnificent. Now they have little in them save chrysanthemums and geraniums.

The road dips somewhat when the twin railroads of the beaches Brighton and Manhattan are reached[19]. They run side by side like the constellation Gemini in the signs of the Zodiac, in a very loving fashion, but they may not be so friendly as they seem, and if railroads were properly comprehended as nothing more than highways, one of these would be closed up. Would the common sense of the community suffer two highways running side by side and going to the same places? The essence of a railroad is a highway, but the details are so complex and multifarious that people forget that essential fact. By people, the writer means tenderly and gently to refer to the Legislature and other charter-giving bodies. The road now trends upward and becomes absolutely delightful walking. The view on either side is more or less open, and there are hedges of young sweet gum trees, whose foliage has become a deep, rich purple. There are oak trees standing all alone in fields of corn, with leaves of a red-

---

[18] Six florists operated between Fort Hamilton Parkway and Greenwood Avenue, Gravesend Avenue (now McDonald) and East Fourth.

[19] A spur of the Prospect Park & Coney Island Railroad crossed Fort Hamilton Avenue at about 37th Street, near where the MTA keeps a train yard today. It was briefly two tracks wide, and it's possible one of these was reserved for trains that made a convoluted connection to the Manhattan Beach line via the modern-day LIRR freight tracks, but it's unclear from an 1888 map.

dish brown, with a peculiar glow in them, coming doubtlessly from the reflection of the colors of other leaves. Men and women are in these uplands with wagons, plucking the deep yellow ears from the gray shocks and bringing in orange-colored pumpkins. Further on, the road is lined on both sides with deep woods, filled with birds, chiefly thrushes and black-and-white creepers and woodpeckers[20]. They are very restless, and will not stay to be looked at, which is not to be wondered at when one learns from the notes of the Audubon Society that 70,000 bird's skins were sent abroad from Long Island alone, butchered for bonnets. It is most deplorable that women who have such tender hearts in concrete things seem incapable of comprehending abstract propositions. The bonnet is a bonnet, and the feathers are "just lovely," but they cannot be made to connect those feathers with a bird shot down ruthlessly because it ventured near the habitation of man. The prolific power of nature cannot stand this fearful drain. If this inhumanity goes on, we shall drive all our small birds into the woods, on mountain sides and in the Adirondacks. As well be deprived of flowers as of small birds. Here in this part of the road the maples begin to show their glorious colors, their yellow fires and golden reds. Here goldenrod lingers, and here and there is a digitalis flower, or a belated cinneraria, lying low down among the sumachs, and poking its beautiful pale purple star through the red leaves, like a little bashful child looking at a stranger from the shelter of its mother's skirts.

---

[20] Most of Fort Hamilton Avenue, between Green-Wood Cemetery and about 60th Street, ran through fields and woodlands. In 1886, there were just a handful of people living or working along it, including H. Webster's Son Open-Air Carpet Cleaning Works, at about 50th Street. In modern-day Dyker Heights, Fort Hamilton Avenue ran alongside what locals called Highlawn Woods, a natural boundary separating Bay Ridge from the rest of New Utrecht. Part of this popular picnic ground became McKinley Park, a triangle formed by Seventh Avenue and Fort Hamilton Parkway, 73rd to 78th streets.

How foolish are those little birds, the titmice. They fly before the approaching footsteps of the pedestrian and push themselves in lines upon the fence rail only twenty feet ahead of him. They wait until he gets within six feet of them when they bustle up in a terrible flurry, fly about twenty feet and perch upon the rail as before, and they continue to do this for a mile until, out of sheer compassion, the wanderer goes to the other side of the avenue. Here he starts another gang of the same kind of birds, who behave with the same precipitation and want of thought. The English sparrow is permitted to associate with these foolish things, and, though sparrows are the most familiar of feathered creatures and under ordinary circumstances will not get out of anybody's way and can almost be kicked, yet now they pretend to be as frightened as the titmice, and fly whenever they do. This proves that birds can be disingenuous. The sparrows are so pleased that the titmice admit them to companionship that they give them the lead and do as they, though they know perfectly well that the heavy foot tread means nothing dangerous to either of them. Just when one sees the tall liberty pole and flagstaff combined of the Village of Fort Hamilton, and can discover the gleaming silver of the ocean mingling with the horizon line, the ground becomes broken and has mounds and hummocks. Ascending one of these, one sees as in a map the whole beautiful picture of the Narrows and the southern shores of Long Island and the ridged back of Staten Island. This scene has a certain mournfulness in the Fall, for in the distance the woods of Staten Island have a melancholy purplish gray tone, and the silver of the sea is cold, though brilliant, and the white sails increase the general coloristic effect. Nothing is more difficult to account for than the emotional power of colors. Hitherto the whole route of Fort Hamilton Avenue has been one of exhilaration and cheerfulness. Suddenly, when the grand panorama of the end of Long Island opens before the contemplation of the pedestrian, the feeling impressed upon the spirit is one of sadness, and one realizes what the poet meant when he spoke of the Fall as the melancholy days[21]. This melancholy is not because the year has come to an end, for that is nothing to us, but it is the effect of masses of gray and purple tones.

E. R. G.

---

[21] William Cullen Bryant's "The Death of Flowers" (1840) begins, "The melancholy days are come, the saddest of the year, /
Of wailing winds, and naked woods, and meadows brown and sere."

SOURCES AND ACKNOWLEDGEMENTS

The book is thoroughly annotated except when I didn't want to spend several pages on, say, the history of Italy in the nineteenth century, or when I had no idea what he was talking about, such as a reference in Chapter 3 to "Schinderian obstinacy." (*Schinder* is German for hide stripper. I suppose hide strippers, by the nature of their work, are obstinate?) In Chapter 24, he mentions a Captain Trent I couldn't identify.

    Primarily, my sources were contemporary newspapers and maps, via the Center for Brooklyn History, the New York Public Library and newspapers.com, though I also relied at times on others' research, especially Suzanne Spellen's work for Brownstoner and Leonard Benardo and Jennifer Weiss's *Brooklyn By Name*. Thanks to Suzanne for reading a draft of this book and giving support, and thanks to all archivists and New York historians for the work they do.

Thanks to Michael, for the cover and the decades of friendship. Thanks to Ben for his edits, and especially to him but also to Jil, Mark and Larissa for politely listening to me talk about this project for the last five years or so. Thanks to Dan for his help and for trying to help even more.

    I began this book before Covid but knocked out most of it during lockdown. I often listened to Side A of Mozart's Requiem, flipped it to Side B, then put on Side A again, all day for days on end. *Lacrimae diebus illae*. Then I stuck the manuscript in the cloud for a while, intimidated by its burgeoning scope.

    Thanks to Sam, for inspiring me to look at it again, for encouraging me and believing in me, for not giving up on me. You are, and have always been, my north star; I would be lost without you.

Made in the USA
Middletown, DE
17 July 2024